UNIONS IN CRISIS?

UNIONS
IN
CRISIS?

THE FUTURE OF ORGANIZED LABOR
IN AMERICA

Michael Schiavone

American Social and Political Movements
Martha Burk, Series Editor

Westport, Connecticut
London

Library of Congress Cataloging-in-Publication Data

Schiavone, Michael.
  Unions in crisis? : the future of organized labor in America / Michael Schiavone.
     p. cm. — (American social and political movements, ISSN 1939–1226)
  Includes bibliographical references and index.
  ISBN 978–0–275–99966–7 (hardcover : alk. paper)
  1. Labor unions—United States. 2. Labor movement—United States.
3. Social movements—United States. 4. Service industries workers—
Labor unions—United States. I. Title.
  HD6508.S333 2008
  331.880973—dc22   2007037945

British Library Cataloguing in Publication Data is available.

Library of Congress Catalog Card Number: 2007037945
ISBN-13: 978–0–275–99966–7
ISSN: 1939–1226

First published in 2008

Praeger Publishers, 88 Post Road West, Westport, CT 06881
An imprint of Greenwood Publishing Group, Inc.
www.praeger.com

Printed in the United States of America

The paper used in this book complies with the
Permanent Paper Standard issued by the National
Information Standards Organization (Z39.48–1984).

10 9 8 7 6 5 4 3 2 1

Copyright Acknowledgments

The author and the publisher gratefully acknowledge permission for use of the following
material:

A portion of chapter 3 was previously published as "Social Movement Unionism and the
UE," *The Flinders Journal of History and Politics* 23 (2006): 57–82.

Portions of chapters 3 and 5 were previously published as "Moody's Account of Social Movement Unionism: An Analysis," *Critical Sociology* 33, no. 1 (2007): 279–309.

A portion of chapter 5 was previously published as "Rank-and-File Militancy and Power:
Revisiting the Teamsters Struggle with United Parcel Service Ten Years Later," *WorkingUSA*
10, no. 1 (June 2007): 175–91.

For Anamaria and Pluto

CONTENTS

SERIES FOREWORD

The social and political landscape of the United States as we know it today is not the result of a benign evolution from a fledgling democracy to a mature one in the short span of 220 years. American society and how we think about what it is and ought to be has always been shaped by movements—some short-lived, others long lasting, some impermanent and others institutionalized.

Books in this series will deal with American social and political movements. Unlike a fad or trend that may attract large numbers of people who are passionate about something for the moment, a movement has a goal, usually related to social, political, or cultural change. Goals can be related to equal rights (or their suppression), changes in societal conditions, or protection of something that cannot speak for itself, such as the environment. Scholars identify both *spontaneity* and *structure* as important elements of movements. This necessary balance distinguishes genuine movements from fads on the one hand, and interest groups (which may represent the goals of a present or former movement, but do not in themselves constitute a movement) on the other. Writers such as Marx have also recognized that structural conditions in a society (e.g., economic collapse, wide income disparity) may contribute to both the spontaneity and success of social and political movements.

While some books are proclaiming (and either lamenting or debating) the death of liberal America, this series will demonstrate that liberal America is in fact alive and well. Because many social and political movements are conservative, the series will not necessarily be limited to liberal or progressive movements. When such movements are explored, however, it will always be from a liberal perspective.

The history of political and social movements in the United States is rich. Political realignments have come from social movements, and social change has come from political realignment. From the early anti-slavery movement to modern day gay rights, progressive movements (and counter movements to stop them) shape change affecting far more than their immediate participants or contemporary environments.

One such movement, the labor movement beginning in the 20th century, is the subject of this book. Michael Schiavone provides the reader with a robust history of the U.S. labor movement. But far more importantly, he gives us an astute analysis of policies, practices, and trends in that movement that have contributed to both its success and stagnation. Using concrete examples from other labor movements and organizational tactics in a variety of settings, he provides a blueprint for revitalization of one of the most significant social movements of the 20th century.

Martha Burk
Series Editor

ACKNOWLEDGMENTS

While my name is on the cover, many people have helped me along the way. The following people either read portions of the manuscript or offered invaluable advice; I cannot thank them enough: Rick Kuhn, Dennis Deslippe, Kim Scipes, Steve Early, Nelson Lichtenstein, Ruth Milkman, Peter Rachleff, and Immanuel Ness.

This book would have never seen the light of day without Hilary Claggett, formerly at Praeger Publishing, believing in it from the outset. Her unwavering belief in the importance of the book led to its publication.

Finally, my heartfelt thanks go to Anamaria and Pluto. No matter what mood I am in, they can always make me smile. Without Anamaria and Pluto, I would have abandoned this project long ago. Thus, I dedicate the book to them.

ABBREVIATIONS

ACORN	Association of Community Organizations for Reform Now
AFL-CIO	American Federation of Labor-Congress of Industrial Organizations
CAW	Canadian Auto Workers
CLCs	Central Labor Councils
CNA	California Nurses Association
CUAW	Canadian United Auto Workers
CWA	Communication Workers of America
GE	General Electric
GM	General Motors
IBT	International Brotherhood of Teamsters
NAFTA	North American Free Trade Agreement
NGOs	Non-Governmental Organizations
NLRA	National Labor Relations Act
NLRB	National Labor Relations Board
NUP	New Unity Partnership
NYTWA	New York Taxi Workers Alliance
SEIU	Service Employees International Union
TDC	Teamsters for a Decent Contract
TDU	Teamsters for a Democratic Union
TNCs	Transnational Corporations
TUEL	Trade Union Educational League
UAW	United Auto Workers
UE	United Electrical Workers
UFCW	United Food and Commercial Workers
UNITE-HERE	Union of Needletrades, Industrial, and Textile Employees-Hotel Employees and Restaurant Employees
UPS	United Parcel Service

1

THE IMPORTANCE OF THE LABOR MOVEMENT

THE STATE OF WORKING AMERICA

Whatever one may think about defining a person by his or her paycheck, a person's paycheck often determines what kind of life he or she will lead. For a majority of Americans, their paycheck limits their quality of life. Weekly wages of nonsupervisory private sector workers today are lower in real terms (adjusted for inflation) than in the early 1960s, and they are 17 percent lower than their peak in 1972. During this time, productivity has increased by 80 percent. In other words, people are working harder for a lot less money. The minimum wage is 33 percent lower now than it was in 1968 in real terms.[1] The good news is that the federal minimum wage will increase by $2.10 over a two-year period so that in 2009 it will be at $7.25 an hour. However, the minimum wage increase was tied to tax cuts for small businesses—further proof that politicians cannot do something solely for the benefit of workers.[2] There is also rising wage inequality. In the early 1970s, European countries had greater wealth inequality than America. Since then, however, inequality in America has skyrocketed. Today, 5 percent of the American population owns 59 percent of the wealth, with CEOs receiving, on average, 245 times the amount that an average worker receives; in 1980 this figure was 42 to 1. A full-time job does not guarantee a person a good income: 58.4 percent of the working poor work full time.[3] The situation is not just confined to the current generation. A group headed by a member of the Federal Reserve Bank of Chicago claims that approximately 60 percent of a person's wage is based on the income level of their father.[4] For the majority of Americans, such a situation is clearly unacceptable. This is why a strong union movement is essential.

In purely bread-and-butter issues (wages and working conditions), unions help ordinary Americans in a number of ways:

1. *Wages:* Union members receive higher wages than nonunion workers. In 2004, the average union member received $781 gross per week, whereas nonunion members received $612 per week, a 27 percent difference. Likewise, women who belong to a union earn, on average, an extra $170 per week compared to women who are not union members; African American union members

earn an extra $150 per week compared to their nonunion brethren; and Latino union members earn an astonishing $225 extra per week compared to Latinos who are not union members.

2. *Health care:* While only 50 percent of families have job-related health care, 81 percent of union members do, and nonunion members pay 43 percent more for family coverage.

3. *Better pensions:* 72 percent of union members have a guaranteed defined benefit pension. In comparison, only 15 percent of nonunion members have such a pension.[5]

Union members receive better wages, better health care, and better pensions compared to nonunion members. Moreover, the decline in the average American's weekly wage corresponds with the decline in unionism. Unions are essential to the livelihood of the American people. Nonetheless, unions are in crisis. Union membership is currently 12 percent of the workforce, but union membership in private industry fell from 7.9 to 7.8 percent in 2006. While there were 50,000 new union members in private industry in 2006, almost 2 million jobs were created. In other words, union growth was negligible. Without a strong union movement, ordinary Americans' quality of life will suffer.

THE IMPORTANCE OF LABOR

Despite evidence that unions help ordinary Americans, among the Left, and especially among the newer generation of activists, it is argued that the labor movement is a dinosaur. They also argue that non-governmental organizations (NGOs) and new social movements can rise up and challenge unfettered capitalism, which will lead to workers once again receiving a fairer slice of the economic pie. They argue that social movements

> nurture both heroes and clowns, fanatics and fools. They function to move people beyond their mundane selves to acts of bravery, savagery, and selfless charity. Animated by the injustices, sufferings, and anxieties they see around them, men and women in social movements reach beyond their customary resources of the social order to launch their own crusade against the evils of society. In doing so they reach beyond themselves and become new men and women.[6]

Hyperbole aside, one must ask why the majority of new social movements, which currently have no desire to support working people, will support working people in the future. Is it realistic that an environmental or human rights group would start to argue that there is a necessary link between the free market and environmental degradation or human rights abuses throughout the world? There is nothing to suggest that capitalism results in new social movements rising up against it. As Boris Frankel claims, "Most organizations in new social movements actually accept to a lesser or greater extent the prevailing public and private political processes, rather than advocate a total dismantling of the whole state institutional system."[7]

While nothing suggests that new social movements are compelled to struggle against capitalism, the same is not true for the labor movement. This is because of the workers' position in the production process. Workers do not like struggling against the system for higher wages and better working conditions, but the system in place forces them to do so. According to Francis Mulhern,

> [The] working class is revolutionary, Marxists have maintained, because of its historically constituted nature as the exploited collective producer within the capitalist mode of production. As the *exploited* class, it is caught in a systematic clash with capital, which cannot generally and permanently satisfy its needs. As the main *producing* class, it has the power to halt—and within limits redirect—the economic apparatus of capitalism, in pursuit of its goals. And as the *collective* producer it has the objective capacity to found a new, non-exploitative mode of production. This combination of interest, power and creative capacity distinguishes the working class from every other social or political force in capitalist society.[8]

Nevertheless, because new social movements are the driving force behind the antiglobalization protests from Seattle to Davos, Switzerland, and beyond, it is necessary to analyze their potential in some detail.

Many people believe that there is a difference between the new politics of social movements and the old politics of the current labor movement. However, the evidence does not support this proposition. New social movements are plagued by so-called old political problems: bureaucracy, conflicts between rank-and-file members and leaders of the movements, political differences, and co-option.[9] Verity Burgmann claims that while new social movements believe they are better than the "old" movements, they are politically weak.[10]

Nevertheless, activists claim that many new social movements have decentralized structures with an apparent absence of leaders (unlike unions). Stephanie Ross states that new social movements make up a large proportion of the antiglobalization movement and that the most important value of the movement is a rejection of hierarchy. This rejection of hierarchy has a major negative implication for the antiglobalization movement and hence new social movements. The movements are ill equipped to deal with long battles because of their institutional structure or, more to the point, because of their lack of one.[11] Historian Barbara Epstein notes that a parallel exists between the nonviolent direct action movement in the United States in the 1970s and the antiglobalization movement. Both movements were based on consensus decision making and a refusal to acknowledge leadership. However, the decentralized structure led to the decline of the nonviolent direct action movement. As Epstein claims, "Anti-leadership ideology cannot eliminate leaders, but it can lead a movement to deny that it has leaders, thus undermining democratic constraints on those who assume the roles of leadership, and also preventing the formation of vehicles for recruiting new leaders when the existing ones become too tired to continue."[12] Likewise, in an analysis of the US women's liberation movement, Carol Hanisch argues that "more structured forms are necessary to assure the development of the organised strength needed to accumulate and eventually take power—assuming the goal is to take women's fair share of power to meet the needs of all, not just to 'empower' individuals."[13] In other words, a decentralized structure with an apparent absence of leaders is not necessarily something that should be lauded.

Nevertheless, some claim that the current crisis of trade unionism is due in part to the structure of unionism: capitalism and new social movements have embraced the network form. They argue that networking and decentralization are more democratic than current union structures.[14] This is not necessarily true. Decentralization may encourage participation, but there is no guarantee that it is more democratic. While on the surface a decentralized structure seems to result in greater democracy, domineering individuals within the group and unequal power relations between groups can easily undermine democracy. Indeed, Ross claims that "it is not entirely clear that the structures of decentralized coordination are sufficient to ensure equal and effective participation. Consensus produces its own tyranny, that of *endurance,* in which 'the last ones left at the table get to make the decision.' The conditions and resources required to engage in consensus decision-making—especially time and energy—are themselves not equally distributed."[15] The organizational structure of new social movements, where the focus is on consensus decision making and an absence of leaders, means that they are difficult to sustain over time. Furthermore, while the network structures of new social movements could lead to an increase in participation, this does not necessarily result in greater democracy. There is no reason to suggest that a networking structure is preferable to the traditional union structure with considerable rank-and-file involvement.

Unlike NGOs and the labor movement, civil society advocates often praise new social movements for not selling out. It is true that new social movements rarely sell out to capital and governments, but is this a sign of their strength or a sign of weakness? In a study on the effect that new social movements have on Australian politics, Burgmann came to the following conclusion: "The relative purity and incorruptibility of the leaders of new social movements attests not to their moral superiority but to their relative powerlessness. If they have no price, it is because the powers that be are not interested in making them an offer. You cannot sell out if you have nothing to sell.... The corruptibility of the labour movement is evidence of its real political power, for good or evil."[16] Gail Omvedt came to the same conclusion. In an analysis of Indian new social movements, she argues that they were unable to implement any significant changes in government policy.[17] This is not to argue that new social movements have never achieved any success. However, the likelihood of new social movements achieving major change on their own is not as great as some would have you believe.

Furthermore, while workers can strike to achieve their demands, new social movements lack this power. Protests and demonstrations can achieve change, but they are not as powerful as strike action. Strike action, in addition to leading to major change, has led to workers shutting down cities; new social movements lack this type of power.[18] This is not to argue that the labor movement should not form alliances with new social movements. New social movements alone will not lead to workers getting a fair share of the economic pie. This is also true for those who pin their hopes on NGOs.

NGOs are movements that belong to neither the state nor the market. They have an institutional structure that seeks to influence government policies and the way people live and react to the world. The number of international NGOs rose dramatically in the 1990s. There were 6,000 NGOs in 1990, but 26,000 by the end of 1999. Membership has also substantially increased. The World Wide Fund for Nature demonstrates this. It now has 5 million members, compared to 570,000 in 1985. In addition, the spending power of NGOs is very impressive. NGOs spend over $10 billion per year, which equates to approximately 10 percent of the official aid for all Organization for Economic Cooperation and Development (OECD) countries.[19] There is a growing body of literature that sings the praises of NGOs: NGOs are "becoming the last hope of angry students, of embittered workers driven to despair by their impoverishment, of lonely old people, of the sick and homeless, of abandoned children, of minorities deprived of their rights. They are spurring a revival of civilized values, of the progressive traditions of community-mindedness, of collective leadership and mutual support. They are giving strength to the powerless."[20]

There is a diverse range of NGO structures and practices, including very democratic organizations. Amnesty International allows all members to vote for state delegates, who in turn vote for national delegates. Any Amnesty member can become a delegate of the International Council, Amnesty's highest policy-making body. It is argued, however, that while NGOs do seek to influence government policies, a majority of them are undemocratic and unaccountable organizations. They are primarily interested in their own particular causes, with some NGO directors being more concerned with their own comfort than with the poor and the environment. Examples of misdeeds by particular NGOs include fabricating environmental research that led to the US delaying ratification of the Convention on Biodiversity, and subsidizing warring factions in Sudan and Somalia. Moreover, while the majority of northern countries allow individuals the right to vote, many individuals in NGOs do not participate beyond paying their membership fees.[21] A self-perpetuating hierarchical group often determines the policies that many NGOs pursue, with no input from the majority of the members; Greenpeace is the most obvious example of this.

These are major problems, especially if NGOs are to be crucial agents of progressive change and help ordinary Americans. NGOs that are more concerned with themselves rather than the poor and the environment are like business unions: as long as they are strong and powerful, it is largely irrelevant if others are suffering. It is highly unlikely that such NGOs will contribute to working Americans receiving an equitable reward.

In addition, there is a common perception that there are few or no formal links between NGOs and states. But this is not the case, especially in relation to NGO income. State funding of NGOs ranges from approximately 10 percent in Austria, 34 percent in Australia, 66 percent in the United States, 70 percent in Canada, and 85 percent in Sweden.[22] Although there are NGOs that refuse to accept government funding—such as Amnesty International—the majority of NGOs depend on state funding for their survival or, at the very least, for the majority of their income. This has led to many NGOs being unwilling to disagree with government policy for fear that their funding will be reduced or cut altogether. As the majority of NGOs rely on government funding to survive, it is unlikely that they will advocate the winding back of neoliberalism and push for workers' rights. Indeed, northern governments may use NGOs to implement neoliberalism in the developing world.[23]

For example, a structural adjustment program in Bolivia in the mid-1980s led to a massive increase in poverty. In an attempt to alleviate this, the World Bank and the American government provided massive aid. On the surface, one would assume this was a good gesture. However, the majority of this aid was channeled through NGOs. This led to a dramatic increase in the number of NGOs.

> Of the tens of millions allocated to the NGOs, only 15 to 20 percent reached the poor. The rest was siphoned off to pay administrative costs and professional salaries....The absolute levels of poverty stayed the same and the long-term structural causes—the neoliberal policies— were cushioned by the NGOs. While not solving the poverty problem, the NGO-administered poverty programs strengthened the regime and weakened opposition to the...[government]. The NGOs, with their big budgets, exploited vulnerable groups and were able to convince some leaders of the opposition that they could benefit from working with the government.[24]

Attacks by NGOs on international financial and trade institutions have led to these institutions engaging in a sustained dialogue with the NGOs and attempting to co-opt them. While international financial and trade institutions have co-opted NGOs, in return, NGOs have often had a major influence on the institutions' policies. For example, following the "Fifty Years Is Enough" campaign by NGOs in 1994, the World Bank engaged in dialogue with them. This led to over 70 NGO specialists working within the World Bank's field offices, and, not surprisingly, there is now very little criticism of the World Bank by NGOs. Indeed, following the World Bank's lead, the International Monetary Fund and the OECD believe that it is important to talk to NGOs.[25] While this can lead these international institutions to modify their neoliberal policies, it is equally likely, as seen in the example of the World Bank, that NGOs will moderate their criticisms of these institutions.

Of course, not all NGOs have the same characteristics, but there must be serious doubt about the emancipatory potential of many NGOs. In other words, a strong union movement is the best, and quite frankly the only, hope for working Americans. At this stage, that hope is fading fast. Unless the union movement makes some fundamental changes, not only will union membership continue to decline, but the chance for ordinary Americans to receive an equitable reward for their labor will potentially be lost for good.

OVERVIEW

In order to understand whether organized labor has a future, it is important to understand its past. Chapter 2 provides an overview of the rise and fall of unionism in America. It looks at what led to labor's success as well as the factors that led to its decline. I also discuss strategies and tactics that unions can use to revitalize themselves. Chapter 3 analyzes a range of proposed strategies: value-added unionism, union democracy, labor-community alliances, organizing the unorganized, and labor internationalism. I argue that the majority of these strategies will help unions, but in isolation they will not stem the decline. Chapter 4 examines a success story among American unions, the Service Employees International Union (SEIU). I argue that while the SEIU has been very successful, it also contains some unsavory aspects that unions seeking to revitalize themselves should avoid. The chapter also examines the breakaway labor federation Change to Win. I argue that while Change to Win's commitment to organizing should be lauded, it is one of the few bright spots in its manifesto. Chapter 5 looks at social justice unionism. By analyzing the Teamsters negotiations/collective bargaining agreements with the United Parcel Service, and the Canadian Auto Workers and the United Auto Workers negotiations/collective bargaining agreements with General Motors as well as the internal structures of the unions, I argue that social justice unionism has been successful in a variety of situations and should be adopted by all unions. Chapter 6, to use a cliché, thinks outside the box. I examine more obscure organizing strategies that can help unions. In some cases these strategies directly involve unions (as in the case of central labor councils), and in other cases unions are not necessarily direct participants (worker centers and the Trade Union Educational League). Finally, Chapter 7 examines outside factors that may hamper union revival efforts, as well as what may lead to unions adopting positive changes. It would be foolish to argue that even with these changes unions will be revitalized and be as powerful as they were in the 1940s. At the very least, these changes will help unions and, more importantly, ordinary Americans. While success cannot be guaranteed, where there is life there is hope.

2

THE RISE AND FALL
OF ORGANIZED LABOR

This chapter provides an overview of the rise and fall of organized labor from the early 1900s until the present day. During this period, unions were on a roller coaster ride. They started at the bottom, climbed for a bit, began to decline, and then hit unimaginable highs. Unfortunately, the highs did not last long. Since the 1950s, the labor movement has been losing strength with no respite in sight. In this chapter I will analyze what led to the highs and lows. To paraphrase George Santayana: It is important to remember the past because those who do not learn from history are doomed to repeat it.

1900–1940s

In 1900, union membership was approximately 5.5 percent of the workforce. Over the next 10 years, organized labor began to grow, so much so that by 1915, union membership had increased to 10.9 percent. Moreover, from 1914 until 1920, union membership grew to 17.5 percent, an astonishing 88 percent increase.[1] President Woodrow Wilson supported all workers in their efforts to unionize and receive an equitable reward for their labor.

> The question which stands at the front of all others amidst the present great awakening is the question of labor...how are the men and women who do the daily labor of the world to obtain progressive improvement in the conditions of their labor, to be made happier, and to be better served by the communities and the industries which their labor sustains and advances.... The object of all reform in this essential matter must be the genuine democratization of industry, based upon full recognition of the right of those who work, in whatever rank, to participate in some organic way in every decision which directly affects their welfare.[2]

However, the support for workers and unions did not last long. There was soon a backlash against them by the government and employers: "In the anti-radical post-Palmer [anti-Communist] Raid era of the 1920s, both unions and the left found themselves in a steep decline. Between 1920 and 1923, union membership decreased by more than 28 percent. By 1929, after a decade of ascendant monopoly capitalism that successfully employed the 'American Plan' to smash unions and reestablish the open shop, organized labor represented just 10.3 percent of the workforce. Membership had dropped to under 3.5 million." In a similar situation that occurs today, there was growing inequality between the rich and the poor, with the largest corporations owning the majority of business assets.[3] A weak labor movement in addition to a system that favors the leading corporations is not good for everyone.

The 1930s and 1940s witnessed a turnaround in labor's fortune. Indeed they were the glory years for organized labor and working people. Richard W. Hurd argues that

> during the 1930s workers' passivity gave way to militance and collective action as they flocked to the industrial unions of the renegade Congress of Industrial Organizations. Union expansion was aided by a friendly federal government which first facilitated union organization with the Wagner Act of 1935 and then promoted collective bargaining during the War to assure industrial peace under the watchful eye of the War Labor Board. In the ten years from 1935 to 1945, union membership exploded from three million to over fourteen million, from 13.2% of the non-agricultural workforce to 35.5%.[4]

The Wagner Act allowed workers the right to strike and the right to choose their own union by a majority vote. It listed a range of unfair labor practices by employers, such as blacklisting and intimidating union members, that were outlawed. The act also led to the formation of the National Labor Relations Board (NLRB), which had the power to rule on employee complaints against management and to oversee union representation elections. Moreover, the act banned company unionism, as employers were not allowed to participate or even encourage a particular union.[5] This favored unions and all working people alike. The massive growth of organized labor is illustrated by the fact that in 1937 alone, unions organized 2.5 million new members. Unions were helped by politicians who recognized people's rights to a job and a decent wage. During World War II, President Franklin Roosevelt stated that the "one supreme objective for the future...can be summed up in one word: Security, and that means not only physical security....It means also economic security, social security, moral security."[6]

The formation of the Congress of Industrial Organizations (CIO) was fundamental to labor's growth. Unlike the American Federation of Labor (AFL), whose affiliates were still organized by craft and had no idea how to organize workers in large-scale industry, the CIO embraced industrial unionism (organizing by industry). Moreover, the CIO utilized rank-and-file–intensive tactics. As a *New York Times Magazine* report on the United Mine Workers stated:

> Seizing plants by sit-down strikes regardless of their legality and massing thousands of pickets from other C.I.O. unions in other cities and States in front of the gates, it has defied the police and the courts to

dislodge them and return the property to the owners until their demands are met....

[The CIO's centralized form of organization] enables...[it] to bring all its resources of men, money and machines to bear upon any given situation....

The same resources enable it to hire intelligent, well-paid organizers, [and] to send experienced men from the United Mine Workers wherever they may be needed...[including] to any place where mass picketing is necessary to help one of the C.I.O. unions.[7]

The number of sit-down strikes clearly demonstrated the CIO's militancy; there were 477 sit-down strikes that involved more than 400,000 workers in the first half of 1937 alone. Labor's massive growth was fueled by strike action to force companies to recognize unions. The United Electrical Workers (UE) was very successful in this regard. The middle-to-late 1930s saw many major UE successes. After a long struggle, the UE organized the General Electric (GE) Schenectady plant, and within four months of this triumph, GE agreed to the UE's request for a national contract, which led to 29 new UE Locals at GE plants. Likewise, Westinghouse agreed to a national contract with the UE in 1941, covering 19 plants after a long struggle and following an NLRB ruling that Westinghouse defied the legal responsibility to bargain. This helped the UE to gain great success in organizing Westinghouse plants.[8]

Workers engaged in all forms of strikes, not just those for their own gain. Union members supported each other, and there was solidarity between all workers; a popular tactic was for unions to engage in sympathy strikes and secondary boycotts. Unfortunately, this solidarity has largely been lost. While bread-and-butter issues were important for CIO unions and their members, the unions also emphasized workers' control. Using a broad definition of "workers' control," Robert Zieger claims that "such practices as union participation in job evaluation, careful regulation of seniority lines, closely calibrated pay scales according to job content, protection from arbitrary discipline, and so forth, external control—'workers' control'...was indeed at the heart of the CIO."[9] In other words, CIO unions challenged employers' unfettered authority to arbitrarily control workers' lives, thus contesting the unequal power relationship between employers and workers.

Further aiding labor's growth was the Left. Communists, Trotskyites, the Socialist Party, and independent radicals were at the forefront of organizing unions. They sought to revitalize all organizations of social struggle and help the local community. Indeed, the Communists were at the forefront of the struggle for racial equality. They wanted racial integration not only in unions and in the workplace, but in every social and political situation. This was such a "radical" position that almost no other group fighting for racial equality had such a forward-looking agenda. Labor historian Nelson Lichtenstein beautifully summed up the importance of the radical Left: "Only those individuals with an intense political or religious vision, only those radicals who saw the organizing project as part of a collective enterprise, and only those who understood the unions as a lever with which to build a new society could hope to calculate that the hardships they endured might reap such a magnificent and political reward."[10]

A WAVE OF STRIKES

During World War II, wages were closely regulated. Following the end of the war, unions went out on strike in record numbers to get a fair share of the economic pie. The United Auto Workers (UAW) demanded wage increases of 30 percent. In 1945, 3.5 million workers went out on strike; the numbers increased to 4.6 million in 1946. The example of the UE demonstrates labor's might at that time.

The Big Three CIO unions (the UE, the UAW, and the Steelworkers) demanded substantial wage increases, with the UE seeking $2 more per day (25 cents per hour), a 24 percent increase. The UE had overwhelming support from its workers at GE, General Motors (GM), and Westinghouse to strike if the companies did not meet its demands. That September, in a precursor to the upcoming strike, Westinghouse briefly locked out 36,000 workers who were demanding wage increases from its East Pittsburgh, Lima, Cleveland, and Sharon plants.[11] GE and GM offered the UE an increase of 10 cents an hour, which was promptly rejected. GM offered 13½ cents an hour in December 1945, which the UE also rejected. UE members at GE, GM, and Westinghouse overwhelmingly voted for strike action if the parties could not reach an agreement.[12] As there was no settlement before the strike deadline, in January 1946 some 200,000 UE workers went on strike at GE, GM, and Westinghouse, with the UAW on strike at GM, and 800,000 steelworkers striking a week later. As Ronald Schatz notes, the "1946 strikes were the first national strikes in the electrical manufacturing industry and the first major strikes GE and Westinghouse had known since 1918."[13]

On February 12, the UE negotiated a wage increase of 18 cents an hour for its GM workforce. As the UAW sought an increase of 19½ cents an hour at GM, it condemned the UE for selling out. In January, however, the UAW agreed to increases of 18 cents and 18½ cents from Ford and Chrysler, respectively. Thus, it is difficult to conclude that the UE sold out, as the UAW had already agreed to the same amount with the other two big automakers. A month later, the UE also achieved an 18½ cent increase for its GE workforce. Two months later, the UE was victorious at Westinghouse. The company, after initially refusing to table any offer and then offering only approximately a 9 cent an hour increase, finally agreed to a 19 cent increase.[14]

GE's insistence that men receive an 18½ cent increase while women receive only 15 cents complicated the UE's negotiations with the company. UE secretary-treasurer James Matles noted that GE "said we'll improve our offer but we will not give the bobby-soxers [GE's name for women] the same as we give the men. ... So the fight then was for equality in the settlement in cents per hour. So we stayed out another four weeks. Then [in the final settlement] it was eighteen and a half cents across the board for everyone in the plants including the bobby-soxers."[15] Likewise, in the UE's settlement with Westinghouse, the 19-cent-an-hour increase included a fund of 1 cent per hour per worker, which was to be distributed to the women in an attempt to bring their pay closer to the men's pay. The GM settlement included the same starting rate for both men and women in the electrical division.[16] The strikes were a success for the UE. While the UE did not achieve its initial demand of a $2-a-day increase, it achieved substantial pay raises for both male and female members, and the result was a step toward equal pay.

The success of the unions led to an employer and government backlash. For example, the Wagner Act allowed employees the right to strike, but in 1938 the US Supreme Court ruled that during strikes the hiring of scabs (individuals who cross picket lines and go to work when other workers are on strike at a company) was allowed and employers hiring scabs did not undermine employees' right to strike.[17] However, the biggest threat to labor under US law came from the Taft-Hartley Act, which was passed despite President Harry S. Truman's veto.

THE BACKLASH AGAINST UNIONS

Politicians and employers were not happy with the increasing power of unions. They wanted to halt this power and transfer it to themselves. This led to the Taft-Hartley Act. As Hurd argues,

> Reeling from the spread of unionization and retaining their hostility, employers sought ways to restrict unions and to stabilize relations in order to reclaim managerial authority in the workplace. A central part of this initiative was a political campaign which contributed to the election of a Republican Congress in 1946 and then culminated in the enactment of the Taft-Hartley Act in 1947. The Taft-Hartley amendments to the Wagner Act placed strict limits on workers' organizing rights, on strikes and other forms of direct action, and on unions' mutual aid tactics, while enhancing the role of collective bargaining in part by buttressing the legal status of negotiated agreements.[18]

The Taft-Hartley Act banned closed shops, thus allowing nonunionized workers to be employed with union workers—a move that gave employers greater influence. The act also allowed individual states to enact laws that dramatically curtailed the rights of unions. Companies could now move their operations to these states and be free from the scourge of unions. Twenty-three states, mostly in the southern part of the country, have passed so-called right-to-work laws, which makes it very difficult for unions to get a foothold in these states. Right-to-work laws outlaw all union security provisions in collective bargaining agreements. Such provisions can include new workers being able to join the union after a certain time period and employers deducting union dues from workers' wages. The laws also force unions to represent all employees, whether or not they pay dues. Such laws have a negative effect on union-organizing drives: if a worker does not have to join a union and pay dues yet still receives the same rewards as a unionized worker, then what incentive is there to join? The right-to-work laws not only adversely affect unions, they are also damaging to workers. The average salary in right-to-work states is $5,333 lower per annum than in other states, and the workplace death rate is 51 percent higher.[19]

Another provision of the Taft-Hartley Act banned sympathy strikes and secondary boycotts, two tactics that were very successful for unions.[20] This was obviously a major problem for unions. Indeed, the general strikes of the 1930s and 1940s that were so successful would have been illegal under such laws.

Moreover, the act had a range of anti-Communist provisions, such as all unionists having to sign affidavits that they were not Communists. However, unions such as the UAW and the United Mine Workers already had anti-Communist provisions in their constitutions.[21] The act led to a purging of left-wing union members and a major negative effect on unionism, as the Left-led unions were the most successful CIO unions. Judith Stepan-Norris and Maurice Zeitlin conclusively demonstrate that the collective bargaining agreements negotiated by Communist-led unions were more pro-labor than agreements by center and right-wing unions.[22] The left-wing unions may have been able to stave off the attacks if other unions had given them aid. However, the growing anti-Communist hysteria not only affected the general public, it was prevalent within the union movement.

> The CIO was revving up to expel the Communists in its midst. The process took a few years, for the organization's president, Philip Murray, was initially loath to split the movement. He reached the decision to oust the leftwing unions only when he felt that their opposition to the Truman administration, as evidenced by their support for the third-party candidacy of Henry Wallace in 1948, conflicted with the CIO's growing dependence on and support for the Democratic Party. The CIO's 1949 convention voted to expel the most important left-led union, the United Electrical, Radio, and Machine Workers of America...and to bring charges of communism against ten others.[23]

Of course, that was not the end of it. The left-wing unions were attacked by all and sundry, from enemies and former friends.

> A single union, like the International Union of Mine, Mill, and Smelter Workers, was not only expelled from the CIO, but was also targeted for decertification by the NLRB on the grounds that Maurice Travis, its secretary-treasurer, had falsified his Taft-Hartley affidavit. Those same charges were repeated before the Subversive Activities Control Board a few years later when the attorney general sought to register the union as a "Communist-infiltrated" organization. Travis himself had to endure several perjury prosecutions, including a conspiracy charge that involved about a dozen other Mine-Mill officials. And, of course, Travis and his colleagues were subpoenaed by congressional investigators. In 1952 they were questioned by the McCarran Committee, as the Senate Internal Security Subcommittee was called.[24]

The example of the UE during this period shows that a left-wing union was powerless to prevent the onslaught. The UE sustained a massive anti-Communist attack by the government. In addition to the anti-Communist clause in the Taft-Hartley Act, the Atomic Energy Commission ordered all companies not to "recognize unions that were labeled as security risks; the UE thereby lost its bargaining rights at the Knolls Atomic Power Laboratory in Schenectady, New York." The US government scheduled House Committee on Un-American Activities sessions at the same time that union representation elections were planned. It forced UE leaders and members to testify about their alleged Communist Party links, while local newspapers reported on the "Red UE."[25]

The UE did not accept the Red-baiting campaign without a fight. It argued that McCarthyism was Hitlerism, as it was "an attack on the freedom of religion, the freedom of belief, the freedom of speech... [and] the freedom of people to freely associate together." Moreover, at a government "executive session," Matles told McCarthy that "when you accuse me of spying, and when you accuse decent working people [in UE-organized plants] in Lynn and Schenectady of spying and sabotage, you are lying, Senator McCarthy. You are a liar."[26]

However, as the left-wing unions were no longer members of the CIO, other unions conducted raids on the expelled unions. Union raids badly hurt the UE: "Between the passage of Taft-Hartley in the summer of 1947 and the withdrawal of UE from the CIO in the fall of 1949, rival unions conducted more than 500 raids on UE locals." Among the unions that conducted raids were the UAW; the International Brotherhood of Electrical Workers; the International Brotherhood of Teamsters; the AFL Jewelry Workers; the Glass, Ceramic and Silica Union; and the AFL Carpenters. In an attempt to stop the raids, UE leaders decided to sign the anti-Communist affidavits as required by the Taft-Hartley Act. Nevertheless, because of the attacks by the government, the raids by rival unions, and its internal conflict due to the anti-Communist hysteria, the UE's membership declined rapidly. By 1954, it was only 164,000.[27] Out of the unions expelled from the CIO, only two survive: the UE and the International Longshore and Warehouse Union. It is hard to disagree with Rick Fantasia and Kim Voss, who argue that the Taft-Hartley Act had a major effect in both limiting the power of the union movement and leading to the rise of business unionism.[28]

1955 ONWARD: THE FOLLY OF BUSINESS UNIONISM

Following the merger of the AFL and the CIO in 1955, the stage was set for labor's eventual decline. After the CIO's expulsion of the Left-led unions, there was virtually no difference between the AFL and the CIO. Thus, there was very little reason for the two bodies not to merge. The president of the AFL, George Meany, who once claimed that he never led a strike or stood on a picket line, became the head of the AFL-CIO.[29] The merger led to the rise of business unionism. Business unionism is concerned only with narrowly defined bread-and-butter issues, such as union members' wages and working conditions. Robert Hoxie defines it as follows:

> Essentially trade-conscious rather than class-conscious... it expresses the viewpoints and interests of the workers in craft or industry rather than those of the working class as a whole. It aims chiefly at more, here

and now, for the organized workers of the craft or industry, in terms of mainly higher wages, shorter hours, and better working conditions, regardless for the most part of the welfare of the workers outside the particular organic group, and regardless in general of political and social considerations, except in so far as these bear directly upon its own economic ends.[30]

Meany endorsed this type of unionism. He claimed that the role of unions is to intervene where management decisions affect workers directly, but unions should not care about things that do not have any direct bearing on a union member.[31]

A dominant tendency of business unionism in the period after World War II was the servicing model of unionism. The servicing model concentrates on taking care of the existing membership as opposed to organizing new members. While taking care of the existing membership is a worthwhile endeavor, the effects were to "demobilize the members and turn the relationship between members and their unions into one analogous to that between lawyers or insurance companies and their clients."[32]

Business unionism was quite successful during and after World War II, especially during the golden years of American capitalism (1947–73) as workers' wages increased quite dramatically in a number of industries. Average hourly earnings for workers in meatpacking rose 114 percent between 1950 and 1965, those in steel 102 percent, in rubber tires by 96 percent, and in manufacturing 81 percent.[33]

However, not all workers were better off. The South was largely ignored, and women and African Americans were generally thrown on the "working scrapheap" following the end of World War II. The AFL-CIO did not get involved in the civil rights movements of the 1960s. While the left-wing unions and leaders of the Left fought for so-called minorities and were generally successful, women and African Americans suffered following the purge. This would soon be true for all organized labor.

All unions were under siege. Beginning in the 1950s, the NLRB, which was meant to protect worker rights, began to continually favor employers over unions in any dispute. Moreover, at the same time that union members' wages were increasing, union membership was declining. Yet, the AFL-CIO argued that organizing new members was not a priority. In 1972, Meany spoke candidly about the AFL-CIO's position on organizing new members: "Why should we worry about organizing groups of people who do not want to be organized?...Frankly, I used to worry about the membership, about the size of the membership. But quite a few years ago, I just stopped worrying about it, because to me it doesn't make any difference.... The organized fellow is the fellow that counts."[34]

In addition, advocates of business unionism believe that unions are in partnerships with companies and with the state to achieve competitiveness for business, with workers receiving higher wages as a flow-on effect.[35] Thus, business unionism accepts the status quo. However, by concentrating on the existing membership and bread-and-butter issues, and not organizing new members, business unionism could not deal with the attack on the social contract by employers and the government beginning in the late 1970s following the ascendancy of neoliberal ideology. The social contract was

> characterized by management's willingness to live with the labor movement where it was already organized and its continued resistance to and avoidance of unions outside labor's well-organized core sectors. Unions...accepted managerial prerogatives that conceded control over production, the labor process, and technology, as well as other strategic business decisions. They also accepted productivity bargaining....Both parties accepted (or tolerated) substantially greater government intrusion into what had been the private sphere of labor-management relations.[36]

At one stage, there was such a good relationship between employers and unions that they actively helped each other. For example, the UAW struck at GM in 1970. As the strike continued, the UAW's strike fund was steeply declining. GM agreed to loan the UAW the money the union needed to pay workers' health benefits. The loan only had to be repaid at the conclusion of the strike.[37] Following the attack on the social contract, there was a significant decline in workers' wages and conditions in real terms (see the following section).

1979– : THE MADNESS OF CONCESSION BARGAINING

In addition to business unionism, the late 1970s brought about one of organized labor's most idiotic strategies ever: concession bargaining. As Hurd argues: "The twin recessions of 1980 and 1981–82 triggered a shift in collective bargaining, ushering in a period of concessions by unions first to firms in economic trouble and then to other employers determined to take advantage of the situation in a reversal of traditional pattern bargaining. Once concessionary bargaining had taken hold, it proved difficult for unions to halt the trend especially given economic pressures which persisted beyond the recessions of the early 1980s."[38]

The 1979 negotiations between Chrysler and the UAW began the era of concession bargaining. Chrysler claimed that if it was to stave off bankruptcy, workers had to accept wage and benefit concessions amounting to $203 million per year for three years.[39] While the UAW accepted the concessions, the Canadian United Auto Workers (CUAW) was initially against them. However, following a brief strike in Canada, the CUAW reluctantly accepted the concessions because it did not want to break the uniformity of contracts between Chrysler's US and Canadian workers.[40] However, less than a month later, Chrysler demanded that the UAW renegotiate their contract in the hope of winning more concessions. The American government demanded these concessions because it made its $3.5 billion bailout of Chrysler conditional on workers accepting additional concessions. The UAW agreed to Chrysler's demand, which amounted to an additional $230 million over and above the original concessions, because it believed the concessions would prevent Chrysler from declaring bankruptcy.[41]

The CUAW, however, rejected Chrysler's demand for concessions. This stance put the CUAW at odds with Chrysler and the UAW. Doug Fraser, president of UAW at the time, issued an ultimatum. Fraser stated that the "Canadians would either accept the concessions, or else they would be denied coverage under future international Chrysler master-collective agreements which would leave the small Canadian Chrysler section (Chrysler had only 14,000 workers in Canada) to the mercy of the large corporation in 1982," when the current contract expired.[42] In an attempt to resist the concessions, the CUAW lobbied the Canadian government to make a loan to Chrysler (Chrysler asked for a loan during the initial round of bargaining) conditional on no additional concessions. The CUAW's position was enhanced when the ruling minority conservative government lost office after only being in power for less than a year. The CUAW spent a substantial amount of time and money in the subsequent election campaign. "It set up eighteen phone banks, through which forty-five thousand autoworkers were reached and twenty thousand NDP [New Democratic Party; a left-wing Canadian political party] supporters were identified." The election result saw the NDP gain four seats overall and the conservatives lose power to the Liberal Party, which campaigned on increased government involvement and "Canadianization" of the economy.[43] The Canadian government eventually reached a deal with Chrysler, after the government sought the CUAW's input in the negotiations. Chrysler received a $250 million (Canadian) loan on the following conditions:

1. "An agreement by Chrysler not to close any existing facilities without approval of the minister of industry."
2. "Corporate commitments to invest approximately $1 billion [Canadian] in Canada between 1980 and 1985."
3. "Job guarantees."[44]

Thus, while the US government tried to force UAW workers to accept concessions, the Canadian government forced Chrysler to protect workers' jobs, to further invest in Canada, and to have no additional concessions.

The 1979 negotiations marked a turning point in relations between the UAW and the CUAW. Chrysler and the US government pressured the UAW to accept concessions, but the UAW did not attempt to fight and almost automatically accepted the concessions. Moreover, as Lichtenstein argues,

> The Chrysler bailout...had a twofold consequence: the concessionary bargaining in what had once been a flagship firm of American industry offered a powerful model that quickly spread to other firms, where blue-collar wages fell; of equal importance, the fragmentation of the collective-bargaining process implicit in the bailout gave to many union-management relationships a quality not far different from that of Japanese enterprise unionism, in which workers are given powerful incentives to identify their economic well-being with the fate of their own firm and its management.[45]

The differences between the contracts also highlight that a strong union willing to stand up for its members (even if it has only a relatively small number of members) can be successful even in dire economic conditions. Moreover, a government often has a say on whether a union will be successful in its fight. I return to these points in later chapters.

Today, in almost every industry imaginable, employers demand that unions engage in concession bargaining: "From the makers of agricultural implements, aluminum, automobiles, buildings, glass, newspapers, oil, processed meats, rubber, steel, to airlines, mine owners, supermarket chains, trucking companies, to local and regional governments and school districts, came demands for wage cuts, wage and pension freezes, reduction or elimination of automatic cost-of-living adjustments, and the establishment of permanently lower pay scales for newly hired workers."[46] Employers demand concessions irrespective of the company making or losing money; they just want increased profits (although they have no hesitation in paying management multimillion dollar bonuses).

Another factor that contributed to labor's decline was then-president Ronald Reagan's decision to load the NLRB with lawyers who were openly hostile to unions, further demonstrating the power of governments to hinder unions. The NLRB not only disregarded the law in making rulings against unions, but it also reinterpreted the law in favor of employers.[47] Furthermore, Reagan performed the one decisive act that put organized labor on its knees. In 1981 the Professional Air Traffic Controllers Organization (PATCO) engaged in a national strike. There was very little support from other unions and workers, as the strikers were viewed as the non-working class. As the strike was causing national turmoil, Reagan proceeded to fire all the striking workers and replace them with scabs. He then decertified PATCO as the legal bargaining agent of air traffic controllers. Despite promises made, organized labor did not come to the defense of the PATCO workers. It was a very sad day, and it was the beginning of open warfare on unions. The union movement has never recovered from Reagan's act.

GLOBALIZATION

The final factor that led to labor's decline was the rise of neoliberal globalization. There is debate whether globalization is an old or new phenomenon, but neoliberalism, which is the ideology behind the current version of globalization, is a revival of laissez-faire liberalism. Proponents of neoliberalism argue that removing government interference from almost all aspects of managing the economy and allowing the market to perform its "natural" role results in economic prosperity for a country and its citizens. Thus, governments should privatize all public enterprises, slay the inflation dragon, and liberalize trade and finance. An important neoliberal policy is monetarism. The basis of monetarist policy is that controlling inflation is the number one goal. Neoliberalism has become such a dominant ideology that political parties across the spectrum have adopted neoliberal reforms in both developed and developing countries.[48]

Many northern governments argue that they are powerless to stop the forces of globalization and consequently have to adopt neoliberal deflationary and fiscally conservative policies to please the global economic players. However, in the realm of trade and the financial markets, governments have contributed to the globalization process.

From the 1960s, the American government recognized that its dominant global financial position would entice foreigners to finance the ever-expanding US current account and fiscal deficits.[49] In the 1980s, the Reagan administration viewed the global financial markets as being able to play a major role in financing the deficits that reemerged in 1982. The US Treasury fought for the decision to abolish the US withholding tax on foreign holdings of US bonds, as this made US financial assets a greater investment to overseas investors. While successfully encouraging Japanese financial liberalization, this also allowed Japanese investors to become the major foreign funding contributor of US fiscal and current account deficits in the 1980s.[50] In addition, the neoliberal beliefs of the new Thatcher government directly influenced Britain's 1979 decision to abandon its exchange controls. Likewise, neoliberal thinking Treasurers Paul Keating and Roger Douglas strongly influenced Australia and New Zealand's decisions to abolish their respective capital controls.[51]

In relation to financial markets, the US decision to abandon various capital controls in 1974 had the resultant effect of internationally enhancing the attractiveness of New York as a financial capital market. Moreover, Britain's decision to eliminate its capital controls in 1979 was partly due to an attempt by the British to retain London's competitiveness compared to New York. This pattern continued throughout the 1980s. For example, the US decision to abolish the withholding tax on foreign holdings of US securities in 1984 led to West Germany implementing the same policy, which was its first major deregulatory move in the 1980s.[52] In other words, northern governments facilitated the globalization process.

Neoliberal globalization had a massive effect on organized labor; combined with an increasing range of imports available in the American marketplace, trade liberalization was promoted by all US administrations from Reagan onward.[53] As a result, cheaper imports began to flood the American market, which had a negative effect on American-made goods (and as a result, US jobs), as well as production plants moving overseas and the outsourcing of US jobs. In the following chapter I will analyze the effect that neoliberal globalization has had on labor and look at international strategies unions should embrace.

What does all this mean for an average worker? Following the attack on the social contract and the rise of neoliberal globalization, there was a significant decline in workers' wages and conditions in real terms. Between 1980 and 1996, the total share of income of the bottom 60 percent of Americans fell from 34.2 percent to 30 percent. This represents a transfer of approximately $160 billion from the poorest 60 percent to the richest 5 percent. The working class has suffered a dramatic decline in wages. The average weekly earnings of the 80 percent of workers, adjusted for inflation, decreased from $315 a week to $258 per week. Moreover, an increasing number of workers have two or more jobs. In 1999, 5.9 percent of the workforce had two or more jobs, which were often low paying. In addition to declining workers' wages, there has been a dramatic decline in union membership. Unions represented only 12 percent of the workforce in 2006 compared to 26 percent in 1973.[54]

THE FUTURE

Taking these figures into consideration, one must seriously ask whether there is a future for organized labor. For most people the answer would be no. However, this would be the worst thing to happen to ordinary Americans. Nevertheless, this is the path that labor will remain on if it does not make major changes in the near future. In the following chapters I will analyze strategies for labor's revitalization. Some of the strategies will help unions, some will have a minor effect, and some will hasten labor's decline. At any rate, changes have to be made, as a strategy of doing more of the same will see labor and ordinary Americans' downward path continue.

3

STRATEGIES TO STOP THE DECLINE

The decline in unionism and the plight of ordinary Americans have led both academics and individuals within the labor movement trying to devise strategies for unions to regain their former strength. It is important to note that activists since the 1960s have been devising ways to prevent the declining union density. In contrast, until the election of John Sweeney as president in 1995, the AFL-CIO either ignored or paid lip service to the decline in union strength. Value-added unionism, union democracy, labor-community alliances and alliances with social movements, organizing the unorganized, and labor internationalism have been suggested as ways unions can regain strength.

VALUE-ADDED UNIONISM

Value-added unionism can be considered an updated version of business unionism. Advocates of value-added unionism argue that an adversarial relationship between labor and business does not benefit either party. Instead, labor and business should work together. The Economic Policy Council states that a "'them and us' system of workplace relations [is] simply inadequate in today's social and economic environment. Finding the common interests of employees and employers, of unions and managers, and developing a process for overcoming the division between workers and managers...[is] the critical challenge that labor and capital must address in the decade ahead."[1] The main difference between value-added unionism and business unionism is that a value-added union works more closely with management and has a greater say in decision making than a business union does. Advocates of value-added unionism claim that it is pointless for unions to have a hostile relationship with business. Rather, unions should work with management to help businesses achieve their goals.[2] Value-added unionism is an "ongoing formal process where workers and their immediate supervisors or union and management leaders bear *joint* responsibility for making decisions. The scope of decision making may be narrow (i.e., it may involve a single issue), or it may be broader, covering a whole range of issues. In addition, there may or may not be formal procedures for resolving disputes that arise in the joint decision-making process."[3] The purpose of joint decision making is for the union to add value to the company and to the economy. In this way, the union gains "legitimacy" in the eyes of business and the government. As labor academic Bruce Nissen notes: "By creating greater efficiency or quality or responsiveness (a public and private good) and higher profits (a private good for employers), unions add legitimacy unavailable under their traditional goals."[4] Examples of value-added unionism include the relationship among Harley-Davidson, the International Association of Machinists, and the Paperworkers, Allied and Chemical Employees; between Shell (Sarina Plant) and the Energy and Chemical Workers' Union; between Xerox Corporation and the Union of Needletrades, Industrial and Textile Employees; and arguably the highest-profile American example of value-added unionism, the relationship between Saturn and the UAW.[5]

Saturn, which is a division of GM, and the UAW entered into a partnership in 1983 where the UAW has a voice in design and manufacturing operations. Saturn's production facility at Spring Hill, Tennessee, produces small cars for the American market. As Nissen states,

> Similar to other unionized large work sites with "high performance" practices, Saturn features self-directed work teams, off-line problem solving teams, labor-management committees, and the like. But all levels of staff and line management are filled with dual union and management personnel, making Saturn a co-management partnership example unlike any other. Four hundred union members (jointly selected by union and company) do managerial duties and 700 additional elected team leaders boost the total engaged in running the operation to almost 20 percent of the membership.[6]

Moreover, wages and job security were different from other GM-UAW contracts. Saturn employees' base wages were only 88–95 percent of those of other GM employees. But by achieving mutually negotiated goals, Saturn employees often earned more through bonuses than other GM workers did. However, such things as seniority rights and the right to transfer to a new plant if Saturn closes are not included in the Saturn-UAW contract. Thus, Saturn employees have to rely on the company's survival for them to retain their jobs within the GM network.[7]

Saturn was an almost instant success story, with high customer satisfaction, quality, and productivity. Indeed, the goal of Saturn is to achieve productivity and quality levels higher than those at other GM-UAW production plants. Beginning in 1997, however, productivity declined in absolute levels and in comparison with other GM plants. Following the defeat of the original Local union leadership in 1999, the Saturn-UAW contract incorporated more features of other GM-UAW contracts, as some aspects of the contract were modified.[8]

The benefit of value-added unionism is that unions can organize workers where they otherwise might not have been able to do so if they did not have cooperation from business. Value-added unionism has to rely on employers agreeing to partnerships and to union representation for their employees.

In other words, value-added unions attempt to organize employers and not employees. This is an unviable strategy to organize the unorganized, and with union density dropping at alarming rates, this is the biggest challenge facing unions. It is unlikely that value-added unionism will succeed, because employers in America (and mostly around the world) are generally hostile to unions, whether they add value or not. Indeed, when President Bill Clinton's Dunlop Commission suggested such a strategy, business was not in favor of it.[9] As noted labor historian David Brody argues:

> The labor movement will not prevail by trying to persuade nonunion employers. It is their employees that have to be persuaded, and if and when that time comes, what will persuade them will be the only kind of appeal that has worked with American workers since the days of Samuel Gompers: namely, the identification of the union with their demand for industrial justice. The source of that appeal is the abiding job-consciousness of American trade unionism.[10]

Whether business unionism or value-added unionism, any type of unionism that has to rely on the willing cooperation of business in this era of neoliberal globalization, where both business and governments are openly hostile to unions, is bound to fail.

THE ROLE OF THE RANK AND FILE

Advocates of union democracy, labor-community alliances, organizing the unorganized, and labor internationalism see labor not as an ally of business, but in the main, hostile to it. They argue that if unions undertake one of these strategies, this will contribute to their revitalization. It is important to note that while these efforts are an attempt to strengthen and support the labor movement, they are not consciously tied together or part of a larger program. Moreover, while some union leaders now argue that unions adopt these strategies, activists have been pushing unions to implement these strategies for a number of years.

A strategy touted to revive organized labor is the belief that democratic unions with extensive rank-and-file involvement will lead to more militant and successful unions. A study noted that where the rank and file were the organizers, unions were successful in 73 percent of NLRB representation elections, compared to only 27 percent when professional organizers took charge. With an active rank and file, the leaders of the union movement in the future would be able to say, "We are the leaders we've been looking for."[11]

The notion that union democracy and rank-and-file participation lead to unions becoming militant is supported by C. Wright Mills. He states that for the "union to become an instrument of social transformation ... [its members must] think of it as their creature; they must want to know all about it and want to run it in as much detail as possible." Through rank-and-file participation, there is a transformation of the union into a political community that does not necessarily readily agree with the accepted order.[12]

In their analysis of CIO unions, Stepan-Norris and Zeitlin conclude that union democracy leads to unions being more militant. They state that a "union with a democratic constitution, organized opposition, and an active membership tends to constitute the workers' immediate political community, sustaining both a sense of identification between them and their leaders and class solidarity; as a result, the union also tends to defy the hegemony of capital in the sphere of production."[13]

Militant left-wing North American unions throughout history have more often than not been very democratic with extensive rank-and-file involvement. Whether the UE, the Longshoremen, the Knights of Labor, or the Industrial Workers of the World, they all had one common characteristic: union democracy combined with rank-and-file participation.[14] A recent example is the Canadian Auto Workers (CAW). While not as militant as the unions just cited, the CAW is much more democratic and confrontational than the UAW (see chapter 5). Likewise, in a study of an International Longshoremen's and Warehousemen's Local, David Wellman argues:

> The experience of community teaches San Francisco longshoremen to be moral, not just economic actors. The principled behavior called for by their ethical code applies to all workers, not just brothers on the docks. The "us" that this community practices, which is reinforced by the daily fights with employers, is sometimes extended beyond the waterfront to workers in other industries and nations....
>
> Disagreements with management also extend considerably beyond job issues to questions of personhood, citizenship, and authority. The process of defensible disobedience teaches longshoremen how to argue with their employers, how to act when they think they are right and have been wronged. They are taught not to accept an order simply because it is issued by powerful people. They learn to ask the powerful, by what right is an order issued?[15]

In other words, union democracy and rank-and-file participation result in workers' questioning the existing order and becoming more militant and therefore a powerful tool to revitalize the union movement.

It is important not to underestimate the contribution of professional organizers. For example, the Union of Needletrades, Industrial, and Textile Employees (UNITE) is successful in organizing drives using *both* rank-and-file and professional organizers. Eve S. Weinbaum and Gordon Lafer note that

> UNITE succeeded through a range of tactics and strategies. Approximately 70 percent of its southern staff are ex-rank-and-file members, while 30 percent come from other backgrounds. While the union is known for its efforts to involve rank-and-file members in organizing drives, it is also known as the union that perfected the "blitz," in which a large group of organizers (in UNITE's case, a mixture of rank and filers and outside staff) kick off the campaign with intensive house visits to sign up a majority of workers.[16]

Moreover, they argue that their case studies of UNITE, the Longshoremen, and the Hotel Employees and Restaurant Employees International Union (HERE) "show the false dichotomy between bottom-up and top-down organizing models. It is often hard to tell if an organizer—or a union staff person—is an insider or outsider. Someone who is rank and file in one workplace can be a carpetbagger in another environment."[17]

Weinbaum and Lafer's main argument is that the crucial role for organizers was to empower local activists. They state that their case studies "all demonstrate that, no matter who the organizers are, their ultimate goal should be to equip local activists to become strong leaders themselves. Strategically, it is almost impossible to defeat an antiunion initiative unless the workers have a high degree of internal organization. And in the long run, the goal of organizing is to transform power relations, to empower workers over their own working conditions."[18] In other words, professional organizers, as well as the rank and file, have a crucial role in organizing drives.

Likewise, it is wrong to assume that the so-called union bureaucracy cannot greatly contribute to the positive transformation of unions. Kim Voss and Rachel Sherman analyzed what led to the progressive revitalization of particular Locals within the SEIU, HERE, and the United Food and Commercial Workers (UFCW). They concluded that "three factors in conjunction distinguish the fully revitalized locals from the others:...the experience of an internal political crisis, which facilitated the entrance of new leaders into the local, either through International Union intervention or local elections; the presence in the local staff with social movement experience outside the labor movement; and support from the International Union."[19] They go on to argue:

> International union leadership was crucial in leading to full revitalization. The International initiated or supported much of the change in local unions; this process was not one of "bottom-up."...[P]rogressive sectors of the International exerted varying degrees of influence over locals in crisis, which led to full revitalization. Furthermore, IU [International Union] influence helps explains the differences among the partially revitalized locals; those that have made more changes...acknowledge significance influence by the IU.[20]

Voss and Sherman's research shows that the transformation of unions is not necessarily just a "bottom-up" process; the top union leadership can greatly contribute to revitalizing unions.

Moreover, these examples of the International Union leadership helping to revitalize Locals in a leftist direction indicate that it is not necessarily the case that the rank and file are more militant than the union leadership (either at the Local or International level). John Kelly supports this position. In an analysis of British unions, he came to the following conclusion: "There is no convincing evidence that union officials, on the whole, are more 'conservative' than their memberships....Clearly there are 'conservative' officials and militant workers, but there are also militant officials and conservative workers, and the precise balance between these groups is likely to vary with circumstances."[21] One can easily point to unions such as the International Brotherhood of Teamsters and the UAW in certain periods of their existence to illustrate that the rank and file are more militant than the union leadership. However, the opposite is also true. Union leaders of the UE and the Longshoremen have often been as militant, if not more so, than the rank and file. Admittedly, these unions were/are known as Communist-led unions, especially during the 1930s and 1940s. This is because of their militant policies and alleged ties to the Communist Party. Nevertheless, they demonstrate that union leaders can be militant. Likewise, there are numerous examples of British union leaders being more militant than the rank and file.[22]

Indeed, the UE is a classic example of a union with militant leadership. Throughout its history, the UE leadership has been ready for a fight with business. A UE Local leader summed up the UE's position as follows: General Electric has "been trying to tell...[the workers]...there are three separate groups in GE: the company, the employees, and the union. That's what they've based themselves on. We have to show them they're wrong. The UE represents the workers. The workers are the union. We have to show them there are not three groups but just two: the company and the union. Them and Us."[23]

Thus, it is wrong to ignore the role played by union officials in organizing campaigns and in revitalizing unions. As Ruth Milkman argues: "Given the hostile environment that unions face...[i]t matters little whether the top-down or bottom-up component of the organizing effort is deployed first...so long as both eventually emerge and are coordinated and sustained over the course of the campaign."[24] While the rank and file do have a crucial role in revitalizing unions, it is important not to underestimate the role played by professional organizers and the union bureaucracy. By doing so, you are painting only half a picture.

IRON LAW?

A potentially damaging problem for those who advocate union democracy and rank-and-file involvement to revive organized labor is the iron law of oligarchy. Robert Michels famously argued that there is an iron law that prevents organizations such as unions from being truly democratic. There are two components to this. First, even if unions have democratic practices, they develop an oligarchical leadership. This is because the rank and file accept leaders' right to office; leaders gain experience and knowledge in their position and therefore are difficult to replace; and leaders become tied to their position. Thus, leaders formulate policies and impose them on the union, irrespective of the workers' wishes. In relation to workers' demands for a wage increase and whether to strike, leaders "claim the right to decide the merits of the question on the sole ground that they know better than the workers themselves the conditions of the labor market throughout the country and are consequently more competent to judge the chances of success in the struggle."[25]

The second aspect of the iron law of oligarchy is that there is a transformation of union policies and practices in a conservative direction. Michels stated that workers become "petty bourgeois." In addition, and more importantly, he claimed that the union leader,

> inspired with a foolish self-satisfaction...is apt to take pleasure in his new environment, and he tends to become indifferent and even hostile

to all progressive aspirations in the democratic sense. He accommodates himself to the existing order, and ultimately, weary of struggle, becomes even reconciled to that order. What interest for them has now the dogma of social revolution? Their own social revolution has already been effected. At the bottom, all the thoughts of these leaders are concentrated upon the single hope that there shall long continue to exist a proletariat to choose them as its delegates and to provide them with a livelihood.[26]

If Michels is to be believed, even if the rank and file manage to defeat the incumbent conservative union leaders (which is difficult in itself), eventually they will become conservative officials themselves. Thus, the belief that the rank and file will transform unions can be called into question if there is an iron law of oligarchy.

Not surprisingly, advocates of union democracy reject the thesis of the iron law of oligarchy. Kim Moody argues that the "rise of democratic unions in the more industrial countries of the South and the partial reversal of bureaucratization in the US Mine Workers in the 1970s, the Teamsters in the 1990s, and, to a lesser extent, other unions in the US brings Michels' 'Iron Law of Oligarchy' into question."[27] Moody is correct to criticize the so-called iron law. In relation to unions developing an oligarchical leadership, Alvin W. Gouldner argues:

> When . . . Michels spoke of the "iron law of oligarchy," he attended solely to the ways in which organizational needs inhibit democratic possibilities. But the very same evidence to which he called attention could enable us to formulate the very opposite theorem—"the iron law of democracy." Even as Michels himself saw, if oligarchical waves repeatedly wash away bridges of democracy, this eternal recurrence can happen only because men doggedly rebuild them after each inundation. Michels chose to dwell on only one aspect of this process, neglecting to consider this other side. There cannot be an iron law of oligarchy, however, unless there is an iron law of democracy.[28]

The continual reform efforts by rank-and-file groups within the International Brotherhood of Teamsters, most recently by Teamsters for a Democratic Union, support Gouldner's findings. Despite a seemingly never-ending number of setbacks, union reform caucuses within the Teamsters continually strive for union democracy and transforming the union into a militant organization. While achieving only partial success at best in relation to the latter, the Teamsters for a Democratic Union greatly contributed to union democracy and militancy in collective bargaining within the Teamsters in the 1990s.

However, even if the rank and file are successful in their attempt to gain office by ousting the conservative union leaders, they will become like the old officials under the second aspect of the iron law of oligarchy. Nevertheless, in a comprehensive study of CIO unions, Stepan-Norris and Zeitlin clearly show that oligarchy is not the only path; another path is democracy.

> Which path a union takes is determined not by any "iron law," but by specific, relatively contingent, political struggles among workers' parties and factions over the aims, methods, and uses of union power, and by

both the resultant pattern of the unions' internal political relations and the political consciousness, radical or conservative, of their leadership. Where these struggles are waged through insurgent political practices, resulting in durable internal bases for opposition factions and allowing radicals to put down deep roots and win and hold their leadership, the union tends, consequently, to be democratic. But where the opposite political constellation prevails, they tend to be oligarchic.[29]

In addition, there are numerous examples of even bureaucratic oligarchical unions being partially or fully transformed into a "radical direction."[30] In other words, there is considerable doubt over the iron law of oligarchy. While oligarchic practices may emerge within a union, it is equally possible that a union will be democratic and militant. Thus, union democracy and active rank-and-file involvement in the union can help in labor's revival.

LABOR-COMMUNITY ALLIANCES

One of the most popular strategies to rejuvenate unions is labor-community alliances. In the past, there was often a link between unions and the local community. However, in recent years this link has been largely broken in many communities. In 1935,

> workers lived in close proximity to one another, and most of them worked close by.... Turn the clock ahead to 1995. There is a glass factory near Meadville, Pennsylvania, and some of the employees there want a union. The plant is located in an isolated area, and the company plans to hire people from a widespread area. When the shift ends, workers scatter in their vans and trucks to their rural and suburban homes. There is no sense of community.[31]

While labor-community alliances used to happen naturally, unions now have to specifically attempt to form alliances with the local community and community groups. These alliances are in part advanced by solidarity, social justice, and the fight against oppression.[32]

In relation to unions regaining strength, there are four main ways that community alliances can benefit unions. First, community groups can assist union-organizing drives. Community groups can reassure workers "who often feel isolated and powerless—that the community stands behind them... [and] also help by using their influence to insist that employers respect the free choice [of workers] to form a union."[33] Second, community groups can aid unions in gaining a first contract. This is done by threatening to boycott the companies' products and using the groups' influence more generally to force a company to agree to a first contract. Third, unions can benefit from community alliances during collective bargaining, especially if workers are on strike. By having alliances with community groups, unions generally benefit through more positive media coverage as well as the government looking more favorably on the strike.[34] Fourth, community alliances can help prevent plant closures. They can do this by pledging to boycott the companies' products, by appealing to their local politicians, and by using their influence more generally.

Indeed, union alliances with social movements and community groups have greatly benefited the labor movement worldwide. In Brazil, these alliances have strengthened unions. Community groups had a large role in the success of the Metalworkers Union in São Bernando do Campo. They helped striking workers by providing donations and refusing to become scabs. This support prevented the Brazilian government from removing the Metalworkers Union leaders during a strike in 1980, with religious groups allowing meetings to occur in churches.[35] A major factor in Brazilian unions incorporating nonclass issues (issues that do not affect working people) was the increasing number of women joining unions in the 1970s. Between 1970 and 1978 over two times as many women joined unions compared to male workers. Corresponding to the increase in female union membership was an increase in women joining social movements. Gay Seidman notes:

> Women participated actively in the movement for amnesty for political exiles and in the small, but visible, feminist movement; women from pri-marily working-class backgrounds led the Cost of Living Movement, as well as local campaigns for daycare centers and health clinics. Perhaps for the first time in Brazilian history, working-class women entered into public debate and successfully mobilized community support, as visible leaders in Christian based communities, in Catholic Mother's Clubs, and in campaigns for improved social services.[36]

The increasing number of women joining unions and social movements in Brazil accompanied the rise of progressive unionism as unions began adopt-ing nontraditional demands as part of their agenda, which benefited everyone in the community.

In South Africa, the rise of radical unionism also coincided with the in-creasing number of social movements. As Philip Hirschsohn states, social movements "thrive during periods of social and political instability, when the political system is seen as having lost its legitimacy, and the status quo is vulnerable to outsiders demanding inclusion in the polity."[37] By the 1980s, social movements engaged in widespread protest against the state in a bid to end apartheid. The formation of the United Democratic Front clearly illus-trates the huge number of social movements: "Over 600 grassroots SMs [social movements] and organizations, united more by their opposition to Apartheid and the state's reform agenda than by an adherence to a particular ideology, formed a broad alliance to coordinate mobilization."[38]

Stayaways (a mass general strike) illustrate the benefits unions receive from alliances with social movements. The November 1984 stayaway in South Africa saw approximately 800,000 workers and 400,000 students not attending work and school, respectively. This stayaway led to the strengthening of alli-ances among unions, students, and community groups and to unions forsak-ing their previous strategy of not getting involved in community struggles. The South African Labor Monitoring Group's analysis of the stayaway notes that the stayaways were most effective where unions and community-student organizations combined their efforts.[39] Thus, alliances with social movements and community groups strengthened unions and led to unions adopting non-traditional demands. This further contributed to the rise of progressive unionism in Brazil and South Africa.

One could argue that the examples from Brazil and South Africa are not relevant to America. However, there was a similar situation in the United States. There was a link between the dramatic increase in public sector union membership after World War II and the rise of new social movements.

President John F. Kennedy's celebrated Executive Order 10988, granting bargaining rights to federal employees, did contribute to the rise of public sector unionism. However, it is only a partial explanation. It ignores the fact that many governments did not want to implement such a policy. It was the resolve of union organizers, who were inspired by the civil rights movement, that led to many state and local governments enacting similar legislation. As Stanley Aronowitz argues:

> The brilliant move of many who led the organizing drives was to link traditional union appeals to public issues, especially civil rights and the feminist movement. In the post offices and many state municipal agencies, blacks and Latinos invoked the iconography of these movements—Martin Luther King was the patron saint of the New York Hospital Workers and, more fatefully, of the Memphis Sanitation Workers—integrated minority and women's issues into bargaining, and encouraged members to participate in peace, feminist, and civil rights demonstrations.[40]

Likewise, Voss and Sherman, in a study that analyzed factors that revitalized American unions, argue that union organizers and leaders who were social movement activists had a large role in transforming unions. As a union organizer stated about what differentiates progressive unions from business unions:

> I would say a big part of it is a lot of activists from the '60s....Similar to [former CIO President] John Lewis saying "let's bring in the Communists 'cause they know how to organize."...I think SEIU realized that let's bring in these activists who were involved in the civil rights movement, the anti-war movement...some sort of political organization, some sort of socialist organization, even, who are actively committed to building the union movement, and have some new ideas about how to do that, and will use the strategies developed in the civil rights movement, and the welfare rights organizations, the women's rights movements, all these different organizations, and get them plugged in and involved....And where unions have done that, there's been more militancy.[41]

Likewise, a study of union leaders in California further determined the importance of social movement activists in unions. It found that 54 percent of future union leaders joined a union with the express goal of engaging in social transformation, while a further 16 percent joined to improve their local communities. The majority of social reformers did not directly move into the labor movement, but first became involved in other social movements.[42]

A recent example of unions adopting nonclass issues to help all concerned is the Stamford Organizing Project. The project is a multiunion drive that not only cares about bread-and-butter issues, but also fights for adequate housing for the local community. Stamford, Connecticut is an affluent suburb that is the third most expensive place in the country for housing costs. While there is public housing, the Stamford Housing Authority decided by the mid-1990s "not to build more affordable housing, but rather to 'rehabilitate' existing units: remove the tenants and improve the buildings, then privatize, rent at market rates, or convert housing to 'moderate-income' units." This would have resulted in rents dramatically increasing.[43] For low-income workers, it was increasingly difficult to find affordable accommodations.

The four unions involved in the Stamford Organizing Project (HERE, the New England Health Care Employees Union District 1199, the SEIU, and the UAW), while not always successful in the fight to keep affordable housing, have become valued members of the community. This has helped them in their organizing drives. Janice Fine argues:

> Because unions have acted boldly to block the demolition of housing, they are seen as advocates for the poor and the working class, and have built a good name for themselves among those they seek to organize. In a field where the work force is tightly segregated by immigrant group and where people live in tightly condensed areas, word about the union travels fast. Indeed, organizers have found that residents they encountered during the housing fight are also working at facilities they are organizing.[44]

Likewise, the reputation the UAW gained in the fight for affordable housing helped in its campaign to organize childcare workers. A UAW official notes:

> We go in and talk to a group of workers in the child care center for example, who are mostly African American and poor and live in the projects, and they know who we are....They've heard their pastors talk about the union and unionization for months, and they've seen the fights, very public fights, that union members have waged around public housing, and it's all fresh, they've seen it happen. So that's been a slam dunk.[45]

The Stamford Organizing Project demonstrates the benefits to unions in adopting nonclass issues and forming alliances with social movements and community groups. Not only are the unions involved in attempting to keep affordable housing for all, but also the fight improves their standing in the community, which can then result in a greater chance of success in organizing drives and during collective bargaining.[46] In addition, the campaign managed to win union recognition for 4,700 workers, which led to increased wages, benefits, and better working conditions. The Stamford Organizing Project was a victory for all concerned.

Likewise, the UE has a long history of benefiting from alliances with community groups. For example, in St. Louis during the 1930s and 1940s, UE Local president William Sentner claimed that while the UE was interested in the livelihood of its members, it was also interested in the economic well-being of the local community.[47] In other words, where workers received higher wages, it was likely that the local community would be vibrant. The UE Local's belief in the benefit of labor-community alliances helped in a campaign to prevent the Emerson Electrical Company from moving its production plant out of St. Louis in late 1939/early 1940. The *St. Louis Star-Times* claimed that the UE "deserves a full measure of credit for its civic spirit and initiative in starting a campaign to keep Emerson...from leaving St. Louis....Its attitude, as shown in its literature, is intelligent, sympathetic and constructive."[48]

The UE's campaign was eventually successful, but at the cost of agreeing to cooperate with management. Nevertheless, the UE's campaign led it to become a respected organization in the community. This helped the Local during a five-month strike at Century Electric in 1940, which led to a good settlement. Likewise, during World War II, the Local hosted a convention involving UE members, business representatives, and prominent figures in St. Louis public life that debated the course industrial relations should take following the end of the war.[49]

In more recent times, the UE's campaign to keep Stewart-Warner's Chicago plant open in the 1980s, and the campaign for union recognition at Steeltech in the 1990s further highlight the benefits of such alliances. Nevertheless, they also demonstrate that despite the best efforts of unions and community groups, sometimes this is not enough.

The International Brotherhood of Electrical Workers was the certified bargaining agent at the Stewart-Warner Chicago plant. However, following worker dissatisfaction with the union, the UE eventually gained certification at the plant in 1980. In 1985, following financial difficulties at Stewart-Warner, the UE formed the Coalition to Keep Stewart-Warner Open (CKSWO). Among its members were the UE, labor activists, aldermen, religious groups, and academics from the University of Illinois at Chicago. In 1986, Stewart-Warner announced that it was to transfer 150 jobs to its Johnson City plant. But, as the UE demonstrated, this was just the tip of the iceberg, as 2,500 jobs were under threat. In 1987, Stewart-Warner merged with the British multinational British Thermoplastics and Rubber. Reverend Jesse Jackson urged all Chicago workers to help in the fight to keep Stewart-Warner in Chicago. He claimed that the reduction of US jobs was "just another form of economic violence that must be ended the same way we ended racial violence about 20 years ago."[50] Later that year, Stewart-Warner announced that in 1988 it would axe approximately a quarter of its Chicago workforce. In June 1989, the company revealed that its Chicago plant may close due to high operating costs.[51] Andrew Jonas notes that the "campaign to save Stewart-Warner was built around a well-organized community base and was linked to a wider political movement to transform economic policy in Chicago. In this respect, the CKSWO's concerns and goals fed into a broader program of action to protect inner-city neighborhoods from manufacturing displacements....Opportunities to link with political movements beyond the city limits also came up during the course of the struggle."[52] Moreover, in an attempt to keep the plant open, Stewart-Warner workers agreed to concessions that would have saved the company $2.5 million per year. Stewart-Warner's management rejected the offer as inadequate.[53] On November 4, 1989, Stewart-Warner announced that it was shutting its Chicago plant and would move its production plants to Mexico in two years. However, the Stewart-Warner Chicago plant remained open until mid-1995. During this time, the UE managed to achieve a contract without concessions, and wage raises for the few remaining employees.[54] But despite alliances with the local community and politicians, the UE was unable to keep Stewart-Warner's Chicago plant open.

Steeltech had a similar outcome. Steeltech Manufacturing commenced operation in Milwaukee in 1990 and received more than $15 million in public funding and loan guarantees. In November 1993, the UE announced that it wanted the NLRB to conduct a certification election at Steeltech. The UE narrowly lost the election in December. However, in June 1994, the NLRB ruled that because of election violations by Steeltech, another certification election would be held. In the second ballot, and following rank-and-file solidarity and community involvement, the UE was successful.[55] However, Steeltech did not recognize the union, as the company claimed that the UE forced workers to vote for it. The UE received community support in its fight to obtain recognition. Eight Milwaukee aldermen wrote a letter to Steeltech, which stated: "[we] urge management to enter into negotiations with the UE local....[B]ecause public funding is involved in Steeltech operations, including significant investment by the city of Milwaukee, we are concerned about these investments being used by Steeltech to stop its workers exercising their rights to unionize and negotiate a contract." Likewise, the mayor of Milwaukee wrote to Steeltech imploring the company to negotiate with the UE.[56] In the campaign for recognition, the UE utilized rank-and-file tactics: "Community participation was anchored in a broad range of organizations and groups. More significant than the array of organizations, however, was the fact that involvement took place as much through the direct participation of individuals as through the organizations themselves. Union members showed the extent to which they were 'in their communities' by speaking to friends, relatives, fellow church members, and allies about the Steeltech struggle."[57] In a great victory for all, in June 1995, Steeltech recognized the UE as the bargaining agent for its employees. Furthermore, there was hope that Steeltech would turn a profit. But in February 1996, Steeltech laid off workers because of a cash-flow crisis, and by February 1998, despite finally being profitable, Steeltech had a mountain of debt. Nevertheless, in June 1998, the UE Local negotiated a 4 percent wage raise effective July 1 and an additional 3 percent from January 1, 1999. After it held meetings with several politicians and company officials, the Local claimed that the short-term future of Steeltech was ensured. In 1999, however, Steeltech was on the verge of bankruptcy and had not paid its workers for two months. It was no surprise that the company declared bankruptcy later that year, with workers losing their entitlements.[58]

The UE's experiences at Stewart-Warner and Steeltech were not isolated events in the 1980s and 1990s. For example, in 1982 UE Local 610 defeated a concessionary contract and achieved contract gains following a 205-day strike at American Standard's Westinghouse Air Brake and Union Switch and Signal, in which the striking workers received strong community support. However, by 1985, and despite strong labor and community support, American Standard decided to shut the plant.[59]

Morse Cutting Tools witnessed a similar situation. The UE defeated a concessionary contract in 1982, but management decided to close the plant in May 1987. Two months later, and following a UE-community campaign, Morse Tools reopened amid much fanfare. But there was not to be a happy ending. Morse finally closed its operations for good a few years later.[60] Nevertheless, that the UE and community groups managed to reopen a closed plant and provide UE members with good wages for a few extra years was a substantial achievement.

The rise of social movements accompanied a dramatic increase in US public sector unionism. In addition, union organizers and leaders who were (or still are) members of social movements partly contributed to the revitalization of some American unions. Likewise, unions adopting nonclass issues have seen tangible benefits, as well as benefits to communities as a whole. It is possible that the current wave of antiglobalization movements and the increase in new social movements more generally will correspond with a revival of organized labor. However, labor-community alliances and alliances with social movements are not enough. The UE was unable to keep Stewart-Warner in Chicago, and eight months after recognizing the UE as the bargaining agent for its workers, Steeltech laid off part of its workforce, with the company declaring bankruptcy three years later. These events demonstrate that while these alliances are beneficial, sometimes they are not enough to stop the decline of organized labor.

ORGANIZING THE UNORGANIZED

Another strategy suggested by activists as well as union leaders for helping unions to regain their strength is for unions to organize the unorganized.[61] One of the most popular "new" organizing strategies is the organizing model of unionism. While not neglecting existing members, the organizing model allocates a substantial portion of union resources to organizing new members, with the rank and file having an active role. A crucial component of the organizing model is organizing the so-called minorities, such as women and immigrants, who have joined the workforce in increasing numbers. These groups are more likely than white males to join a union, and they can lead to the revitalization of unions.[62] Moreover, as labor activist Khalil Hassan argues: "The quintessential practice of the organizing approach was the *contract campaign,* an all-round activation of the members to participate in collective bargaining. As adopted by several unions, the contract campaign entailed the creation of contract action teams, coalition building, and member education.

The same technique could also be used to organize new members."[63] Indeed, the AFL-CIO would like all affiliated unions to spend 30 percent of their budget on organizing. Following his election as AFL-CIO president, John Sweeney made organizing new members his number one priority.

> A new Organizing Department was created with a $10 million annual budget.... The Organizing Institute's program was expanded with the goal of recruiting and training 1,000 new organizers within two years. Internships in organizing for 1,000 college students and young workers were established for the 1996 Union Summer. The AFL-CIO MasterCard agreement was renegotiated with much of the additional revenues earmarked for organizing. A $5 million organizing fund was established to assist innovative multi union organizing campaigns.[64]

The organizing model has led to an increasing number of workers joining unions than what otherwise would have been the case. Labor academics Kate Bronfenbrenner and Tom Juravich studied factors that contributed to unions' victories and defeats in NLRB certification election campaigns. They concluded that unions were more successful in organizing campaigns by using rank-and-file–intensive tactics.[65] Obviously any focus on organizing the unorganized is one that all unions should embrace. Unions that have adopted the organizing model, such as the SEIU and the Communication Workers of America, have been able to organize new members despite tough times. In other words, it is still possible to organize the unorganized (see chapter 4 for analysis of the organizing model).

LABOR INTERNATIONALISM

Another popular strategy for strengthening unions that scholars, activists, and unionists believe unions should embrace is labor internationalism.[66] The argument advanced by many is that if a business is located in just one geographic region, it is possible for unions to achieve their goals through just a national campaign. However, because of neoliberal globalization and the international nature of capital, there must be alliances between unions and workers worldwide.[67] Neoliberal globalization "simultaneously challenges the power of organized workers and offers the opportunity to transcend national concerns. Relatively secure labor in developed countries has been threatened by globalization as it has led to an undermining of the welfare state and intense competition from low wage producers. Globalization has been used as an ideology to justify economic retrenchment and the dismantling of social welfare provisions.... This has facilitated the forging of transnational coalitions and networks."[68]

In *Revolution and World Politics*, Fred Halliday argues that by their very nature, revolutions and uprisings are in some sense international. There are four reasons for this. First, revolutions appeal to general abstract principles such as equality and justice. For example, in relation to the battle against hostile employers and governments, labor movements argue against the increasing gap between the rich and the poor. Second, the "oppressors" or enemy is international. In relation to the labor movement's fight against capital, the enemies include the World Trade Organization (WTO), the International Monetary Fund, and transnational corporations. Third, all protest movements have a practical need to build alliances internationally. As Halliday argues, "In a situation of continuing domestic conflict, and with threat from abroad . . . revolutionary movements and regimes seek to strengthen their own position: they aim to weaken that of their enemies, by building international alliances, and, if possible, assisting such movements to come to power." Finally, the realm of revolutionary ideas is international. Long before the Internet and globalization, many uprisings had their bases in previous revolutions and struggles. In Latin America alone, these include the Cuban revolution and uprisings in Bolivia, Mexico, Nicaragua, and Peru.[69]

It is impractical to believe that labor movements will form internationally without first having a strong national base. The first phase of the revitalization of the labor movement must occur at the national level because this is where individuals live and work. It is important to remember that while capital may be very mobile, labor is almost the exact opposite. Only 1.5 percent of individuals work in countries where they are not citizens, with 50 percent of these individuals working in sub-Saharan Africa and the Middle East.[70]

Moreover, contrary to the popular globalization literature, the increased economic integration of the world's economy has not led to the state becoming powerless: the idea that businesses can relocate offshore in an instant "is largely globalonely."[71] The nation-state is still crucial, as business needs the state to protect its investments. The state in capitalist society is required to introduce laws to protect private property, to have a police force to enforce the laws, to have courts to prosecute offenders who break the laws, and to provide services such as education. Moreover, economic globalization has led to an increase in some state functions. These include the basic "infrastructure of the world market, its ports, airports, . . . the countless bilateral and multilateral trade and commercial agreements that facilitate the world market, . . . and when capital gets in trouble abroad, it is its 'home' nation-state that comes to the rescue through negotiations, pressure, or military threat or intervention."[72] It is hard to disagree with this assessment: "Most of the struggle against the structures and effects of globalization necessarily occurs on a national plane. That, after all, is where workers live, work, and fight. . . . The most basic feature of an effective internationalism for this period is the ability of the working class to mount opposition to the entire agenda of transnational capital and its politicians in their own backyard."[73]

Concentrating on national struggles while developing international linkages was an issue that Karl Marx and Frederick Engels argued. An exclusive focus on the last lines of *The Communist Manifesto* ("Working men of all countries, unite!") suggests that Marx and Engels' concerns were primarily international. However, sections of the *Manifesto* clearly indicate a struggle at the national level is paramount: "Though not in substance, yet in form, the struggle of the proletariat with the bourgeoisie is at first a national struggle. The proletariat of each country *must, of course,* first of all settle matters with its own bourgeoisie."[74] In addition, as Halliday claims, just as *fraternite* "was at that time used to denote solidarity *within* France, the 'unite' at the end of the *Manifesto* refers not to any international action, but to the organisation of workers within each state. The German original '*Arbeiter aller Welt, vereinigt euch*' could as well be rendered 'Workers of Each Country, Get Organised.'"[75]

Nevertheless, some argue that the growth of transnational corporations (TNCs) means that labor should concentrate on international struggles. The size of TNCs is impressive: the 35,000 largest TNCs have 150,000 affiliates, and they have foreign investments worth $1,700 billion. However, TNCs still rely heavily on their home state. For example, over two-thirds of TNC sales go to their home country. In the manufacturing sector, US TNCs in 1993 sold 65 percent of their products locally; in Japan it was 75 percent, while UK and German TNCs sold 65 and 75 percent, respectively, of their products locally. In the services sector, the figures are even higher, with US TNCs selling 79 percent and Japanese and the UK TNCs selling 77 percent of their services to their respective domestic markets. Moreover, most industrial output is produced by and targeted to Locals.[76]

Likewise, TNCs retain most of their assets in their home country. In the manufacturing sector, US TNCs had 73 percent of their assets locally, which is an increase from 66 percent in 1990. UK TNCs had 62 percent of their assets locally, up from 48 percent, and Japanese TNCs had 97 percent of their assets situated locally. In the services sector, US TNCs had 77 percent of their assets locally, and the UK and Japanese TNCs had 69 percent and 77 percent, respectively. These figures illustrate that TNCs largely rely on their home country.[77] In the retail industry, only six of the largest TNCs have more than 20 percent of their sales outside their home regions, and only one is considered truly global. Even Wal-Mart has only 9.6 percent of its stores outside the United States, Canada, and Mexico, with its international sales accounting for only 16.3 percent (although both figures are on the rise).[78]

Globalization advocates argue that TNCs over time will abandon their home countries and move their production facilities offshore. As Susan Strange claims: "The offers from governments in newly industrializing countries (NICs) are likely to be more generous and seductive than those from governments of developed countries...[and] the competition among the [NICs] is apt to have an eroding effect on two important sources of state authority: the power to tax and the power to regulate markets, including labor and financial markets."[79] Thus, TNCs, which are presumably concerned only with profit margins, will relocate their production plants overseas.

This argument is mistaken in a number of important respects. First, new technology reduces the importance of variable costs, such as wages, while adding extra importance to fixed costs, such as equipment and machinery. Moreover, as international economy expert Linda Weiss notes, knowledge-intensive labor is increasingly being treated as a fixed cost, and new technology reduces the savings to be made by relocating offshore.[80] In other words, new technology can reduce labor costs so that they compose only a fraction of the total cost of a product.

Second, time is often more important than labor costs in deciding where to produce, especially in the textile, clothing, and retail industries. Nike's misadventure highlights this. Because Nike orders shoes from its Asian retailers months in advance, it has to rely on fashion remaining stable for a period. In 1997, teenagers abandoned sportswear. Nike was then unable to sell hundreds of thousands of sneakers.[81] While Nike could take the economic hit, many other companies would not be able to do so.

Third, TNCs benefit from being located in major industrialized countries. Important export sectors in the United States profit from research and development assistance, from being in key districts such as Silicon Valley, where major industries are situated, and from having the protection of commercial law for patents and trademarks.[82]

Fourth, many major companies have been protected by trade barriers or have been saved by their home government. For example, despite the North American Free Trade Agreement (NAFTA), US sawmills, through a lumber accord, still receive protection from cheaper Canadian producers.[83] In addition, as Winfried Ruigrok states, "among the top 100 [companies in the 1993 *Fortune* Global 500 list] virtually all appeared to have sought and gained from industrial and/or trade policies at some point. At least 20 companies...would not have survived as independent companies if they had not been saved in some way by their governments."[84]

While it would be a mistake to deny that many TNCs depend on overseas markets and production facilities, their level of involvement overseas is not as pronounced as some would have us believe. As Robert Wade argues:

> The point is not just that [T]NCs do have a home base to which they are closely tied and generally more loyal than to other locations. It is also that, except for the most routinized assembly operations, they are much less than perfectly footloose with respect to *any* location once they have invested there. They face a variety of sunk costs, which constitute barriers to exit. These include initial startup costs, the costs of learning over time about a particular environment, and the costs of building reputation, gaining acceptance among government, and other firms regarding their ability as producers, employers, and suppliers in each market. Knowledge and information are not fully codifiable or completely fungible between places; trust and reputation are even less so.[85]

The latest figures further show that TNCs continue to rely on their home state. In 2000, the 100 largest US TNCs sold 69 percent of their products locally, with local employment accounting for 61.4 percent of their total employment.[86] Likewise, in 2004, out of the 100 largest TNCs worldwide (based on foreign assets), 25 were US companies (the next highest country on the list was France, with 15 TNCs in the top 100). The Transnationlity Index ([TNI] which is calculated as the average of the following three ratios: foreign assets to total assets, foreign sales to total sales, and foreign employment to total employment) of American TNCs is 48.2. In other words, even the largest TNCs in the United States that are based on foreign assets still have the majority of their assets, sales, and employment in the United States. Obviously, US TNCs not in the top

100 will have much more of their assets located in the United States. Moreover, the United States is also the most favored location for affiliates of TNCs from both the developed and developing countries. Indeed, the United States has a TNI ranking of 29th for developed countries (its TNI is approximately 6, well below the average of approximately 24 for developed countries).[87] In other words, the United States and its companies are very home-centric, and TNCs from other countries want to have affiliates in the United States. Thus, despite claims of a globalized world, unions can still target TNCs with the sound knowledge that TNCs want to be based in the United States.

While TNCs still largely rely on their home bases, this is not to argue that TNCs are not powerful or large and influential employers. A successful international campaign against TNCs would have a flow-on effect to workers worldwide because of the size and number of the TNC affiliates. TNCs "dominate many nominally independent employees, set the world-wide trend in working conditions, and preserve the unequal wage levels that perpetuate completion among workers even in the same TNC."[88] Different unions that have members within a TNC should conduct coordinated bargaining. The idea behind this is not a single contract or even similar contracts for workers in different countries, but to help facilitate international solidarity. Thus, a successful campaign against TNCs would benefit many workers worldwide and contribute to international solidarity.[89]

However, while TNCs are very powerful players in both the national and international economy, it is important to remember that most people are employed by medium and small firms; such firms are generally not able to move their operations overseas.[90] Moreover, in an analysis of the impact of globalization on the US economy, Dan Clawson concluded:

> Not only is two-thirds of employment...relatively insulated from globalization, but that is even more true of the fastest growing jobs. Of the thirty occupations with the largest job growth, I would classify only four as vulnerable to globalization....Excluding general managers and top executives as not relevant to a union analysis, the other twenty-five occupations with the largest job growth all appear to be relatively insulated from the pressures of globalization....Job growth for these occupations was projected to be 6.9 million.[91]

The industries relatively protected from globalization include the government sector, retail, health services, the financial industry, and legal, educational, and social services. It is a major mistake to totally blame globalization for the decline in union members and the growth of outsourcing. While employers often threaten workers that they may move their production plants overseas if the workers agree to a union or demand a decent contract, this is just a threat in most cases. For example, during collective bargaining, employers use this tactic 36 percent of the time in industries such as construction, health care, education, and retail. It is a hollow threat; what is an employer going to do—move the nursing home to Mexico? Likewise, there has been a decline in unionism in vulnerable industries such as the auto and steel industries, but construction unions have declined at similar rates.[92] This is not to say that neoliberal globalization has had no effect on American workers and unions, but its effect is vastly overstated.

It is not that TNCs are leading to a fragmented labor force or relying on their home country to a lesser degree. Thus, a strategy that focuses on building strength at the national level, while not neglecting international struggles, is a strategy that the labor movement should undertake. While there are many different strategies for unions and rank-and-file workers to forge effective labor internationalism, Kim Moody and Mary McGinn outline an effective six-step proposal. The first step for effective international alliances is for local unions to form an international solidarity committee. The committee would educate its members on the benefits of international solidarity and form alliances with overseas unions and workers. Second, there is a need for a grassroots network on free trade that would coordinate campaigns and help facilitate international contacts. Third, International Union conferences could begin to turn abstract internationalism into an effective internationalism by helping workers realize that overseas workers are just like them. Fourth, unions should engage in industry-wide networks since many industries have production facilities in different countries. These networks could exchange information on such things as wages and working conditions while developing common demands. Fifth, unions that operate within TNCs should engage in internationally coordinated bargaining. The purpose of such coordinated bargaining is not to achieve a single contract for workers in different countries, but to help facilitate international solidarity. A successful campaign against TNCs would benefit many workers worldwide and contribute to international solidarity. The final step for an effective international solidarity is for rank-and-file workers to change their unions so they are member-controlled and militant.[93]

The AFL-CIO's international strategy demonstrates the shift in policy of American unions and labor federations since the end of the Cold War. During the Cold War, the AFL-CIO was an ally of the US government in its fight against Communism. This led the AFL-CIO to attempt to destabilize leftist overseas unions. As David Bacon notes, in "developing countries—from Vietnam to Brazil to Chile to El Salvador—the AFL-CIO subsidized unions that supported US policy and attacked ones that didn't. Sometimes, as in Chile and Brazil, it even helped organize fascist coups, which left thousands dead and entire labor movements in ruins."[94]

However, since the late 1980s, with the collapse of Communism and the new era of globalization, the AFL-CIO is starting to develop an international focus. For example, the AFL-CIO sent a delegation to South Africa to meet union officials who, in the past, would have been accused as being Communists. Likewise, since the election of John Sweeney as president, the AFL-CIO has begun to support the independent, and not government-sponsored, Mexican trade unions—something that would have been unthinkable under the previous administration. AFL-CIO secretary treasurer Rich Trumka argues: "The cold war is gone.... It's over. We want to be able to confront multinationals as multinationals ourselves now. If a corporation does business in fifteen countries, we'd like to be able to confront them as labor in fifteen countries. It's not that we need less international involvement, but it should be focused towards building solidarity, helping workers achieve their needs and their goals here at home."[95] Labor internationalism advocates argue that if the American labor movement embraces internationalism, not only will this help local unions gain strength, but it will benefit workers and unions worldwide.

STRATEGIES TO STOP THE DECLINE: AN ANALYSIS

Labor-community alliances, the organizing model of unionism, and labor internationalism are all important strategies that unions should undertake. Labor-community alliances have assisted in organizing drives, in unions gaining a first contract, and during collective bargaining. Additionally, they have prevented, or at least delayed, plant closures. The organizing model of unionism has led to an increase in membership in unions such as the SEIU and the Communications Workers of America. Likewise, unions achieve a higher NLRB certification election win rate through adopting the organizing model.[96] Labor internationalism, in addition to forging solidarity among workers worldwide, has led to American unions achieving better collective bargaining agreements (see chapter 5 for examples). Furthermore, workers worldwide, particularly in Mexico, have benefited because of the increasing international activities of American unions (see chapter 5 for examples).

There are, however, inherent problems with unions using labor-community alliances, the organizing model of unionism, and labor internationalism in isolation from other progressive strategies. Labor-community alliances can help unions in particular struggles, but they do not change a union's organizational culture and structure. Unions can use these alliances only to achieve better wages and working conditions for their members. Likewise, the organizing model can increase union membership, but it is silent on issues such as militancy in collective bargaining and rank-and-file involvement in the union apart from organizing. Finally, labor internationalism can help in particular union struggles and build worker solidarity worldwide, but it does not necessarily encourage militancy and rank-and-file involvement. Admittedly, very few, if any, of the advocates of these strategies claim that labor-community alliances, the organizing model of unionism, and labor internationalism will solve all of the problems facing American unions.

These strategies are used to help not only union members but all workers, whether or not they belong to a union and/or social movements and community groups. However, business unions can undertake all three strategies only for the benefit of themselves and their members. For example, business unions can have labor-community alliances and only implement such a strategy to achieve better wages and working conditions for their members, but they may not care if the community groups benefit from the alliance. They can also use the organizing model of unionism to organize workers, but they may continue business union practices of limited rank-and-file involvement in the affairs of the union, apart from organizing. The organizing model in isolation can strengthen other forms of unionism, such as business unionism. This is because unions can use the organizing model to recruit new members but continue business union practices of limited rank-and-file involvement in the affairs of the union (apart from organizing) and an exclusive concern with bread-and-butter issues. It is foolish to believe that you can activate people for a particular campaign and then deactivate them once the campaign is over. For the majority of people, once they become involved, they want to stay involved.[97]

Furthermore, business unions may form international alliances only for their own self-interest. For example, despite the positive changes within the AFL-CIO, it still primarily focuses on American workers irrespective of the effects on workers worldwide. As part of its internationalist strategy, the AFL-CIO has begun to address the role of international economic institutions. The AFL-CIO argues that the WTO should be transformed into an organization that would enforce workers' rights by the use of side agreements. This is a somewhat surprising position because the labor side agreement in NAFTA has been unable to prevent the exploitation of workers. Sweeney's belief in the positive future role of the WTO led him to sign a letter from President Bill Clinton's "Advisory Committee for Trade Policy and Negotiators, endorsing administration goals for the WTO talks, including greater access for US corporations and investors abroad."[98] In other words, Sweeney hopes great market access for US corporations will benefit US workers. This expression of business unionism demonstrates that the AFL-CIO has not entirely broken away from its past.

Likewise, in its opposition to NAFTA, the AFL-CIO argued that the agreement would result in US job losses to Mexico. It is examples like these that have led some overseas unions to question the AFL-CIO's internationalist stance. A Mexican union leader asked a US union leader: "Why all of a sudden are you calling us 'brothers'? Is it because today you realize you need us, because you are about to lose your jobs—even perhaps your unions—and because you think we stand to gain from your loss? Where have you been for the last 40 years, when many times we were in need of you?"[99] Moreover, the AFL-CIO still undermines overseas unions and governments. For example, in Russia in 1999 the AFL-CIO's Free Trade Institute collaborated with the US coal industry to weaken Russian trade unions in an effort to broker a new coal policy that would benefit US corporations. More recently, since 2003 the AFL-CIO through its "Solidarity Center" has been attempting to destabilize the Venezuelan government.[100]

This is not to argue that these strategies will not benefit unions. Indeed, they have all been successful in one way or another in helping unions. Nevertheless, labor-community alliances, the organizing model of unionism, and labor internationalism have not and will not dramatically change the business union culture or lead to the revitalization of American unions.

4

THE SEIU AND CHANGE TO WIN: PROGRESSIVE OR MORE OF THE SAME?

The SEIU is constantly praised as being a progressive union and a model for other unions to follow. Likewise, the breakaway labor federation Change to Win has been lauded due to its commitment to organizing and its preparedness to take action rather than patiently waiting for labor's rebirth. There are things to admire about the SEIU and to a lesser extent Change to Win, but as is often the case, looks can be deceiving.

THE SEIU

The SEIU formed in 1920 as a janitors' union. It expanded in the 1960s to cover workers in health care and the public sector. As these were growing employment sectors, this allowed the union to strengthen as other unions were losing members. Moreover, the SEIU has a long history of organizing the unorganized. Even in the 1970s when most of the union movement did not care about organizing, the SEIU focused on organizing the unorganized. Arguably its greatest single victory occurred in February 1999 when the SEIU organized 74,000 home care workers in California; this was the most successful organizing campaign since 1937. The SEIU's commitment to organizing the unorganized sees it spend approximately 45 percent of its revenue on organizing.[1] The SEIU's focus on organizing includes forging ties with nontraditional unions and worker organizations (see chapter 6 for more details on nontraditional worker organization). Today, the SEIU is the fastest-growing union in North America, with over 1.8 million members (plus 50,000 retirees). The SEIU is

- The largest health care union, with 900,000 members in the field, including nurses, doctors, lab technicians, nursing home workers, and home care workers
- The largest property services union, with 225,000 members in the building cleaning and security industries, including janitors and door persons
- The second-largest public services union, with 850,000 local and state government workers, including public school employees, bus drivers, and child care

providers (The total number of members exceeds 1.8 million due to overlaps in public/health care).

Moreover, the SEIU has political power. The *National Journal* argued that among 20 grassroots organizations, the SEIU ranked highest at mobilizing grassroots supporters and getting voters to the polls.[2] Arguably the best known and most influential SEIU campaign is Justice for Janitors.

JUSTICE FOR JANITORS

The Justice for Janitors campaign is the classic example that advocates of the organizing model use as a case study to demonstrate the potential benefits for rank-and-file workers and unions if they adopt such a strategy.

Janitors have predominantly been African American. However, because of natural job attrition and the influx of immigrants, Latino immigrants were replacing African Americans at such a rate that by 1990 the percentage of Latino janitors was 61 percent compared to just 7 percent in 1970.[3] A major reason for the change in the ethnic origins of the janitors was that as African American janitors retired or changed jobs, building owners deliberately replaced the African American unionized workforce with nonunionized Latino immigrants on lower wages. This resulted in the average wage for a janitor in Los Angeles to decrease from $7.07 per hour with full health insurance in 1983 to approximately $4.50 per hour with no health insurance in 1987, with union membership declining dramatically.[4]

The Justice for Janitors campaign, an initiative of the SEIU, began in Denver in 1985. It hit its stride with SEIU Local 399 in Los Angeles in 1987, focusing on Century City, an LA business district. Realizing that electoral success through the NLRB was next to impossible, the union "devised a strategy which relied on direct action, public pressure, aggressive worker mobilization, community support, legal tactics, and corporate strategies." These tactics included sit-ins, civil disobedience, blocking traffic, marches, and focusing on the whole building service industry rather than individual companies.[5] A crucial component of the campaign was that the union relied on the militancy of immigrant workers. As David Bacon explains: "Local 399's organizers mobilized them again and again, bringing them into the streets to win contracts. They drew on the traditions and experiences of workers who faced down government terror in El Salvador or Guatemala. They appealed to workers who learned, as children in Mexico, that while they have a right to a fair share of the wealth of society, they have to fight to get it."[6] The workers were not afraid to fight. As a Salvadorian worker stated: "There [in El Salvador], you were in a union, they killed you. Here, you [are in a union] and you lost a job at $4.25 [per hour]." It is a big difference. The campaign got national coverage when janitors in Los Angeles were beaten by police during a peaceful demonstration against a cleaning contractor in 1990. The public outrage generated from this incident resulted in the contractor agreeing to recognize the union.[7]

The Justice for Janitors campaign demonstrates the success of the organizing model of unionism. Union membership for janitors in Los Angeles in the late 1990s was 90 percent, compared to only 30 percent in 1987. The success of the campaign has seen its adoption throughout America.[8] Over 225,000 janitors in 29 cities have joined the union, further demonstrating the success of the campaign. The latest major victory for Justice for Janitors occurred in Houston in 2006. Ercilia Sandoval, a janitor in Houston, claimed: "This is an incredible victory for our families and for all families.... When I go back to work, I will go back proud of what we have accomplished, not just for us and our families, but for all of the workers in this city who work very hard but are paid very little. We showed what can be done, what must be done to make America a better place." Indeed, the victory was remarkable. According to the SEIU, the agreement benefits the janitors in four areas:

- Higher wages: Janitors will see their wages rise by 126 percent over the course of the contract-with an immediate 21% increase on January 1. Janitors pay...increase[d] to $6.25 an hour on January 1, 2007, [and will increase to] $7.25 an hour on January 1, 2008, and $7.75 by January 1, 2009.
- More hours: The new contract will increase work hours for janitors currently provided with only 4 hours of work a night to six hours a shift in two years. The additional hours and the wage increase mean that janitors who make $5.15 an hour will see their income more than double by the end of 2008.
- Quality, affordable health insurance: At a time when many employers are shifting health care costs on to workers, Houston janitors won individual health insurance at a cost of only $20 per month. Family insurance will also be available for a cost of $175 a month. The health insurance will become available starting January 1, 2009.
- Paid holidays and vacation time: The contract will allow workers—many for the first time in their lives—paid time off from work. Janitors will receive six paid holidays per year and be able to accrue paid vacation time beginning the first year of the contract.[9]

The Justice for Janitors campaign is absolutely amazing. Before the campaign began, it was considered almost impossible to organize immigrant janitors. Not only has the SEIU managed to organize more than 225,000 janitors, it has improved the janitors' lives through better wages and working conditions. Thus, the lesson the rest of organized labor can learn from the Justice for Janitors campaign and the SEIU is that militancy matters.

Moreover, the Justice for Janitors success in Houston demonstrates that although it may be difficult, it is possible to organize workers in right-to-work states. One would assume that organizing low-pay workers, who are mainly immigrants (and may well include undocumented workers), in a state where the law makes organizing difficult would be next to impossible. However, the SEIU, to its credit, not only managed to organize 5,300 workers, but also secured an outstanding contract. Organizing over 5,000 workers in a right-to-work state is a great achievement, but being victorious in a contract fight that led to workers' wages being more than doubled, additional hours, paid holidays and vacations, and low-cost health care is spectacular. How did the SEIU secure such a victory in Houston, as well as in other cities across the country?

As noted, the campaign relied on such things as direct action, public pressure, and aggressive worker mobilization. This led the janitors to engage in sit-ins, civil disobedience, traffic blockades, and marches. Such tactics are quite successful.

Another lesson from the campaign is that even in the face of a hostile NLRB, it is possible to circumvent it and still organize workers. The Justice for Janitors campaign often tries to get employers to agree to card-check neutrality. Under this method, if a majority of workers sign a form stating that they want a union to collective bargain for them, and, most crucially, an employer agrees to voluntarily recognize the union, the union is deemed the bargaining agent for the workers. Thus, unions avoid dealing with hostile antiunion campaigns by employers and a pro-employer NLRB that makes it difficult for an organizing campaign to succeed. This increases the chances that workers are able to join a union. Obviously, a majority of employers do not agree to the card-check procedure. Nevertheless, as the Justice for Janitors campaign demonstrates, it is possible to organize workers through circumventing the NLRB. Indeed, certification elections are not the main way people join unions. Twenty years ago, 95 percent of workers joined through NLRB certification elections. In contrast, currently 70 to 80 percent of workers join unions by alternative means.[10]

The campaign further demonstrates that so-called minorities are crucial to labor's future. Latinos and African Americans largely contribute to reforming the union movement. For example, in the 1970s and 1980s, African American workers played a major role in the union reform movements from New Directions in the UAW to New York City Transit Authority workers in the Transport Workers Union. In addition, Latino and other immigrant workers had a crucial role in militant resistance, the revival of rank-and-file unionism, and the development of alternative strategies for unions in many struggles in the 1980s.[11] Furthermore, the increasing numbers of African Americans, Asians, Hispanics, and women do not necessarily divide the workforce. It is true that many unions have done nothing to combat discrimination against minorities, but these groups can revitalize a union. For example, between 1960 and 1975, public sector unionism went from 5 percent to almost 40 percent, with a disproportionate number of the workers being female and/or African American or Latino.[12] When there is more than 75 percent of women workers who are African American, Latino and/or immigrants in an organizing campaign, unions are successful in 82 percent of certification elections. Conversely, when women are in the minority, a union wins only 31 percent of elections and is victorious only 40 percent of the time when African American, Latino, and/or immigrant workers are in the minority.[13]

Another lesson from the Justice for Janitors campaign is that it is possible for unions to overcome labor laws. Erickson and others argue that the "antiunion effects of the law can be neutralized by creative tactics and that small changes in the law regarding picketing can have a very significant effect on the ability of firms to squelch strikes and protests." For example, mass protests during the day via marches are likely to have a much greater impact than simply picketing buildings. While the union still picketed buildings, it did so only at night. The Taft-Hartley Act prevents unions from picketing buildings other than the workers' employer. With the workers picketing at night, the employer could not claim that the union was pressuring building owners (who are not the janitors' employer) or the tenants of the building.[14] Obviously, some of the tactics used by the campaign are not applicable to other industries. Nevertheless, by using a diverse range of creative tactics and not just assuming that labor law prevents the use of certain organizing and campaigning methods, a union can still be very successful in spite of the law. The Justice for Janitors campaign clearly demonstrates that it is still possible to organize workers and achieve good contracts even in these antiunion times. However, the SEIU is far from perfect.

DEMOCRACY?

One of the SEIU's main problems is that it allows union democracy in its organizing campaigns (such a tactic is crucial in Justice for Janitors), but it is not too fond of union democracy in other aspects of the union. For example, as members in SEIU Local 399 were not happy that they did not have a bigger voice in how the union was run and wanted greater democracy, it led them to challenge for 21 out of 25 positions on the Local 399 union board. The group known as the Multiracial Alliance wanted more Latinos in positions of power in order to reflect the new makeup of the Local following the success of the Justice for Janitors campaign (as did other Latinos in the Local), and for more Justice for Janitors organizers to come from within the Local.

In a triumph for union democracy, the Alliance won every seat it contested. However, the Local president refused to work with the Alliance. Among other criticisms, he was not happy that the board tried to fire a number of Local employees and tried to form a grievance committee. Following a period of instability, John Sweeney, then head of the SEIU and current AFL-CIO president, placed the Local into trusteeship. Members of the Multiracial Alliance were then relocated, without their consent, to SEIU Local 1877.[15]

Unfortunately, this was not the only time that the SEIU has shown distaste for union democracy. Other Locals in Atlanta, San Francisco, San Jose, and Washington, DC, have encountered similar problems, with the SEIU leadership often placing dissident Locals in trusteeship.[16] Another recent example of the SEIU being distasteful toward union democracy was in Massachusetts in 2003. There was a merger of four different SEIU Locals at the University of Massachusetts into a single Local: Local 888. Members in Locals 509 and 285 were worried whether the democratic practices and rank-and-file involvement would continue in the new super Local. The fears were well founded. The new president of Local 888 argued that members should not be concerned with how the Local is run, only about the results. Thus, initiatives proposed by members were ignored. Dissidents within the union pushed for a range of democratic measures, such as a bill of rights and for members to be able to have a say in formulating Local policy. The SEIU leadership was not happy with the push for democracy and eventually allowed the dissidents to leave and join the Massachusetts Teachers Association in 2005.[17] In a sad state of affairs, the SEIU preferred workers to leave the union and join a rival union rather than granting greater democracy and rank-and-file involvement. The example of the SEIU demonstrates the challenges facing union reformers. The SEIU, despite using the organizing model to attract new members, still has unsavory practices in the union.

CHANGE TO WIN

In addition to being the fastest-growing union in North America, the SEIU played a major role in the breakup of the AFL-CIO and the formation of the new labor federation Change to Win. The impetus for the split occurred in 2003 when a group of union presidents, including SEIU president Andy Stern, formed a reform group known as the New Unity Partnership (NUP). The partnership argued that the organizing strategy of Sweeney and the AFL-CIO was a failure. It claimed that there were too many small unions covering many diverse industries. As a result, unions had no power. The NUP argued that unions should merge into one powerful organization that would cover a single industry, sector, and labor market. It wanted the 58 unions affiliated with the AFL-CIO to merge into 20 unions. The NUP believed that "central-ising power in a single organization would not only give unions a sharper strategic focus, but would also create economies of scale. Such an organiza-tion could mobilize hundreds of full-time organizers, thousands of volunteer union members, tens of thousands of volunteers in unorganized workplaces, hundreds of thousands of community allies, tens of millions of dollars in dues money, and billions of dollars in union-controlled pension investments."[18]

However, the AFL-CIO also argued that it would "implement a proac-tive, industry-based strategic merger policy, through a process (currently in the Constitution) of voluntary agreement or voluntary merger."[19] The differ-ence between the two strategies is that the NUP wanted to force the unions to merge, while the AFL-CIO's strategy was voluntary. Because the AFL-CIO is only a loose federation and not a binding organization, it is highly unlikely that the AFL-CIO could force unions to merge, as unions could simply leave the AFL-CIO if they did not want to merge.

The architect of NUP policy, Stephen Lerner, who is an SEIU staff member, argued that the revival of the labor movement should come from above, that is, the AFL-CIO. However, since the AFL-CIO has no real power to force its affiliates to do what it wants, it is impossible for real change to come from the AFL-CIO (although how he expected the AFL-CIO to force union mergers is a mystery). The NUP unions wanted a major change in the AFL-CIO. As Stern stated, "We need to talk about should the AFL-CIO be revolutionized, should its role be drastically increased or decreased."[20] The NUP believed that by organizing and spending sufficient resources on the task, the labor movement would be revitalized and everything would be right in the world once again.

It is important to note that questions of union democracy were ignored. Lerner argued:

It is too narrow to limit the discussion about union democracy only to the question of internal union governance. If we are truly committed to meaningful democracy we need to talk more broadly about how unions are strong enough locally and nationally to win economic justice for workers. If only 10 percent of workers in an industry are unionized, it is impossible to have real union democracy because 90 percent of the workers are excluded. If unions are weak, there is no democracy at the work site. If unions don't dominate industries, there is no power to challenge the dictatorial power of corporations. If unions don't represent a significant percent of the workforce workers won't have political power in our communities or nationally.[21]

However, the dissident unions could not gather enough support to change AFL-CIO policy. The majority of AFL-CIO unions argue that because of labor law, it is impossible to undertake the massive organizing efforts proposed by the dissident unions. Instead, they believe the AFL-CIO should concentrate on electing Democrat politicians who will implement labor-friendly policies and allow organizing campaigns as envisaged by the NUP. One flaw in this line of thinking is that there have been Democratic congresses and presidents since the enactment of the Taft-Hartley Act, and the politicians have done very little to support unions and workers. The Democratic Party has never failed to disappoint organized labor. While unions believe their decline is due to the Reagan and Bush Sr. administrations, the election of Clinton and Democratic control of Congress led to no favorable labor laws being enacted. Why the AFL-CIO and certain unions believe that the Democrats are the savior is a great mystery. The Democrats keep breaking labor's heart. This is certainly not to argue that there is no difference between the Democrats and the Republicans when it comes to labor issues. Yet, it is certainly true that the Democrats promise the world and deliver a lot less.

Stern disagrees with the AFL-CIO strategy that a Democratic-controlled Congress and president would reverse labor's fortunes. He states: "Other than when jobs are going overseas...there's not an employer where—with enough time, money, and [a good] strategy—you don't have a legitimate shot at building a union. Others think you have to legislate ourselves out of the problem—elect friendly officials, pass labor-law reform. We think you have to grow your way out of the problem."[22] The dissident unions believed that the AFL-CIO's political strategy was so flawed that in April 2005 they withdrew their members' names from the Federation's political files. This action prevented the Democrats from accessing the names of members who belonged to the NUP unions for voting mobilization campaigns.

The dissident unions also wanted Sweeney not to be reelected AFL-CIO president. The preferred candidate was UNITE-HERE president John Wilhelm. Before the NUP came into existence, it was likely that Sweeney was not going to seek reelection, because when he was elected in 1995, he claimed he would only stay in the presidency for 10 years. However, Sweeney was upset by the criticisms of the AFL-CIO by the NUP, and other union presidents pushed Sweeney to seek reelection, as they were also angered by the dissidents.

After the NUP unions realized that it was likely that Sweeney would be reelected AFL-CIO president, they disbanded the NUP under the assumption

that things would remain the same, with no transformation along the lines
they were pushing for. Almost immediately, the NUP unions formed a new,
similar coalition called Unite to Win. A few months later, Unite to Win became a formal grouping, Change to Win, on June 15, 2005. Its press release
stated: "While the founding unions [of Change to Win] hope their proposals
are passed by the delegates to the AFL-CIO Convention, it will put them into
practice immediately through the structure and activities of the Change to Win
Coalition. Regardless of the agenda adopted in Chicago by the AFL-CIO, the
Coalition will move forward with its reform program after the Convention."[23]
In other words, regardless of the outcome at the AFL-CIO Convention, the
Change to Win unions were going to do what they believed was right, no
matter what. Indeed, one SEIU staffer claims that the Change to Win unions
were "moving the goal posts each time [the AFL-CIO] got close."[24] As they
were unable to persuade other unions to support their proposals, less than
two months later, on July 25, the SEIU, Teamsters, United Food and Commercial Workers International Union (UFCW), and UNITE-HERE boycotted
the AFL-CIO Convention, and at the start of the convention the SEIU and the
Teamsters withdrew from the AFL-CIO. Teamsters' president Jimmy Hoffa Jr.
stated: "We have reached this decision as a matter of principle. Our differences are not about words, but are deep and fundamental....Unfortunately
the Federation has refused to embrace the progressive measures that we believe are necessary to accomplish their goals." Likewise, Stern stated: "We
know that all leaders of the AFL-CIO would like to see a world where workers' efforts are valued and rewarded. But for many years, and particularly in
the past nine months, our members and leaders have concluded that there
are sincere, fundamental, and irreconcilable disagreements about how to accomplish that goal."[25]

They were eventually joined by other unions. The initial members of Change
to Win were the SEIU, the International Brotherhood of Teamsters, Laborers
International Union of North America, United Brotherhood of Carpenters and
Joiners of America (UBC), United Farm Workers, UFCW, and UNITE-HERE.
The loss of the unions to Change to Win resulted in the membership of the
AFL-CIO shrinking by 48 percent, which meant a reduction of the AFL-CIO's
per capita dues falling from $91 million to approximately $48 million. Moreover, as the Teamsters and the SEIU were the two largest unions, this led to a
massive decline in AFL-CIO membership. The loss of the two unions, plus the
other Change to Win unions, meant that the AFL-CIO's share of the unionized
workforce dropped from 82 percent to only 43 percent.[26]

Proponents of Change to Win argue that there is one main reason why the
new labor federation will reverse labor's declining fortunes; namely, it has
a much more serious commitment to organizing than the AFL-CIO. On the
surface, a massive increase in funds committed to organizing is laudable and
should be embraced.

The AFL-CIO argues that unions should devote 30 percent of their funds
to organizing—a figure very few unions reach. Indeed, five unions employed
48.9 percent of the total organizers in the entire state of California in 2002, with
the SEIU accounting for 22 percent. It is estimated that, on average, unions

devote only 5 percent of funds to organizing. This means that only $422 million out of $8.5 billion in revenue received by unions actually goes to organizing. Considering the decline in unionism, it is truly a pitiful figure. The AFL-CIO recently proposed that "$22.5 million [be devoted to the] Strategic Organizing Fund—a $10 million increase over the current fund...[and] $15 million would go back to unions for organizing if they meet standards established by the Executive Council and Organizing Committee, including dedicating at least 30 percent of their annual revenue to strategic organizing."[27] In contrast, Change to Win proposes that 75 percent of its dues will go to organizing. This will undoubtedly benefit unions and, more importantly, workers. However, while the AFL-CIO per capita dues are 65¢ per member per month, Change to Win charges only 25¢.[28] Change to Win is sacrificing a substantial amount of money that could go toward organizing. Moreover, while the federation is planning to devote 75 percent of dues to organizing, the amount devoted to organizing by Change to Win unions depends on the particular union, and the amount of revenues received by Change to Win unions is only 21.4 percent of total revenue for all unions. If all unions spent 75 percent on organizing, this would mean $6.3 billion would be devoted to organizing new members. What would this mean to union organizing? Masters et al. argue:

> If [union] density is to increase from the current 12.5 percent of the workforce to 16.9 percent...[by] 2012, unions need a net gain of slightly more than 10 million members. Assuming an attrition rate of five percent per year, the total number of new recruits needed to reach almost 25.8 million members by 2012 is about 18.6 million, or roughly 2.33 million per year. With an annual organizing budget of $6.335 million, this gives unions $2,726 to spend per recruit to reach the goal.[29]

In other words, even if Change to Win unions adopt a massive increase in spending on organizing (at this stage it is highly unlikely that the Change to Win unions will devote anything close to 75 percent of revenue to organizing), this will have only a limited impact on union density. While it will help unionization rates in particular industries, for there to be even a modest rise in union members there has to be a total commitment by the majority of unions.

Furthermore, the Change to Win unions do not have the greatest record when it comes to organizing. From 1993 to 2003, union membership and density decreased in the majority of industries that Change to Win unions are involved in. These include

> textiles, clothing, and laundry (UNITE); restaurants and hotels (HERE); and building services and nursing homes (SEIU). The only industry with increased density over the past five years is hospitals (SEIU), although unionization is lower than in 1993. Looking at selected occupations, the picture is mixed. Density is lower among janitors (SEIU), carpenters (UBC), and construction laborers...but it is up over the past five years for registered nurses (SEIU) and nursing aides (SEIU). Membership is up in four of the occupations, which in part may be attributed to higher employment levels, accounting for some of the growth experienced by [the] unions.

External factors such as globalization have affected organizing efforts in the clothing industry and in the depressed hospitality sector following the September 11, 2001, terrorist attacks.[30] However, external factors affect all industries, not just the industries that Change to Win unions attempt to organize. Thus, while the Change to Win unions criticized the AFL-CIO and its member unions for not doing enough to organize workers, they have also not been that successful apart from the SEIU. Nevertheless, Change to Win's commitment to organizing is something all unions should adopt. But, like the SEIU, there are unsavory elements to the Change to Win manifesto.

The Change to Win unions argue that labor should cooperate with management. In other words, they argue that unions should embrace a form of value-added unionism. However, as I argued in chapter 3, it is unlikely that value-added unionism will succeed, because employers in America are generally hostile to unions, whether or not they add value. Whether business unionism or value-added unionism, any type of unionism that has to rely on the willing cooperation of business in this era of neoliberal globalization, where both business and governments are openly hostile to unions, is bound to fail. Indeed, in regard to organizing new members, unions have generally achieved growth not by cooperating with management, but by conflicting with management. The Justice for Janitors campaign has succeeded not by working with business, but by putting enough pressure on management that it eventually gives into the SEIU's demands.

However, the SEIU also proposes that an adversarial relationship between labor and business will generally not benefit either party. Instead, labor and business should work together. Stern states that the "1930s adversarial type unionism isn't going to apply to nurses and reporters and childcare workers.... We need to create a lot of different models of unions."[31] He further adds that the militant unionism of the 1930s was a problem: "It was sort of a class struggle kind of... [unionism], but workers in today's economy are not looking for unions to cause problems, they're looking for them to solve them.... We need team America to really work together if we're really going to reward American workers' work.... We need to be partners with our employer."[32] In other words, sometimes it is necessary to work with employers. For example, the SEIU has a partnership with Kaiser Permanente Health Care. Although a number of Kaiser workers are happy with the partnership, others claim that working conditions have not improved. One Kaiser worker argues that "it's as bad as it ever was... people call the business agents and don't hear back from them, sometimes for days, sometimes for weeks. Business agents don't show up at the worksite—people never see them." Nevertheless, Stern claims that unions should have a partnership with employers, with unions being an "intermediate force in an industry to make these increasingly rapid changes (outsourcing and globalization) less painful."[33]

Of course, having an alliance with management comes at a price. The SEIU and Kaiser lobbied the state of California to prevent patients suing their health maintenance organizations (HMOs). The SEIU used its influence within the LA County Federation of Labor and the LA Central Labor Council (CLC) to lobby Democrats in the state legislature to not support a bill that would have allowed patients to sue their HMO's over medical malpractice or denial of adequate care. The HMO industry wanted to continue to insist that patients agree in advance to a system of compulsory arbitration in such disputes. Marc Cooper argued that the labor groups opposing the bill "often lionized as the linchpin of local progressive politics [were] smack dab in bed in the most compromising of positions with the HMO lobbyists and a kinky trio of spineless local Democrats."[34] This is hardly supporting ordinary Americans. As the California Nurses Association (CNA) executive director Rose Ann Demoro argues: "You can't be on the side of the public and the side of the corporation at the same time.... The agreement places the union in the position of being a special interest, while we should be the strongest advocates for patient care." Moreover, while gaining better wages and working conditions for their members, the SEIU in return cooperated with Kaiser in replacing registered nurses with less qualified staff. Although the SEIU managed to organize workers due to its partnership with Kaiser, one must ask at what cost. The CNA argues: "If you look at what SEIU and Kaiser agreed to, it is insidious for the public.... They agreed to gag their employees on any criticism of Kaiser. They were silent when Kaiser closed hospitals, made cuts in patient services and cooperated with Kaiser on reductions in care."[35] Another such partnership operates in the state of Washington. In the agreement, the SEIU agreed to "no strikes and ... to let the nursing home operators—not the union or workers—decide which homes are offered up for organizing. The union also agreed not to try organizing more than half of a particular company's nonunion homes." If workers in other nursing homes try to organize with the SEIU, the SEIU must prevent it from happening. The SEIU has also agreed to push for more state funding for nursing homes (increased profitability), and in return the nursing home operators "allow" the SEIU to organize homes it may not have been able to otherwise.[36] Thus, the SEIU is throwing some workers to the wolves, so it can save others. Every worker who wants to join a union should be able to, irrespective of any labor-management partnership. As Rose Ann Demoro succinctly argues about the benefits of labor-management partnerships:

> When conservative magazines ... [write] glowingly about CTW's [Change to Win] embrace of labor-management partnerships—with their corporate-friendly cost savings schemes, worker speed-up programs, and explicit endorsement of globalization, deskilling, outsourcing, and privatization ... [and] [w]hen a key CTW leader appeared on the cover of Human Resource Outsourcing Today magazine embracing globalization and endorsing proposals that would only further alienate U.S. workers from the labor movement and further erode labor's power [there is cause for alarm].[37]

Another problem with Change to Win is that the federation, like the SEIU, does not place much credence on union democracy and rank-and-file involvement. Indeed, as I previously noted, Lerner, who was the main architect of the NUP policy (which later became the Change to Win policy), argued that union democracy was not important. Indeed, three unions within Change to Win—the Teamsters, the Laborers Union, and the Hotel union (part of HERE)—have had major links to organized crime, and the decision to leave the AFL-CIO and form Change to Win did not come from the rank and file. The rank and file had no say in the matter, nor were there any forums to discuss the changes. A member of the UFCW notes: "Not one time did reps come into stores telling members of the plan to exit the AFL-CIO—no letters, nada. Most members had no clue any of this was even happening until they received their after-the-fact letters from [the Local president]."[38]

Nevertheless, Change to Win has a vision of a centralized labor movement in which the leaders have almost all the power. As Hurd notes:

> All of...[the unions] retain strategic and budgetary control in the office of the national president. At least four of them (the possible exception is...the laborers) have implemented rather drastic internal restructuring in recent years to augment centralization of authority. In three unions (SEIU, UNITE, and HERE) staff can run for office, and the power to impose trusteeship on locals has been used to place in positions of authority key staff members that share the unions' organizing philosophy. This top-down internal restructuring has been an essential ingredient of the drive to move forward.[39]

However, as I argued in chapter 3, union democracy and an active rank and file are essential to unions. Through rank-and-file participation, there is a transformation of the union into a political community that does not necessarily readily agree with the accepted order.[40] In their analysis of CIO unions, Stepan-Norris and Zeitlin demonstrated that union democracy leads to unions being more militant and more successful in collective bargaining.[41] Moreover, the SEIU has suffered because it does not allow its members a big enough say in the affairs of the union.

Furthermore, the Carpenters Union has already reorganized itself into the bureaucratic vision embraced by Change to Win. The results have not been promising, to say the least. Herman Benson sums up the situation well:

> Carpenter locals have been reduced to impotent units. Merged into sprawling regional councils, locals are not permitted to pay any officers or staff members; their main source of income, the work tax, is taken over by the councils. Locals have lost all control over collective bargaining. Business agents are appointed from above. No member can hold any paid staff position in the council or any local without the permission of an all-powerful executive secretary treasurer [EST]. Local delegates, who elect the EST, cannot hold a paid union job without his or her endorsement. If that system were to be applied to public government no member of Congress or staff employee could be paid out of government funds, without permission of the President. It is reorganization carried out to the point of parody.[42]

The Change to Win Federation has also adopted the NUP idea that there should be a single union covering a single industry or sector of the labor market. The Change to Win constitution states that the "affiliate which can best serve the interests of the affected workers in the industry or industries involved considering all of the facts and circumstances shall be awarded the exclusive right to organize the workers involved."[43] This vision is supported by some labor academics. Marick F. Masters, Ray Gibney, and Tom Zagenczyk argue that there has to be a mobilization of money and people to defeat well-funded antiunion companies. However, like Change to Win, they believe that the current structure of the labor movement will not allow this to happen. They state that "overlapping jurisdictions and marginal unions combined with low rates of density reduce organized labor's bargaining and political muscle below even what its dwindling ranks connote."[44] In other words, labor's influence in the political realm and in organizing and collective bargaining is very, very weak.

There will, however, have to be a vast reorganization of the Change to Win unions for them to adhere to the single industry, jurisdiction strategy. For example, the Laborers have 50,000 postal workers as members, UNITE-HERE has members in the clothing industry as well as hotel and restaurant employees, and the Teamsters have members in industries ranging from the university sector and trucking, and rail to public sector employees. It is foolish to believe that any of the Change to Win unions will give up members to other unions. Indeed, Hoffa Jr., responding to the question of whether the Teamsters would stop organizing in other industries, stated: "Absolutely not. We would not give up members.... We have from A to Z in our union, airline pilots to zookeepers.... We will never just be a trucking or transportation union. We will always be a general union, and we are not giving up our right."[45] In addition, the idea that a single union should cover one single sector or industry ignores the fact that many companies are now involved in many sectors. General Electric is a classic example. "The company is a key player in financial services; it manufactures everything from plastics to aircraft engines to washing machines, and is a major player in the entertainment industry through its ownership of NBC and Telemundo. One magazine called GE CEO Jeff Immelt the seventh most powerful person in the U.S. in the health-care industry (because of GE's influence and investments in health insurance and medical instruments technology)."[46]

The criticisms of the proposal for a single union to cover a particular industry do not mean that there should not be coordinated bargaining within a particular industry or company. However, a single bureaucratized union covering one particular industry, company, or sector is unlikely to happen due to the unions involved, and it is a good thing for it to never see the light of day.

Another major problem with Change to Win is in the political arena. While I previously argued that a strategy that relies on the Democrats to change labor law (thus it will be easier to organize workers) is living in a fantasy land, many of the Change to Win unions have a long history of supporting the Republican candidates and the party as a whole. The Republican Party is not a friend to organized labor and working people. The Democratic Party certainly has betrayed organized labor, but it has never come close to being as antiunion as the Republicans. However, this has not stopped many Change to Win unions and leaders from supporting the Republicans. Despite endorsing

John Kerry in the 2004 presidential election, the Teamsters have once again begun to give qualified support to the Republican Party. Additionally, Hoffa Jr. supports George W. Bush's Terrorism Information and Prevention System. Unlike the majority of unions, the Teamsters endorsed Bush's proposal for oil companies to drill in the Arctic National Wildlife Refuge. Hoffa also claimed that the "[International Brotherhood of Teamsters] IBT was working to 'find common ground' with Bush and [US vice president Dick] Cheney." Likewise, the Teamsters endorsed the reelection bid of an antilabor Republican in Michigan because he supported the elimination of federal court supervision of the Teamsters, and the union provides photo opportunities for Bush posing with union leaders at Labor Day events.[47] However, the Teamsters are not alone among Change to Win unions. HERE,

> plus the Carpenters, Teamsters, Service Employees/District 1199, and recent hotel workers' merger partner, UNITE…helped re-elect Republican George Pataki as governor of New York in 2002. Pataki's anti-worker positions included opposition to a minimum wage hike, which was finally adopted by the state legislature last year, over his veto, after intensive organizing and lobbying by New York's feisty Working Families Party.…Pataki promot[ed] right-wing schemes like privatizing the New York State Thruway; meanwhile, his "labor liaison" three years ago, Teamster and [SEIU] 1199 consultant Greg Tarpinian, has just been named executive director of the CTW.[48]

While primarily supporting the Democrats, the SEIU has also given millions to the Republican Party, while the president of the Carpenters union stayed neutral during the 2004 presidential election. During the early days of the NUP, leaked documents showed that the NUP was willing to work with Republican strategists including Karl Rove.[49] Obviously, there are similar examples of unions within the AFL-CIO that also support the Republicans. However, this does not change the fact that supporting the Republican Party in any shape or form is likely to help labor's revival.

SOME GOOD, MORE BAD

The SEIU is a fascinating union. Its success, along with its willingness to lead the fight to help stop organized labor's decline, should be lauded. However, while it believes in democracy in its organizing campaigns, it does not believe in democracy in other parts of the union. Indeed, it is willing to lose members rather than allow them a greater say in the affairs of the union. Likewise, while labor-management partnerships can be successful for particular unions at various times, such a strategy is not going to stop labor's decline. Even Stern admits that "changing non-union employers' attitudes…remains a monumental challenge. They often don't believe that partnerships with unions are possible, nor are they able to overcome their prejudices against unions in order to establish a different kind of relationship that could add value to their bottom line."[50] One might suggest that a far better monumental challenge would be for Stern to concentrate on organizing the unorganized and not bother with trying to convince hostile employers who do not like unions in the first place. Negatives aside, the SEIU, at the very least, demonstrates that it is still possible for unions to prosper, to organize the unorganized, and to secure decent contracts even in these rough times.

At this stage, it is unlikely that Change to Win will reverse labor's fortunes. The increased focus on organizing should help, but at the same time, the federation's distaste for union democracy, its top-down bureaucratized vision, its flirtation with the Republican Party, and its belief in labor-management cooperation have always led to labor shedding blood. Judging from the above, it is likely that Change to Win strategies, apart from its commitment to organizing, are likely to be worse than the current strategies of the AFL-CIO. In other words, labor's decline will continue unabated.

5

SOCIAL JUSTICE UNIONISM: A PATH TO LABOR'S RENEWAL

Social movement unionism has become the new buzzword for both the academic Left and union reformers. As Ian Robinson notes, "analysts and activists have begun applying the concept to organized labor in the United States, as a characterization of some unions within the larger movement, as an ideal towards which organized labor ought to be moving if it wishes to recapture lost economic and political power, or both."[1] An increasing number of people argue that social movement unionism is *the* strategy/ideology that American unions should adopt.[2] While they argue that American unions should adopt social movement unionism, there has been little in-depth analysis of the likelihood of this strategy succeeding and revitalizing the labor movement.

This chapter provides an outline of the theory of social justice unionism (due to the difference between what is labeled social movement unionism in America and social movement unionism in Brazil, the Philippines, South Africa, and South Korea, I prefer to use the term *social justice unionism* although I use the terms interchangeably), and by using case studies of the Teamsters' negotiations/collective bargaining agreements with the United Parcel Service (UPS), as well as collective bargaining in the auto industry, I will argue that social justice unionism greatly benefits unions.

WHAT IS SOCIAL JUSTICE UNIONISM?

Kim Moody is the most influential advocate of social movement unionism, and he has long been a strident critic of business unionism. Indeed, his book *An Injury to All* is mainly a critique of the business unionism of the AFL-CIO. In *Workers in a Lean World* and in other publications, Moody provides another path for unions. He argues that the changing nature of contemporary work undermines old union structures and practices and leads to a new form of unionism. For unions to successfully organize workers and mobilize their current members, they must adopt a new form of unionism: social movement unionism.

> Social movement unionism is one that is deeply democratic, as that is the best way to mobilize the strength of numbers in order to apply maximum

economic leverage. It is militant in collective bargaining in the belief that retreat anywhere only leads to more retreats—an injury to one is an injury to all. It seeks to craft bargaining demands that create more jobs and aid the whole class. It fights for power and organization in the workplace or on the job in the realization that it is there that the greatest leverage exists, when properly applied. It is political by acting independently of the retreating parties of liberalism and social democracy, whatever the relations of the union with such parties. It multiplies its political and social power by reaching out to other sectors of the class, be they other unions, neighborhood organizations, or other social movements. It fights for all the oppressed and enhances its own power by doing so.[3]

The crucial aspects of social movement unionism are as follows: union democracy leads to strong progressive unions; unions should organize the unorganized, with the rank and file playing a key role; unions should be militant in collective bargaining; and unions need alliances with community organizations, as well as with unions and rank-and-file workers across the globe.

As I argued in chapter 3, union democracy with an active rank and file, labor alliances with social movements and community groups, and labor internationalism are important strategies unions should undertake. However, the use of one strategy alone, or even two of them together, will not revitalize unions, as these strategies can be used with unsavory strategies such as business unionism or value-added unionism. It is through social justice unionism that all the strategies combine and form the path to union revitalization. The following case studies of Teamsters negotiations with UPS, and collective bargaining in the auto industry demonstrate the benefits of such an approach.

TEAMSTERS

Founded in 1903, the International Brotherhood of Teamsters (IBT) is arguably the best known and most infamous union, not only in America but worldwide because of corruption and its ties with organized crime. Beginning in the 1930s, the Teamsters were characterized by conservative business unionism combined with rank-and-file militancy. As Dan La Botz claims:

> The Teamsters had been founded back in the 1890s as a craft union . . . made up of local cartage drivers. Under the leadership of Dan Tobin, the Teamsters formed an important part of the American Federation of Labor (AFL). But Tobin was a conservative leader, dedicated to the AFL's craft union model, uninterested in organizing immigrants, African Americans, or industrial workers whom he called riff-raff. The Teamsters' heroic years began in 1934 when rank-and-file truck drivers and warehouse workers from Minneapolis, Minnesota led a series of strikes, culminating in a city-wide truck-drivers' strike. The leader of that strike was Farrell Dobbs, a socialist . . . who went on to organize over-the-road freight drivers and other dock workers and warehousemen throughout the Midwest. In this way Teamsters underwent a transformation from a craft union to a kind of industrial union of the transport industry.[4]

Dobbs's strategy resulted in the union becoming the largest private sector union in America by 1940; it is still one of the largest today. However, the Teamsters expelled Dobbs and other socialists in the lead-up to World War II. The union leadership consolidated top-down control, which resulted in future leaders such as David Beck and Jimmy Hoffa.[5]

Under Beck's and Hoffa's presidencies, the Teamsters were corrupt. Beck was contemptuous of rank-and-file control. He stated that "unions are big business. Why should truck drivers and bottle washers be allowed to make big decisions affecting union policy? Would any corporation allow it?"[6] Moreover, Beck was corrupt. He used Teamster funds for personal gain and had alliances with numerous employers. Eventually, in 1957 under investigation by the McClellan Committee, which was examining union racketeering, Beck announced that he would not stand for re-election. Hoffa replaced him as IBT president.[7] Soon Mafia members and Mafia-connected union officials had prominent places within the Teamsters. In addition, "Hoffa and the corrupt union officials he supported or put into power cut dirty deals with employers, including payoffs for labor peace. He also bought trucking companies in his wife's name and became an employer." During Hoffa's reign, the AFL-CIO expelled the Teamsters in 1957 until they could eliminate corruption from leadership positions. Eventually Hoffa was jailed for jury tampering and misappropriating members' pension funds. However, Mafia influence continued to grow under Frank Fitzsimmons, who replaced Hoffa, and his successors.[8] Nevertheless, as La Botz states:

> Under Tobin, Beck and Hoffa the Teamsters had become the corrupt, bureaucratic institution it was in 1976 when TDU [Teamsters for a Democratic Union] began, dominated by the Mafia, manipulated by the government and collaborating with the companies. Contrary to myth, the corruption of the Teamsters was not due to the fact that Jimmy Hoffa had invited the Mafia into the union. The union had been perverted from its original purpose because along the way Tobin, Beck and Hoffa had come to accommodate employers, adapting to the values of the employers, and to the employers' sense of who should run things.[9]

In other words, the Teamsters were a corrupt business union. This led to a reform caucus within the union, Teamsters for a Democratic Union (TDU), which attempted to democratize the Teamsters and make the union militant.

TDU was formed in 1976 from Teamsters for a Decent Contract (TDC). Teamsters who were members of the International Socialists (IS) created TDC in August 1975. The IS argued: "At this point the forces involved in TDC are far beyond what we could have accrued through patient local work. While many of the individuals and groups involved locally are weak, as a national grouping the sum equals more than its parts."[10] TDC's goal was for the Teamsters to achieve a good Master Freight Agreement in 1976. TDC managed to gain considerable support in a short period of time: it "won thousands of supporters by holding a series of coordinated national demonstrations in cities across the country, including one in front of the IBT's 'Marble Palace' in Washington...that received national media attention."[11] TDC's activism led the

Teamsters' president, Frank Fitzsimmons, to call a four-day official national strike against the freight companies. This resulted in a substantially improved Master Freight Agreement. However, TDC's success infuriated the Teamsters' leadership. Fitzsimmons vowed that a Communist group (i.e., TDC) would never infiltrate the Teamsters. Furthermore, a group of Teamsters physically attacked TDC's only convention delegate during the 1976 Teamster national convention. The success of TDC in helping the Teamsters achieve a good Master Freight Agreement resulted in the IS deciding to form a permanent reform movement within the Teamsters: Teamsters for a Democratic Union.[12]

Since its formation, TDU has emphasized democracy, militancy, and fighting against concessions in collective bargaining agreements, which are key aspects of social justice unionism. Although not always successful, TDU was involved in many fights regarding collective bargaining, protection of members' rights, strikes, and union education.[13] These battles paved the way for TDU's future successes.

In 1986, believing that the Teamsters were corrupt and had ties with the Mafia, the US government began investigating the Teamsters through the Racketeer Influenced and Corrupt Organizations (RICO) Act. Indeed, from 1957 to 1990, every Teamsters' president except Billy McCarthy was convicted of a federal offense. The government considered placing the Teamsters under trusteeship, which would have allowed an appointed government official total control over the union.[14] TDU opposed such a move on the following grounds:

> Big questions are raised about the Justice Department plans to put our union in trusteeship. It is unlikely that it would even be workable. Removing the eighteen top officers of the IBT would leave over 99% of full-time Teamster officials in place. It would also leave in place the current method of choosing top officers and changing the constitution....The power brokers who installed Presser, and have kept him there, would just pick whoever they wanted at the next convention despite the trusteeship.[15]

Instead, TDU argued that the government should monitor Teamster elections, and that members should directly elect the president and other leading union officials. While the US Labor Department continually disregarded TDU, in 1986 the President's Commission on Organized Crime report noted that the Teamsters' election methods for Local delegates were illegal and recommended that rank-and-file members be allowed to vote for delegates at the Teamsters' convention. A *New York Times* editorial also supported this view. TDU campaigned around the United States, gathering 100,000 signatures in support of members directly electing the Teamsters' leadership. It held rallies across the country, and many TDU members persuaded their Locals to adopt TDU's position. The campaign was ultimately successful.[16] In March 1989, the government and the Teamsters reached an agreement. The government dropped the RICO charges in return for the democratization of the Teamsters. The key points were as follows:

1. Government involvement to weed out corruption and mob influence
2. Direct vote for national leaders

3. Direct vote for delegates to the international convention
4. Nominations to be made at the national convention
5. Secure nominations for candidates receiving 5 percent of delegate support through a secret ballot
6. Independent auditor's review of the international books
7. Government-supervised elections in both 1991 and 1996.[17]

Without government intervention, these changes would not have occurred as quickly. Nevertheless, TDU's national campaign against trusteeship and for Teamster members to directly elect the top union officials influenced the government to implement this strategy.

TDU decided not to field a candidate for the 1991 IBT presidential election, instead endorsing Ron Carey because he supported union democracy and militancy in collective bargaining. TDU president Ken Paff argued that TDU backed Carey because he "had been a Teamster official in the capital of Teamster corruption, New York City[,]...had never sought to rise in the hierarchy, had a modest salary, [and] stood up as a militant for his members, including opposing national contract settlements repeatedly."[18] TDU organized meetings in support of Carey; its members provided places for Carey to stay while he toured the country, and did everything possible to ensure a Carey victory. This effort paid dividends. In December 1991, Carey and his entire slate won a three-way race, receiving 48 percent of the vote. In addition, through TDU efforts, the 1991 IBT convention saw 275 reform delegates elected (15 percent of the total delegates). However, this illustrates the extent that old hierarchy remained in office at different levels, as there were 1,900 delegates elected in total.[19]

Under Carey's leadership, the Teamsters supported many of TDU's goals; it moved to the left and acquired more features of a social justice union. Carey spearheaded the campaign against NAFTA, and he increased the organizing budget, while reducing union officials' salaries. Likewise, "he increased education for stewards and rank and file members, putting emphasis on contract campaigns, local unions, and shop floor organizing." These are all important aspects of social justice unionism. In addition, the Teamsters finally endorsed the Democratic Party despite a long history of supporting the Republican Party. However, the Teamsters did not endorse Bill Clinton in the 1996 US presidential election, because Clinton supported NAFTA.[20] In other words, the Teamsters were on the path toward independent political action despite its long ties with the Republican Party. The Teamsters' newfound progressive orientation would eventually pay dividends in its collective bargaining negotiations with UPS.

1997 UPS NEGOTIATIONS/COLLECTIVE BARGAINING AGREEMENT

From small beginnings in 1907, in Seattle, UPS by the 1990s was a transnational company with operations around the world. However, UPS does not provide a happy working environment:

The UPS worker's every move is planned precisely by company managers, from picking up the keys to loading the package.... The day begins with a management pep talk and ends in exhaustion....Workers are pushed to their physical and psychological limits, leading to a high incidence of accidents, injuries and occupational illnesses. The pressure to perform is so great that some workers even donate their unpaid time before and after work or work through their lunch break to meet production goals.[21]

The 1997 negotiations/collective bargaining agreement highlights the benefits of using social justice unionism tactics in collective bargaining. As the 1993 UPS contract failed to meet member expectations, the Teamsters implemented many new campaign tactics. The Teamsters prepared well in advance for the 1997 negotiations. The union decided to implement TDU's idea for a contract campaign: "Bargaining moves on two fronts. One is at the bargaining table. An equally important front is in the field—a contract campaign in which union members support our bargaining committee, work to unite all Teamsters, and show management we won't settle without a fair contract."[22] The Teamsters conducted a survey of its UPS members in the lead-up to the contract negotiations. It asked for a list of contract priorities and activities that workers were willing to undertake, such as passing out leaflets and attending local union meetings, to achieve a good contract. The key issue for 90 percent of part-time workers was the conversion of part-time jobs into full-time positions. This became the Teamsters' number one goal during the negotiations. In addition to the survey, the Teamsters "distributed cards that thousands of individual members, many of them in locals where their leaders [i.e., Carey's opponents] showed little interest in the campaign, mailed back to the international union headquarters, so that they could become directly involved."[23] This allowed the rank and file of all Teamster Locals to become involved even if conservative officials headed their Locals. Another Teamster initiative was to hold rallies in targeted cities just before the union and UPS negotiators exchanged proposals. Six weeks before the old contract was set to expire, "the organization and unity built by the member-to-member networks paid off as more than 100,000 Teamsters signed petitions telling UPS that 'We'll Fight for More Full-time Jobs.'"[24]

The Teamsters' efforts built unity between full-time and part-time workers. This was crucial to the negotiations and subsequent strike. As a UPS driver stated: "Feeder drivers would sit over here and have their own break room and package car drivers would sit over there and part-timers over there. But early on this year we were talking together and I learned about other people's issues. By the end, we had enough reasons that we could all stick together."[25]

The Teamsters fought for three key issues during the negotiations. The first was the number of part-time workers UPS employed. Approximately 58 percent of UPS's employees were part time, and in 1993–1997, 38,000 out of 46,000 new jobs at UPS were part time. The starting rate for part-time employees had not risen in 15 years, with UPS seeking to extend that for another five years. Moreover, while many UPS workers were part time, they worked a full-time schedule. UPS prefers part-time employees, as it pays them less than full-time workers.[26] The second issue was pensions. The Teamsters "wanted increased contributions to its multi-employer pension and health funds. The company responded with a proposal to increase pension benefits for its workers by an average of 50 percent in exchange for pulling out of the multi-employer funds."[27] Under the multiemployer pension fund, all Teamsters receive the same benefits irrespective of the company they worked for. As a very profitable company, UPS did not want to subsidize the Teamsters' pension fund. The third issue was the Teamsters' demand that UPS limit the amount of work that the company could subcontract. In preparation for the negotiations, Carey formed a 50-person UPS bargaining committee. The committee included, among others, officials from Locals that were hostile to Carey, several TDU activists, and UPS rank-and-file workers and part-timers—a very rare occurrence in union bargaining committees.[28]

TDU played an active role in the lead-up to the negotiations. As labor writer Jane Slaughter argues, it was "TDU's plan for a contract campaign against UPS that Carey adopted. Most important, TDU had a strong base at UPS. Over the years, shop floor leaders there had been trained in fighting the boss. In locals where local officials were lukewarm, these rank and filers were the ones who carried the ball."[29] In its contract campaign, the Teamsters sought international alliances, partly because UPS was planning to expand its overseas operations. In the UPS plant in "Gustavsburg, Germany, workers handed out leaflets and stickers, wore white socks as a symbolic show of unity, and blew whistles like those being used by Teamster members at actions in the US." Other international action included a "one-hour strike at half of the UPS facilities in Italy, a two-hour strike in Spain at the Madrid hub, and a protest at UPS European headquarters in Brussels."[30]

While it is difficult to determine the effect campaign tactics had on UPS's management, UPS offered the Teamsters a "last, best and final" contract, which included an extra $1 an hour increase, for a total increase of $2.50 an hour for full-time workers (the company initially offered a $1.50 an hour increase). It would begin a profit-sharing plan and would guarantee 10,000 full-time positions for part-time workers. However, UPS refused to contribute to the Teamsters' multiemployer pension plan. In the 1990 and 1993 negotiations, the Teamsters accepted UPS's "final" offer, with the membership ratifying the agreement on each occasion.[31] This time the Teamsters rejected the offer and conducted a national strike at UPS beginning on August 3.

In an attempt to undermine the Teamsters' position, UPS launched a million-dollar ad campaign portraying the strikers as greedy. However, the issue of part-time workers resonated strongly with the US public. UPS vice chairman John Alden stated: "If I had known that it was going to go from negotiating for UPS to negotiating for part-time America, we would've approached it differently."[32] UPS, however, tried to convince the public that it was a victim; the campaign did not work. A USA Today-CNN-Gallup poll showed 55 percent supported the Teamsters and only 27 percent supported UPS. Likewise, only 25 percent of the public believed that President Clinton should declare a national emergency and force the strikers to return to work.[33]

Helping the UPS workers' public image was that they continued to travel their routes, explaining to their customers why they were on strike, and rank-and-file

Teamsters were often spokespeople in news conferences.[34] In addition, the Teamsters had support from community groups. For example, Jobs with Justice (an organization that attempts to mobilize unionists and their supporters in national campaigns) organized protests against companies that urged President Clinton to order the Teamsters back to work; "Local Coalitions for Occupational Safety and Health planned news conferences and demonstrations highlighting how UPS had paid academics to help attack federal job safety rights for all workers." Women's groups highlighted the effect that a reduction of jobs with decent pension and health benefits has on women.[35] David Moberg claims: "By preparing well in advance, the Teamsters were able to mobilize critical support from the rest of the labor movement: UPS pilots and mechanics refused to cross Teamster picket lines, and AFL-CIO President John Sweeney pledged to raise whatever money was necessary to sustain the modest Teamster strike benefits. Just as the strike was settled, the European UPS unions were preparing for a major meeting and protest that would have included more job actions."[36] The Teamsters announced that it would hold a national Action Day of Good Jobs on August 22.

However, the union and UPS agreed to a five-year contract (the union had demanded a three-year contract; UPS wanted a six-year contract) before the rally took place. UPS pledged to create 2,000 new full-time jobs for each year of the contract. It would subcontract only during peak seasons, and, unlike in 1993, it would consult with the Teamsters before it increased the package weight limit. UPS abandoned its opposition to the Teamsters' multiemployer pension plan and agreed to increase its contributions to the plan. It provided a wage increase of $4.10 an hour for part-time workers, with full-time workers receiving an extra $3.10 an hour over the life of the agreement. The strike was an overwhelming success for the Teamsters as UPS caved in to a majority of the union's demands. Carey stated, "This strike marks a new era. American workers have shown...we [can] stand up to corporate greed. This victory shows that American workers are on the move again."[37]

In July 1998, however, UPS argued that under the terms of the contract it did not have to create 2,000 full-time jobs per year if a reduction in the amount of parcels shipped by UPS forced the company to lay off workers. It claimed that because of the 1997 strike, it had laid off 10,000 workers due to a reduction in parcel traffic. The Teamsters argued that UPS had engaged in speedup and was forcing drivers to work through their lunch breaks to prevent workers becoming full time. This led the Teamsters to file a complaint with the NLRB. In March 2000, the board ruled that UPS was in violation of the 1997 contract. It ordered UPS to create the full-time jobs as outlined in the 1997 contract within 90 days, and provide back pay and benefits to the new full-time workers.[38]

The Teamsters overwhelming success demonstrates the benefits of social justice unionism tactics in collective bargaining. The Teamsters were successful on all fronts and achieved the majority of its demands. Even after UPS tried to avoid creating the new full-time jobs it agreed to, the Teamsters were successful as the NLRB upheld the contract. Admittedly, the Teamsters benefited during the strike through the public identifying with them over the issue of part-time jobs, but the public sided with UPS over the company wanting to withdraw from the Teamsters' multiemployer pension plan.[39] The union did profit from President Clinton's decision not to call a national emergency and order the strikers back to work, a decision that surprised UPS management. Likewise, improved economic conditions, such as the low US unemployment rate (4.9 percent), and the decision of UPS management not to bring in scabs during the strike further aided the Teamsters. Nevertheless, this does not take away from the Teamsters' achievement.

In addition to demonstrating the benefits of social justice unionism in collective bargaining, the Teamsters 1997 UPS campaign is a model that other unions should follow on how to effectively launch a bottom-up contract movement. The Teamsters surveyed members on the demands the union should make in the negotiations (and more importantly, listened to and implemented the members' wishes), included both full-time and part-time rank-and-file workers in the UPS bargaining committee, and kept the rank and file informed on the state of contract negotiations. This led to unity within the Teamsters between part-time and full-time workers (often a problem for unions in collective bargaining), and to the rank-and-file workers believing that they and the union were the same; it was us versus them. The Teamsters' social justice unionism tactics can easily be embraced by other unions, and judging from the success of the campaign, they should be implemented, especially in light of the 2002 UPS agreement.

2002 UPS NEGOTIATIONS/COLLECTIVE BARGAINING AGREEMENT

The 1997 UPS negotiations were Carey's last major triumph. Instead of relying on the rank and file during his successful 1996 reelection campaign, as he did in 1991, Carey hired political consultants. However, the consultants—the "November group"—implemented an illegal fundraising scheme that led to union funds being channeled into his reelection campaign.[40] While Carey was eventually cleared of all charges, during the investigation the Justice Department forced Carey to step down as president and for the Teamsters to conduct a new presidential election. In the election, James Hoffa Jr.—Jimmy Hoffa's son—defeated TDU-backed candidate Tom Leedham to become president of the IBT. This was to have a negative impact on the 2002 UPS negotiations/collective bargaining agreement.

The 2002 UPS collective bargaining agreement proves that top-down campaigns employed by business unions are often not as successful as social justice unionism campaigns that extensively involve the rank and file. The shadow of the September 11, 2001, terrorist attacks on the United States served as a backdrop to the 2002 UPS negotiations. The US economy was in recession, with workers being laid off across the country. Unlike in 1997 when a Democrat was in the White House, an antilabor Republican, George W. Bush, was president. However, UPS was still a very profitable company. In 2001, UPS's profit after taxes was $2.1 billion, which was its second best result ever. Likewise, while net income decreased 3.3 percent during the March 2002 quarter, it was still $563 million. This amount exceeded UPS's expectations. Moreover, since the signing of the 1997 contract, UPS had accumulated profits of almost $8 billion.[41] UPS could not credibly cry poor during the negotiations.

UPS believed it could reach a settlement with the Teamsters without a strike. UPS chairperson and chief executive Michael Eskew stated that a strike was unlikely, as the company was "dealing with reasonable, rational people this time. Ron Carey is no longer here."[42] However, Hoffa Jr. was promising UPS workers that the Teamsters would negotiate the best contract ever. He stated that the Teamsters would "win the strongest contract ever at UPS. UPS is the goose that laid the golden egg, and we will grab that goose by the neck and get every one of those golden eggs." Likewise, he claimed that the Teamsters were "going to be asking for a lot of money.... We think our people are behind for the kind of work they do. Look at the profits...[UPS] is making. The workers should share in that too." While the Teamsters did not release its economic proposals, it did release its noneconomic proposals: one of its demands being that UPS create 3,000 full-time jobs for every year of the contract.[43] In addition to 3,000 new full-time jobs for each year of the contract, the union's other main issues during negotiations were wages, pensions, and health care benefits. Hoffa Jr. stated that the increases would be better than the 1997 contract.

Hoffa Jr. did not actively involve the rank and file in the negotiations. The union did, however, distribute surveys to all UPS employers almost a year before the old contract expired to measure "bargaining priorities, including wage and benefit improvements, time-off improvements, benefits, job security, the grievance procedure and paycheck accuracy, and gauge member positions on issues regarding part-time workers, safety and health and working conditions."[44] In addition to the survey, other campaign tactics included touring two UPS contract caravans across the country to increase support for the negotiations. The only other rank-and-file-intensive tactic the Teamsters employed in the lead-up to the 2002 contract was in June, when it held rallies across the United States. At a rally in New York, Hoffa Jr. claimed that "we will protect Teamster pensions. We will maintain good health benefits. We will win more full-time jobs. And, we will preserve and expand good Teamster jobs."[45]

The caravans and the survey, however, were not used to mobilize members; union officials conducted the campaign with little rank-and-file involvement. For example, the union did not make its opening economic proposal public, nor did it release *any* information on the progress of the negotiations to members. Nevertheless, reports indicated that the Teamsters demanded a $1.25 wage increase for each year of the contract, while UPS offered a 35 cent increase. The Teamsters wanted a three-year contract, while UPS wanted a five-year contract.[46] Although there was some uncertainty about UPS's opening economic proposal, it is clear that Teamster officials were not impressed by it. Ken Hall, who along with Carey was the key architect of the 1997 negotiations/strike, was also the co-chair of the National Negotiating Committee for the 2002 negotiations. He claimed that the two sides "are very far apart on economic terms of the contract. I have urged the company to submit proposals that reflect the contributions of our members to UPS' success."[47]

Two weeks later, however, the Teamsters reached an agreement with UPS. This was very surprising, as the old contract was not set to expire for another 16 days. Hoffa Jr. claimed that the agreement "surpasses any contract ever negotiated at UPS... [and] it is the richest contract in UPS history and will set the tone for all collective bargaining for years to come."[48] The agreement revealed otherwise. The six-year agreement (the longest UPS agreement ever) contained a 3.2 percent wage increase for full-time workers ($5 per hour), and part-time workers received a $6 per hour increase over the life of the agreement.[49] However, there was only a 50 cent increase in starting pay for part-time workers. Thus, by 2008 the starting rate for part-time UPS employees will be $8.50 per hour compared to $22.50 for full-time employees. As TDU noted, "there seems little doubt that by 2008 McDonalds, Burger King and other low wage employers will be paying more than $9 per hour," as does the nonunionized Federal Express. Moreover, there was no increase in the daily minimum hours for part-time workers. UPS agreed to create 10,000 new full-time jobs over the life of the contract (as in the 1997 agreement, but in that agreement, UPS agreed to create 10,000 full-time jobs over five years; the Teamsters wanted 3,000 new full-time jobs per year of the contract), with "annual increases of $.63 per hour in health and pension contributions, compared to $.36 in the 1997 agreement." However, UPS workers in the Central States Pension Fund, which is the largest pension fund, received no pension increase.[50] Likewise, the new full-time jobs were not necessarily real full-time jobs. The contract states that UPS "wherever possible, [would] reschedule part-time employees to make additional full-time jobs or *combination* full-time jobs."[51] In other words, UPS has the option of classifying workers in these new jobs as full time for only part of the day, while for the rest of the day, workers would be classified as part time. There is a substantial difference between full-time and part-time wages. A part-time worker with four years' experience and seniority would receive $11.25 per hour, while a full-time worker would receive $22.50 per hour. Thus, the company would save money by classifying a worker as full-time for only part of the day. Overall, the agreement was good for full-time UPS employees, and average for part-time employees.

It is likely that the Teamsters could have achieved a better contract. Following the 1997 strike, UPS was fearful that another strike would occur. Indeed, UPS volume was decreasing before the contract expired, as customers anticipated another strike. Volume declined by 4 percent in June and 5 percent in the first two weeks of July.[52] This gave the Teamsters bargaining strength. This was in addition to the increased strike fund, which Hoffa Jr. claimed was to allow the Teamsters to "grab that goose [UPS] by the neck and get every one of those golden eggs." However, failure to mobilize the rank and file in advance of the negotiations made threat of a strike less plausible. While the contract was good for some UPS workers, it was only average for others, particularly part-time workers, who make up the majority of UPS's workforce.

TDU campaigned against the contract. It argued that UPS workers should reject the contract because of, among other things, the Central States

Pension Fund freeze, the widening of the gap between full-time and part-time wage rates, and the six-year contract. However, a clear majority of UPS workers (72.1 percent) ratified the contract, although voter turnout was only 38 percent. This was the lowest voter turnout in UPS history and the first time it had fallen below 50 percent.[53] Moreover, Hoffa Jr. imposed the UPS Detroit Area Contract Rider (a local contract in addition to the national UPS agreement) despite a majority voting against the contract. Hoffa Jr. implemented the two-thirds rule as less than 50 percent of UPS members voted, reinforcing Hoffa Jr.'s distaste for union democracy.[54] A recent survey casts further doubts on Hoffa Jr.'s claim that the 2002 UPS agreement is the best contract ever: more than 56 percent of UPS Teamster members claim that conditions are worse today that they were in 2002, with an astounding 95 percent claiming that the Hoffa administration has failed to live up to its promises on benefits.[55]

SOCIAL JUSTICE UNIONISM AND COLLECTIVE BARGAINING

TDU, despite its small size, played a crucial role in moving the Teamsters to the left. It accomplished this through its attempts to make Teamster officials agree to majority rule in contract and strike votes, and by helping to persuade the US government not to put the Teamsters into trusteeship, but to allow the rank and file to vote for top Teamster officials. Moreover, it helped in Ron Carey's successful election campaign, which subsequently led to the Teamsters increasing its organizing efforts. In the political arena, the Teamsters moved away from the Republican Party and toward the Democratic Party. The Teamsters attempted to stop NAFTA and to increase rank-and-file involvement in the union. However, the Justice Department, by forcing Carey to step down as president, which assisted the election of Hoffa Jr., negated much of TDU's efforts. Hoffa Jr. slashed the organizing budget, partly realigned the Teamsters with the Republican Party, and limited the rank and file's involvement in the union. After the Teamsters failed to achieve good collective bargaining agreements with UPS in 1990 and 1993, the union implemented a contract campaign in the 1997 negotiations that had a definite social justice unionism flavor (militancy, rank-and-file solidarity, internationalism, and community involvement). This led to a stunning victory for both full-time and part-time UPS workers. Under Hoffa Jr.'s leadership, with little rank-and-file and community involvement, the 2002 UPS agreement was a disappointment. While the contract was good for full-time workers, it was inadequate for part-time workers.

The Teamster-UPS negotiations and collective bargaining agreements clearly indicate that social justice unionism is an undoubted benefit for workers. Despite overwhelming odds and a history of poor agreements, when the Teamsters embraced social justice unionism it was successful. In the 2002 negotiations, where Hoffa Jr. reverted back to a top-down campaign with little rank-and-file and community involvement, the results were subpar for workers. The benefits of social justice unionism are further seen when looking at the auto industry.

CRISIS IN THE AUTO INDUSTRY

The auto industry is in crisis. Companies are reporting record losses and are in the process of slashing their workforce. In 2003 the UAW agreed to cut wages for new employees at the Visteon and Delphi (a major part supplier to GM) plants by $10 per hour. In 2006 the union agreed to early retirement buyouts for all GM and Delphi workers, with GM announcing plans to eliminate 60,000 jobs. Indeed, 35,000 workers have already accepted the buyout. At Delphi about 12,400 employees, representing almost 85 percent of the retirement-eligible UAW workforce, elected to retire by January 1, 2007, while about 1,400 employees opted for the buyout option. Almost all of the supplier's US hourly employees represented by the UAW were entitled to the buyout program, with about 14,600 eligible to participate in the retirement and preretirement programs. Of course, as GM is demanding this, company officials will receive multimillion dollar bonuses. Furthermore, the UAW accepted concessions in health care for its members at both GM and Ford, with Daimler-Chrysler pushing for the same concessions. At GM, 40,000 workers have had their pensions frozen. In addition, the UAW agreed to health care concessions. For the first time, it will require some retirees, who currently pay nothing for health coverage, to pay as much as $752 a year in deductibles, co-payments, and premiums.

Ford is planning to eliminate more than 30,000 jobs by 2008 (the UAW has 75,000 members at Ford). It has offered buyouts to all 75,000 of its North American factory workers in hopes of cutting its payroll costs by nearly a third. Moreover, UAW-Ford workers will forego future pay increases through the deferral of 17 cents of future quarterly cost-of-living adjustments (COLA) and the 3 percent wage increase that took effect in September 2006.

This is a crisis in anybody's language. However, in many ways the current crisis is just history repeating itself. As noted in chapter 2, the auto companies, in the face of record losses, demanded that unions reopen their contracts and engage in concession bargaining in the late 1970s and early 1980s. By the UAW engaging in concession bargaining, many UAW members lost their jobs, while the workers who remained had their wages and benefits slashed. In contrast, the Canadian United Auto Workers refused to accept concession bargaining, fought for their members, and were overwhelmingly successful.

THE CAW: A CASE STUDY OF SOCIAL
JUSTICE UNIONISM IN PRACTICE

The Canadian Auto Workers (CAW) formed after breaking away from the UAW in 1984 and changing its name from the Canadian United Auto Workers (CUAW). It broke away primarily due to its unhappiness with the UAW's continued willingness to engage in concession bargaining. The CAW is a successful union, and this success is largely due to its embrace of social justice unionism.

The CAW is a very democratic union. A key component of the CAW's Statement of Principles is that "unions are voluntary organizations. We can only be effective if the membership knows the union truly belongs to them. This means a union which reflects the goals of its membership, allows the members full participation, and encourages workers to develop their own skills and understanding."[56] The CAW's organizational structure is a crucial element in its approach to democratic unionism. Under the CAW's constitution, each Local, of which there are over 700, must have "several standing committees including Education, Environment, Women's, and Political Education...[as] a way of encouraging member involvement in their union—either through contested elections to fill such posts or through executive appointments to do the business of these committees."[57] Each CAW Local elects one delegate for a three-year term to sit on the CAW Council or the Quebec Council. The CAW Council and the Quebec Council are parallel organizations. The Quebec Council covers the Quebec region, while the CAW Council covers the rest of Canada. The CAW Council and the Quebec Council meet two times a year. At these meetings there is discussion of all issues affecting the CAW. As Ann Frost argues, "It is through these meetings that the CAW's mission of being a member-driven, responsive organization is realised. They also enable members to share in important ways what the union does. Decisions are made at these meetings by delegate vote and since all delegates are elected by their fellow rank-and-file members, considerable control rests in the hands of the CAW's local members."[58] In addition, the CAW and Quebec Councils provide a forum where the CAW leadership can be kept informed of the rank-and-files response to key issues. It is also used to mobilize the rank and file in any campaign. Directly above the CAW and Quebec Councils in the CAW's organizational structure is the CAW Council Executive. It comprises seven elected members who administer the CAW and Quebec Councils. The seven-member Council Executive is also part of the National Executive Board: the CAW's chief decision-making body. The National Executive comprises 10 part-time members (the seven members of the Council Executive and three other individuals chosen from CAW Council and Quebec Council delegates or the rank and file) and three full-time members (the president, the secretary-treasurer, and the Quebec director). If a union member has a dispute with the National Executive, he or she can ask the Public Review Board to adjudicate on the matter. The Public Review Board oversees the conduct of the National Executive Board and comprises five people who are not members of the CAW.[59]

The UAW provides a contrast to the CAW's democratic unionism. The UAW Executive Board has 24 full-time members, with no representation from the Local level. Since the late 1940s, the UAW leadership has controlled all internal debates. The UAW's Public Review Board argued that "executive board officers had a right to expect absolute loyalty from those below them because the union is 'a one party state.'" The UAW hierarchy's belief that the union is a one-party state led it, for example, to refuse the dissident New Directions movement from speaking at the 1992 UAW Convention.[60] This demonstrates the differing approaches to union democracy of the CAW and the UAW.

An important aspect of social justice unionism is that unions have alliances with the local community. CAW president Buzz Hargrove stated that "social unionism stresses the broad well-being of all working people, not just the narrow economic interest of our own members." A somewhat surprising CAW campaign is the fight against homelessness. With housing prices rising dramatically in relation to people's income, this is an important fight for unions. The CAW noted that a "single worker employed full time in Canada's largest city on a minimum wage of $6.85 an hour will fall about $3,000 short of the poverty line at the year's end."[61] In other words, workers earning minimum wage may have to choose between paying rent and spending their wages on other essentials, such as food or clothing, and the situation is even worse for the unemployed. The CAW argued that urgent steps had to be taken to stem the problem of homelessness. Its recommendations included implementing a national housing strategy, increasing government spending by an extra 1 percent in order to meet basic housing needs, and asking the government to restore effective rent control legislation.[62]

Another community campaign that the CAW is involved in is the fight for adequate child care. On November 14, 2001, *The Toronto Star* leaked a report that stated that the Ontario government planned to cut the managed child care budget by 45 percent. The CAW aligned with the Ontario Coalition for Better Child Care as it attempted to stop the massive cuts. The CAW, which was at the forefront of including child care issues in collective bargaining agreements, stated that "we cannot sit back and watch the system developed over the last 60 years be wiped out in one stroke. The government of Ontario needs to hear NOW that thousands of Ontarians want significant increases to child care funding—NOT CUTS."[63]

Since it seceded from the UAW, the CAW has seen staggering growth. In 1984, a year before its secession, the CAW had 120,000 members; in 2001 it had 250,000 members and, on average, has organized more than 6,000 new workers per year. In contrast, the UAW for the decade after the split lost one-third of its membership, and between 1979 and 1995, it lost half of its members. The recent slashing of jobs in the auto industry will see the UAW's membership decline even further. Nevertheless, the UAW still organizes more new members than the CAW. From 1998 to 2002, the UAW organized 51,782 workers, or about 13,000 workers per year. The UAW has 640,000 members, which is nearly three times the size of the CAW.[64]

Like the UAW, the CAW has not been immune to membership losses. Between 1985 and 1995, the closure of 250 unionized production facilities resulted in a loss of approximately 28,000 CAW members. In addition, because of downsizing, approximately 10,000–15,000 CAW members lost their jobs. This would have resulted in the union membership falling to well under 80,000, but successful organizing drives led many workers to join the CAW. Between 1985 and early 1996, approximately 50,000 workers became CAW members.[65] These new members neutralized the loss of membership due to plant closures and downsizing. While the CAW was successful in organizing a substantial number of workers, the real growth of the CAW came from union mergers. Between 1985 and early 1996, union mergers led to almost 100,000 workers becoming CAW members, and allowing for job losses and retirements, workers who became CAW members since 1985 account for approximately 65 percent of the membership and 50 percent of the activists within the union.[66]

While the majority of new CAW members are from union mergers, the CAW's profile as a social justice union influenced many unions to merge with the CAW. Gindin asserts that the "CAW was an attractive potential partner to many sectors because of its high profile, strong servicing reputation, independence from the Americans, and stance on concessions and fighting the corporate agenda." Thus, in addition to organizing the unorganized, the CAW, through mergers, has brought existing union members under its banner of social justice unionism.[67]

Social justice unions should also have international alliances. As with its commitment to union democracy and organizing the unorganized, the CAW is at the forefront of labor internationalism. The CAW was involved in a noteworthy example of labor internationalism in the telecommunications industry with the Teamsters and the Transport and General Workers Union (TGWU) in Britain during the early 1990s. The alliance formed when, during collective bargaining negotiations, Air Canada threatened the CAW that it would move ticket reservation calls to the United States. At the same time, Air Canada management threatened the Teamsters that it would move US reservations work to Canada. However, instead of accepting Air Canada's demands for concessions, the CAW and the Teamsters formed a pact with the TGWU, and they received help from the transport workers' International Trade Secretariat. The pact stated that the "reservations made in each country were the work of the union workers in that country.... [Moreover,] the three unions agreed that they would refuse to take reservations calls from each other's countries, should the company try to reroute them."[68] By working together, unions in three different countries stood up to management threats while at the same time forging closer links with workers worldwide.

Moreover, the CAW has a long history of forging links with workers in the South, particularly in Mexico. For example, the CAW joined with UAW Local 879 in support of Cuautitlan Ford workers when Ford broke its contract with the Mexican workers. Ford refused to pay a Christmas bonus, which makes up a substantial part of the workers' wages, and to participate in profit sharing. Moreover, it fired over 750 union members. In response to Ford's actions, workers "from all three countries have met on several occasions [and] in a symbolic gesture of solidarity, they have worn black arm bands to commemorate the death of... a Ford worker killed by CTM [Confederación de Trabajadores Mexicanos] goons."[69] In an effort to cover the costs of labor internationalism, the CAW established a social justice fund. Through a clause in a collective bargaining contract, the employer must pay an amount into the fund: three cents an hour in the case of the Big Three automakers, and one cent for smaller companies. This generates approximately $2.5 million (Canadian) per annum and is an ingenious way to make employers contribute to the fight for decent pay and working conditions for workers in both the North and the South.[70]

The CAW is a democratic union with active rank-and-file involvement, organizes the unorganized, and has alliances with social movements, community groups, and workers worldwide. In other words, it is a social justice union.

COLLECTIVE BARGAINING AT GM

The 1996 CAW-GM and UAW-GM negotiations/collective bargaining agreements show that militancy and a union's ideology are crucial in collective bargaining. Since the late 1970s the CAW has achieved better collective bargaining agreements than the UAW, but it is often argued that this is due to the healthier state of the Canadian economy compared to the American economy.[71] However, in 1996, the American economy was in a healthier state than the Canadian economy. For example, the Canadian unemployment rate was 9.7 percent, whereas the US unemployment rate was 5.4 percent. The Canadian gross domestic product (GDP) grew by 2.1 percent in 1996, while the US GDP grew by 2.7 percent for the corresponding period.[72] Thus, while neither economy was buoyant, the US economy was healthier.

The key provision in the UAW's collective bargaining agreement with Chrysler required Chrysler to keep 95 percent of its workforce. The UAW allowed Chrysler to reduce the number of unionized jobs, and the same situation occurred with Ford, as the company had previously agreed to the 95 percent level. The UAW began negotiations with GM following its settlement with Chrysler. Industry analysts predicted that it was unlikely GM could match the contract provision in which Ford and Chrysler agreed not to reduce their workforce by more than 5 percent. The main obstacle during the negotiations was that GM did not want to include in the 95 percent level the 12 plants it was planning to close. Following strikes at key GM production plants, GM agreed to match the Ford contract, including the 95 percent of the existing workforce provision.[73]

While on the surface the contract appeared a victory for the UAW, a closer examination revealed otherwise. Numerous loopholes allowed GM to reduce its workforce by more than 5 percent. The contract provisions allowed GM to do this and not be in breach of the contract if it reduced "jobs as it makes factories more efficient, if market share declines, if it sells uncompetitive plants, or if it goes ahead with previously announced plant closings."[74] Moreover, the UAW agreed to "renew its 'living agreement' approach, whereby top management and the pinnacle of the union hierarchy can change local working conditions (flexibility) at will, and to permit unbounded overtime and outsourcing; they also agreed to introduce a new element of wage flexibility granted earlier to Ford, allowing the pay of workers in its part plants to fall behind those in assembly over time."[75] The contract allowed GM to reduce the unionized workforce by more than 5 percent for the further implementation of lean production methods, and the UAW agreed to an unequal wage level for its GM workers. The collective bargaining agreement was hardly a success for UAW GM workers. Indeed, the UAW's only success was achieving a $2,000 ratification bonus for its GM workforce and a 3 percent increase in the base wage rate for the second and third years of the contract. Thus, it was the first time since the 1980s that the union won annual pay increases in more than one year of the contract.[76] During the same period, in every collective bargaining agreement with the Big Three, the CUAW/CAW had achieved an increase in the base pay rate for each year of the contracts.

The CAW negotiations with GM began after the CAW reached an agreement with Chrysler in which Chrysler agreed not to reduce its workforce. Outsourcing was the main issue during the negotiations, and the CAW was hoping to limit the number of jobs that GM outsourced. While analysts believed that GM could successfully deal with a strike because of the company's financial reserves and the limited CAW strike fund, this did not deter CAW GM workers. The workers voted overwhelmingly (92 percent) to give the CAW leadership strike authorization.[77] GM refused to accept the same deal the CAW negotiated with Chrysler, and the CAW refused to compromise, which led to CAW GM members going on strike.

To help striking workers, a CAW convention approved the doubling of dues for non-GM members for the duration of the strike, and the United Steelworkers provided financial assistance to the CAW.[78] The CAW employed militant tactics as part of its strategy. When GM attempted to move production equipment from a struck plant to resume production elsewhere, CAW members staged a sit-in. This action had widespread community support and was ultimately successful. As CAW official Dave Robertson noted, "We . . . saw solidarity in how the community responded. We were not seen as an isolated aristocracy of labor, but as a social movement that was fighting to preserve communities. And that has to do with how we defined the union."[79]

The two sides eventually compromised after a 21-day strike. Under the terms of the settlement, GM reversed its decision to outsource 814 jobs in Ontario and Quebec. It extended the life of one plant, which led to the retention of 1,000 jobs and the creation of another 400 jobs, but GM could sell two plants that employed 3,500 CAW members.

However, while the CAW allowed GM to sell the plants, the contract stated that the new owners of the plants must abide by the CAW-GM contract. Workers who wished to retire were offered early-retirement packages, and workers who remained at the plants were guaranteed the same pension benefits as GM employees for nine years.[80] GM workers received a 2 percent increase in their base pay rate for each year of the contract, plus cost-of-living provisions. Moreover, GM agreed to provide health care benefits for the live-in partners of homosexual employees. Under the terms of the contract, "same-sex partners of GM's 26,000 Canadian hourly employees can receive the health-care benefits already offered to workers' married spouses or heterosexual partners." This provision in the contract was groundbreaking because in the United States, GM did not provide these benefits to live-in partners of GM workers if they were the opposite sex, let alone the same sex.[81] Ford accepted the same contract without a fight.

Thus, the UAW agreed to grant management greater flexibility and allowed GM to reduce its workforce. Conversely, the CAW achieved an agreement that created jobs and funded redundancies through retirement packages. The UAW allowed wage differentiation between its assembly line and its auto-part plants workers. The CAW, even where it allowed GM to sell two plants, ensured that its contract with GM covered the workers in those plants. There is no comparison between the two agreements. Despite the healthier state of the US economy, the CAW achieved a superior contract from GM (and Chrysler and Ford) compared to the UAW. The UAW's only success in comparison to the CAW was securing higher wage raises for the second and third year of the contracts (3 percent to 2 percent). However, as the CAW achieved a 2 percent increase for each year of the contract, it matched the total increase the UAW gained (6 percent). Moreover, while UAW workers got a $2,000 ratification bonus, CAW workers, through an increase in payments for such things as overtime, cost-of-living allowance, and other benefits, came close to equaling or surpassing the $2,000 bonus through their 2 percent increase in the first year of the contract. The 1996 collective bargaining agreements demonstrate that while the state of the economy has some bearing on collective bargaining agreements, a union's militancy and ideology, along with its preparedness to stand up in the face of threats by employers, are important factors. The CAW's social justice unionism ideology and its militancy in collective bargaining negotiations with the Big Three was an undoubted benefit to its members. As Moody argues, the lesson learned by the CAW's struggle against concessions and lean production while the UAW embraced them was that "resistance matters, particularly when the union leadership is willing to stick to its guns, and that elements of lean production or competitiveness the company sees as essential can be stopped or modified."[82]

SOCIAL JUSTICE UNIONISM:
COLLECTIVE BARGAINING AND ORGANIZING

These case studies reveal that with respect to wages, working conditions, and organizing new members, social justice unions achieve better wages and working conditions and organize more new members per capita than their rival business unions. Likewise, the Teamsters achieved its greatest success in recent years when it implemented a contract campaign that had a definite social justice unionism flavor.

From 1979 onward, the CUAW/CAW consistently achieved better collective bargaining agreements with the Big Three automakers (Chrysler, Ford, and GM) than did the UAW. This was irrespective of the state of the Canadian and US economies. The differences between the contracts were because of the CUAW/CAW's militancy and its refusal to accept concessions. Conversely, the UAW leadership refused to fight for its members, which led it to accept concessions very quickly. Furthermore, since its split from the UAW in 1985, the CAW has increased its membership by 130,000, with it organizing more than 6,000 workers per year. The majority of new members came from mergers between the CAW and smaller unions, but the CAW's social justice unionism influenced many unions to merge with the CAW. In contrast, between 1985 and 1995, the UAW's membership decreased by 33 percent, and between 1979 and 1995, it decreased by a massive 50 percent.[83]

Likewise, the Teamsters achieved its best contract ever with UPS in 1997, with both full-time and part-time workers attaining significant gains. It was during this campaign that TDU's influence was greatest and the Teamsters' leadership implemented a contract campaign, which was initially suggested by TDU. The campaign definitely had a social justice unionism flavor (militancy, rank-and-file-intensive tactics that built solidarity between full-time and part-time UPS employees, international solidarity, and community alliances). In contrast, the 2002 UPS campaign either utilized these tactics only to a limited extent or ignored them for a top-down approach. It was therefore not surprising that these contracts were disappointing to many UPS workers, especially part-timers.

The two case studies demonstrate the benefits of social justice unionism compared to business unionism for workers, purely in regard to bread-and-butter issues. Moreover, they show that social justice unions organize more workers per capita than do their rival business unions. Social justice unionism, at the very least, will certainly benefit both unions and workers and can do no worse than what is currently happening in the auto industry. Years of indifference, business unionism, and concession bargaining cannot be reversed overnight, or even in the midterm. Nevertheless, history has proved that social justice unionism is a successful strategy for unions to adopt in a variety of industries, even in bad economic times.[84] In this period of declining union membership and declining workers' wages (in real terms), social justice unionism would be a great benefit to all concerned.

6

NONTRADITIONAL STRATEGIES

The previous chapter concluded that unions should adopt social justice union-ism in an attempt to revive organized labor. This chapter looks at nontra-ditional organizing strategies unions should adopt. In many cases, these strategies involve forming alliances with nonunion organizations. As with so-cial justice unionism, these strategies will not cure all of labor's woes, but they are certainly a step in the right direction.

Many of these strategies are targeted to immigrant workers, whether they are documented or are in the country illegally. There has been a dramatic in-crease in the number of foreign-born workers in the United States. In 2004, the number of workers born overseas was more than 22 million (only about 8 million are citizens), 14.5 percent of the workforce. Of this, approximately 10.5 million people are in the country illegally. Latinos account for the biggest increase in immigration numbers: 7 million joined the workforce from 1995 to 2004 (46 percent of all immigrants).[1] It is often assumed that the increasing number of foreign-born workers, and especially undocumented workers, is driving wages down, but this is not true. As noted in chapter 1, real wages began declining in 1973, almost a decade before Latinos started coming to the United States in any great numbers. Moreover, while Latinos were coming into the country in record numbers in the 1990s, real wages increased and unemployment decreased from 1995 until 2000 (wages decreased and unem-ployment increased following the recession). As Moody argues:

> What appears to be the case is that there is a strong tendency today, as there was over a hundred years ago, for the various ethnic immigrant groups to concentrate in particular occupations or industries in a given geographic region where jobs were being or had been abandoned by native-born workers. So, in L.A., for example, the building maintenance workers are heavily Mexican and Central American, as are the dry wall installers, and the truckers on the waterfront. In New York, Latino immi-grants are found in greengrocer stores and restaurant kitchens, but also construction, while Indians and Pakistanis are found driving cabs, etc. In these cases, there is little evidence of competition with other groups of workers.[2]

As I have continually argued, immigrant workers have had a crucial role in reviving some unions, and more generally have introduced new innovative and militant union tactics. Immigrants are essential to labor's revitalization. The power of immigrant workers was clearly demonstrated on May 1, 2006.

"A Day without Immigrants" witnessed approximately 4–6 million immigrant workers, their families, friends, and supporters marching in support of immigrant rights. This act of power occurred because of the increasing anti-immigration rhetoric and policies from politicians. A particularly reprehensible bill is HR 4437, which the House of Representatives passed in December 2005. The bill will criminalize undocumented workers and anyone who helps them.

In response, immigrant workers displayed a level of people power comparable to anything seen in American history. While unions were not at the forefront of organizing the protests throughout the country, they played a part. For example, in Los Angeles, unions provided more than $80,000 for the event, as well as coordinating it.[3] The SEIU also had an important role in helping the marches. The union claimed that it had "brought credibility to the demonstrations, making it safe for politicians and other community leaders to participate with grassroots groups they knew little about." The spokesperson for SEIU Local 1877 in Los Angeles stated, "We make sure these organizations are stable and respected players."[4] However, at the same time, the SEIU did not want its workers to go out on strike. The vice president of SEIU Local 1199 claimed that to "call on our lowest-income workers not to go to work would be inappropriate at this time." But not all unions and federations felt this way; the Chicago Federation of Labor encouraged its members to march.[5] The likelihood that organized labor will survive and prosper depends on its ability to organize immigrants.

As Ruth Milkman argues, there are three main reasons why it may be easier to organize immigrants compared to US-born workers:

> First, working-class immigrants tend to have stronger social networks than all but the poorest natives, and typically these networks are deeply embedded in occupational and/or workplace settings, where they can support unionization and political mobilization efforts. Second, class-based collective organizations like labor unions and CBOs [community-based organizations] may be more compatible with the lived experiences, worldviews, and identities of many immigrants...than with those of native-born workers. Finally, the shared experience of stigmatization among immigrants, both in the course of migration itself and even after years of settlement, may foster a sense of unity—especially in employment settings where immigrants make up the bulk of the workforce.[6]

Immigrant workers are a virtual untapped resource for unions. Unions should do everything in their power to organize immigrant workers. In so doing, unions will be revitalized. In return, immigrant workers will receive better wages and working conditions. Moreover, all workers will benefit. Union members receive better wages and working conditions, as well as greater health care coverage. A revitalized labor movement will mean that more workers are organized, not just immigrants, which means that *all* workers are better off. The following strategies are ones that unions should implement to help in organizing immigrants as well as all workers.

CENTRAL LABOR COUNCILS

By effectively utilizing central labor councils (CLCs), unions can increase the number of union members. CLCs are local federations of AFL-CIO unions that "work actively with community groups and academics to educate working people, to create jobs (often for women, African Americans, Latinos, and all immigrants, as in Atlanta during the 1996 Olympics), to improve community life (unionists and environmentalists have cooperated in Los Angeles to stop corporate outlaws from polluting working-class communities), and to organize workers."[7]

The emphasis on organizing began in 1998, when the CLC advisory committee joined forces with Jobs with Justice to demand that workers have the right to join unions. By June, over 70 CLCs were involved in some form of organizing campaign, and by 2000 more than 150 CLCs were engaged in supporting organizing campaigns in some form. The director of the AFL-CIO Field Mobilization Department claims, "This is not just the story of a Seattle, a San Jose, a Los Angeles, or a Cleveland, but places as diverse as Houston, Little Rock, Hartford, Denver and Savannah, Georgia."[8]

One way for unions to use CLCs is to organize workers through living-wage campaigns. In these campaigns, a CLC convinces local governments to implement legislation that forces businesses that receive contracts and/or subsidies from governments to pay their workers a wage that, at the very least, corresponds to the federal poverty line. Stephanie Luce claims that while the majority of campaigns have not resulted in an increase in organizing, there are exceptions. This is through the campaigns' "improving labor's image and educating workers about unions, as well as by creating a chance to get organizing leads during the campaign itself; for example, in Chicago, the campaign helped SEIU find leads for new organizing among home-health-care workers."[9] Moreover, before the living-wage campaigns, workers' received, on average, $6.25 per hour; this figure increased to $8.50 an hour after successful campaigns. This is a huge difference to workers with low pay.

Santa Cruz was the site of a particularly impressive living-wage campaign that led to both increased wages and a successful organizing campaign. The local CLC joined forces with organizers from the living-wage campaign to not only fight for a living wage for workers, but to increase union membership. In a great victory, the "living-wage law that was passed last year not only delivered the highest living wage in the country, it also required that covered employers remain neutral during union-organizing elections and agree to card-check recognition of a bargaining unit. Literally days after the living-wage law went into effect, it was used to persuade a non-profit agency with a history of anti-union behavior to agree to card check and neutrality for a unit of paratransit workers." The workers' wages increased to $11 per hour. Furthermore, the campaign also helped the SEIU organize temporary workers employed by the city of Santa Cruz, who received lower wages and benefits than the full-time unionized workforce. The SEIU involved the temporary workers in the living-wage campaign. Following the campaign's success, the city council agreed to recognize the workers' right to organize, to stay neutral in the organizing efforts, and to card-check recognition.[10] This was not the only time the SEIU gained from a living-wage campaign. SEIU Local 880 in Chicago has greatly benefited from such campaigns. In addition to their members' receiving higher wages, the campaigns help to gain new potential organizing leads. Keith Kelleher of SEIU Local 880 claims, "You can bet that every time we do any action around living wage, we get calls."[11]

Union involvement in living-wage campaigns has both positives and negatives. Union involvement helps the campaigns get media attention and credibility, and the unions can also use their resources (staff as well as money) to benefit the living-wage fight (the use of union resources to produce election day flyers was what led to the success of the living-wage campaign in Detroit). Conversely, due to the long history of business unionism, some community groups and funders of antipoverty campaigns will not become involved in the campaigns if there is union involvement.[12] Nevertheless, as is usually the case, change takes time. As the labor movement increasingly becomes involved in such campaigns and (hopefully) moves away from business unionism and toward social justice unionism, organized labor will no longer be seen in a negative light. Indeed, living-wage campaigns have transformed unions into organizations that care about *all* workers. This obviously helps not only the employees, who are now receiving a better wage, but the unions themselves, as they have a better public image, which is a benefit in any organizing drive. As David Reynolds and Jen Kern succinctly argue,

> When unions join active living-wage campaigns, not only do they help change public policy, they transform themselves. They join efforts that involve many of the core aspects needed to revitalize organized labor as a progressive social force. As living-wage campaigns become more ambitious and as they spread into more conservative areas of the country, they will offer even greater promise as seedbeds of progressive transformation. The future of living-wage organizing is part of the future of American unionism.[13]

There are other ways that CLCs help unions organize workers. First, a CLC can support a union's organizing efforts through mobilizing alliances between labor and community groups, including politicians and by helping rank-and-file workers to become organizers.[14] As I argued in Chapter 3, union alliances with community groups and new social movements are an undoubted benefit to labor. While it is often assumed that living-wage campaigns only benefit workers in the service industry, this is not the case. The building industry in Virginia was increasingly becoming nonunion, with Latino workers becoming the norm. Ironworkers Local 5 understood that building bridges to the local Latino community would prevent employers from causing divisions between the new workforce and unions. Thus, the Ironworkers helped form the Northern Virginia Living Wage Coalition, which led to alliances with a wide range of community groups and religious organizations. The campaign was characterized by an impressive coalition of local labor, low-income and religious activists, and a combination of public pressure tactics and grass-roots lobbying. The coalition was ultimately successful in achieving a living wage for workers in Alexandria, Virginia.[15] While such campaigns may not necessarily lead to organizing victories straight away, they are great building blocks for future campaigns.

Another example where labor benefited through a CLC having a partnership with community organizations was in Arkansas. The Central Arkansas Labor Council joined forces with the Association of Community Organizations for Reform Now (ACORN) to spearhead the drive for living-wage ordinances, to organize workers, and to help elect like-minded politicians. ACORN is a community organization of generally low- and moderate-income families that pushes for social justice and stronger communities. ACORN organizers often help sign up workers for union certification elections and support unions in contract campaigns.[16] Alliances with ACORN help unions immensely. Regarding labor's relationship with ACORN in New York, the *New York Times* reported the following:

The Working Families Party [a union and ACORN initiative] and ACORN, one of its largest affiliated groups, have emerged as a significant policy-making force on the [New York City] Council, working with a loose coalition of about two dozen [city council] members.... They have nudged members to propose laws that would raise to $8.10 an hour the minimum wage that companies receiving public money through subsidies or contracts must pay their employees, regulate training and education for welfare recipients, and prohibit the city from doing business with banks that engage in predatory lending.... Several proposals to generate additional revenue, developed with the help of the Working Families Party, are supported by at least half of the Council's 51 members. They include reviving taxes on stock transactions and on commuters, and raising the personal income tax for the wealthiest commuters.[17]

These are just a couple of examples of alliances between ACORN and organized labor; other examples are in Connecticut, Illinois, Louisiana, Massachusetts, Missouri, New Jersey, and Pennsylvania, just to name a few. In all these situations, the labor movement's alliance with ACORN was a benefit. Obviously, unions' alliances with ACORN are not perfect. Too often unions are happy to receive support from ACORN during such things as organizing drives, but are unwilling to reciprocate the support in nonunion campaigns. Such things will only damage labor's reputation even further, and hasten its decline. There is no such thing as a nonunion campaign. All issues that affect working people deserve and need labor's involvement.

Returning to the issue of CLCs, another way that CLCs help organize workers is through a CLC actually coordinating organizing campaigns. An example of this occurred in California. Taking the lead from the Los Angeles County Federation, which helped organize thousands of workers at the Los Angeles international airport, the San Mateo Labor Council attempted to organize workers at the San Francisco airport. The CLC worked with unions that already had members at the airport as well as the AFL-CIO and academics from the University of California-Berkeley in organizing a campaign. The group received support from San Francisco mayor Willie Brown and the Airport Commission. The mayor passed an ordinance in which the unions promised there would be peace and employers agreed not to interfere in the organizing campaign. The CLC still had a crucial role when the unions involved launched their own organizing campaigns. Shelley Kessler, executive secretary of the San Mateo Labor Council, stated, "Our labor councils were effective because we were able to help individual unions think and act collaboratively even though they have different cultures, history, and negotiating styles." The campaign was a huge success that led to over 2,000 workers joining unions. It was also a success for the workers: their working conditions improved, and their average wages increased from $6 per hour to almost $10 per hour.[18]

The third way that CLCs help organize workers is by initiating organizing campaigns in cases where workers are unsure whether they want a union and a union has doubts about whether an organizing campaign would be successful. The CLC would do all the groundwork, and if over time the workers decide that they need union representation, the CLC would turn its efforts over to a union.[19] In addition, a CLC can help workers who are not allowed to join a union or are unable to engage in collective bargaining. For example, New York City taxi drivers are considered independent contractors. As such, they are unable to engage in collective bargaining. This has led the New York Taxi Workers Alliance (NYTWA)—a nontraditional union—to join the New York Central Labor Council. This is a benefit to all concerned. As the director of the NYTWA argues, "We're not isolated anymore. Next time we protest it won't just be our leaders and members—it will be New York labor leaders too." It is also a benefit to the labor movement because there are "40,000 taxi drivers in New York, and that's 40,000 working families that have joined the labor movement."[20]

Fourth, a CLC can continually harass a company to recognize a union. For example, in a US Midwestern right-to-work state, a CLC picketed a hotel until the hotel agreed to recognize the union.[21] There was a similar situation in Milwaukee. As Enid Eckstein explains,

> The Milwaukee Organizing Roundtable spent several years discussing how to best support local organizing efforts. The council worked with the Hotel and Restaurant Employees union…to win a card check neutrality agreement for a proposed hotel development. In 1998 the council united with a neighboring labor council to hold a major hearing on organizing rights of a part-time college faculty. The council supported the Amalgamated Transit Union…campaign to organize and win a first contract for the workers at Laidlaw, a local bus service. The council recognized that much of the organizing targeted county subcontractors, and it sought to find a way to support organizing that would not disrupt services and to avoid the long, drawn-out fights that characterized previous organizing.[22]

After winning this fight, the Milwaukee CLC helped elect a union member to the Milwaukee County Board of Supervisors. After union members continually met with board supervisors, the board eventually passed a regulation stating that employers must recognize the right of workers to join a union. The Milwaukee CLC president said the campaign was a "great fight for the council because it got everyone on board and united them. It brought all the unions—building trades, public-sector and service-sector unions—together and we built a campaign to win.... We were able to educate our religious allies and then they were able to educate the county supervisors."[23] In 2000 alone, CLCs played a major role in many union victories across the country:

> The Alameda Council helped HERE win recognition and a first contract at the Berkeley Radisson Hotel, Phoenix supported the IBEW [International Brotherhood of Electrical Workers] at Southwest Gas, and Cleveland helped HERE, the...SEIU, and UNITE win significant victories. In San Jose, the South Bay Labor Council and its Workers Rights Board held a community election to allow hospital workers to quickly win a voice at work and avoid lengthy delays designed to avoid unionization. In Philadelphia, the Philadelphia Labor Council built political support for the graduate student organizing campaign at Temple University. The City Council passed a resolution calling for the University to recognize the AFT [American Federation of Teachers] and not to engage in antiunion behavior. The Western Pennsylvania labor councils helped Allegheny General and Beaver Health Systems registered nurses organize with 1199P/SEIU....And the list goes on and on.[24]

However, like the small number of social justice unions in America, only about 23 percent of CLCs engage in any kind of organizing efforts not connected to national unions. While the AFL-CIO is trying to revitalize CLCs through the Union Cities program, similar to the union movement as a whole, there has been limited change, with only 33 percent of CLCs joining the Union Cities program.[25] This is a major problem, yet at the same time it reveals that CLCs are largely an untapped resource that unions can use to organize new members. Another problem that CLCs must confront in their efforts to help organize workers is that unions often view the CLCs as outsiders that should not be involved in organizing. This illustrates the difficulty of transforming unions into social justice unions or, at the very least, more progressive unions. When CLCs are viewed as outsiders, it is an indication of the long road that lies ahead in trying to change the culture of unions.

The Union Cities program clearly identifies the problems for labor's revival. The AFL-CIO and CLCs implemented the program in 1997 with the express purpose of helping CLCs engage in organizing. A city can be considered a Union City if the local CLC devotes one-third of its resources to organizing, implements a "Street Heat" program (a rapid-response group that is willing and able to engage in demonstrations against antiunion employers and governments), pressures local governments to pass labor-friendly ordinances, and has alliances with the local community.[26] If the CLC implements these goals, the AFL-CIO recognizes the city as a Union City. The Union Cities program has been a success for those CLCs that have made changes (as noted above, only a disappointing 33 percent of CLCs have joined the program, although this does equate to 200 CLCs). Union City projects have helped organizing drives in Baltimore; Charleston, South Carolina; Chicago; Kansas City; Milwaukee; New York City; Portland; Seattle; and Syracuse. The successful organizing drive at the San Francisco airport was helped through involvement of a CLC in a Union City. If a city is classified as a Union City, unions are very successful in certification elections. Unions win 59 percent of certification elections when they are held in a Union City; this rises to a massive 82 percent when the unions involved engage in five or more rank-and-file organizing, community-based tactics.[27] The Union Cities program is one of great success; the win-rates are outstanding. Given this, you would think the AFL-CIO would encourage more CLCs to adopt the Union City agenda with the AFL-CIO devoting a lot more resources to the program, but you would be wrong. The AFL-CIO has actually devoted fewer resources to the Union City program than it has in the past. This perfectly sums up the hard road ahead for positive transformation in the union movement. Nevertheless, this does not take away from the importance of CLCs and the Union City program. CLCs are an essential component of labor's revival.[28]

WORKER CENTERS

Just as CLCs can help in the fight to organize more workers, worker centers are another way to organize workers. Janice Fine, the leading expert on worker centers, claims,

> [worker centers] are not quite unions, although they mobilize workers around employment concerns. They are not quite community organizations, although they are involved in community issues. And they are not quite legal services or social service agencies, although they provide some legal representation as well as training and education. They grew out of the enormous unmet needs of immigrant workers who had no organization or representation as they faced tremendous problems in their workplaces. Some worker centers are directly affiliated with unions, but the bulk of them are independent.[29]

The formation of worker centers in the past was mainly due to two reasons: (1) unions were unwilling to organize marginal workers who wanted representation, and (2) traditional organizing techniques, such as certification elections and collective bargaining, were ineffective in organizing the people worker centers cater to.[30] Moreover, there are a number of worker centers that were formed due to conflict with unions. The founder of the Workplace Project argues, "Some centers were founded by workers who had been burned by their experiences with unions. Others started out working with the labor movement but felt that the unions first co-opted the leadership they had fought so hard to build and then pulled out after a campaign lost."[31] The growth of worker centers is due to the changes in America's economic structure, namely, the rise of sweatshops, subcontracting, service industries (especially hospitality), and the informal economy. All of these industries have bad wages and working conditions, with an increasing majority of the workers being immigrants.[32]

The relationship between worker centers and unions varies among worker centers and among unions. In some instances there are close ties between the two, in other instances there is some collaboration, and unfortunately in others there is no relationship, often due to unions. The more progressive the union, or if the union has a majority of immigrants as members, or if the union is in an industry that has a lot of immigrants, the more likely there will be at least some ties between the union and a worker center. There is a growing realization within the union movement that it needs close ties with worker centers.

Three waves of growth have occurred in worker centers. The first wave was in the late 1970s and early 1980s and was started by political activists with some connections to unions. The second wave took place from the late 1980s until the mid-1990s. This wave was associated with immigration from Central America as people fled the war-torn region. The third wave occurred after 2000. What is particularly different about this wave is that there was a greater connection between worker centers and unions than seen in the past, and they were increasingly located in southern states. Organized labor has had some role in forming worker centers: 9 percent of worker centers formed due to the decline of unionism in particular industries, and another 14 percent formed due to connections to unions and organizing campaigns.[33]

Worker centers generally focus on a particular region (whether it is a metropolitan area, city, or neighborhood) or a specific industry. They concentrate on race and ethnicity as the basis of discrimination against their clients. In addition, an increasing number of centers are focusing on the relationship among race, gender, and low-wage work. Worker centers are very democratic, as they involve all workers in the decision making regarding their future. As part of the democratic process, worker centers believe that education is essential to empowerment. Indeed, the board of the Workplace Project in Long Island totally comprises local members. The project's number one principle is that the center should be run by the workers and they should fight for themselves.[34] Moreover, worker centers often have ties to other community organizations and religious groups as well as with similar organizations in other countries facilitated by the immigrants they help. They generally have three main roles:

1. Service delivery: they provide legal representation to workers to recover unpaid wages. Worker centers on average manage to recover approximately $100,000–$200,000 a year in unpaid wages for workers. In 1993, after only a few years in existence, the Workplace Project, with only one part-time employee focused on the issue, managed to win 71 percent of unpaid wages cases, recovering $215,000 for 166 workers. In contrast, the Department of Labor took on 72 cases and won only two. They also work to improve wages as well as conduct English lessons and worker education programs that teach immigrants about employment and social welfare laws. In regards to wages, the Workplace Project increased wages for day laborers by over one-third, from $40 to $60–$70 over a three-year period.

2. Advocacy: They lobby governments to implement and change laws so they are more worker and immigrant friendly, and they take businesses to court over labor violations (the Workplace Project was instrumental in New York legislators passing the toughest unpaid wages law in the country).
3. Organizing: They forge ties among unions, immigrants, and the local community. As Jennifer Gordon, founder of the Workplace Project, claims, the project organizes at different levels: "around individual workers' claims, at particular workplaces, across industries, and around issues that affect all low-wage workers."[35] Thus, worker centers concentrate on workplace issues, as well as challenging power relationships within the community. In this regard, their outlook is very similar to social justice unions.

Obviously, each worker center, of which there are over 135 (122 worker centers can be classified as immigrant worker centers), will have different focuses and may engage in a variety of activities depending on the conditions, obstacles, and context the worker center finds itself in. Worker centers are an invaluable tool to immigrants in a diverse range of areas. I will focus on their efforts to organize workers.

Worker centers often help recent immigrants who are employed in the worst jobs imaginable (indeed, these industries attract many undocumented workers). These immigrants often face a language barrier (to combat this, worker centers often provide English as a second language classes) and anti-immigrant discrimination, and they work in the informal economy. Worker centers are educating these workers about their rights and are helping to protect them from unscrupulous employers. Obviously, if workers are undocumented, they face many hardships that other workers do not endure and they are often greatly exploited. Worker centers help immigrant workers by explaining to them their rights and by helping them to help themselves through collective action and even through legal redress.[36]

While it is very unlikely that these workers will become official union members in the short term, worker centers educate immigrants about how they can stand up and fight. As I have often noted, immigrants are crucial to the revitalization of the labor movement. By helping immigrant workers, worker centers are helping to breed the next wave of activists. The Carolina Alliance for Fair Employment is an example of a worker center representing workers unlikely to be organized by a union. The Alliance started the Worker's Rights Project in Greenville, South Carolina. The project helps organize and provides assistance to recently arrived Latino workers. In addition, the project helped the successful passage of a law that makes it difficult for employers to fire injured employees.[37] Indeed, there is a greater chance that contingent workers, who receive low incomes and are generally immigrants and/or women, will initially approach community-based organizations like worker centers rather than unions. Thus, it is essential for unions to have, at the very least, some form of alliance with worker centers to help vulnerable workers. Indeed, just for purely selfish reasons, by having alliances with worker centers, unions will be able to tap an untouched resource.

Worker centers can be a valuable tool in organizing new union members, especially immigrants, who can then potentially greatly contribute in the progressive transformation of unions. Indeed, undocumented workers are often very pro-union and are not fearful of losing their jobs. This is because they understand that in many places it is easy for them to get another job, and companies that betray their undocumented workers to the Immigration and Naturalization Service (which is now the Department of Homeland Security) quickly get a bad name and jeopardize their chances of employing undocumented workers. Moreover, as they entered America illegally once, they will most likely come back if they are deported. As one worker claimed, "They're not going to kill you! The worse thing they can do is send me home, and I'll come back!"[38]

UNITE has successfully used worker centers to organize workers. Indeed, UNITE formed a worker center in Brooklyn's Sunset Park neighborhood. May Chen and Kent Wong note that the "purpose of the center is to act as a magnet for Chinese garment workers in that community by providing education and a base for organizing and networking." They concluded that the "experience in Sunset Park shows that it is eminently possible [to organize immigrant workers], given the proper resources for educating and training worker leaders, hiring and utilizing bilingual union staff, establishing a labor voice in the ethnic media, and support among community organizations."[39]

Of course, worker centers can organize nonimmigrant workers. For example, African American workers formed the Carolina Alliance for Fair Employment. Their efforts eventually "helped 140 workers at the Daufuskie Island Club and Resort on Hilton Head Island win union recognition and a 13 percent wage increase; it also helped bring NLRB charges against the employer when workers were subsequently fired."[40] Likewise, Black Workers for Justice (BWJ) focuses on organizing campaigns, welfare reform, and workers' rights. The group has worked with unions to help organize workers in the South. A flow-on effect of BWJ is that its organizing efforts have led to the formation of independent unions. One such example is the North Carolina Public Service Workers Union (NCPSWU). The NCPSWU affiliated with the UE under UE Local 150 in 1997, and from humble beginnings with just 300 members, the Local now has over 3,000 members.[41] Likewise, the Chicago Interfaith Workers Rights Center joined forces with the UE to help workers gain union recognition in Illinois, and the Omaha Together One Community (OTOC) worker center and the United Food and Commercial Workers (UFCW) campaigned to win recognition for meatpackers in Nebraska. The campaign was immensely helped by the OTOC convincing the state governor to implement a worker's bill of rights. The bill of rights includes such things as the right to organize, the right to receive remuneration for duties performed, and the right to have a safe workplace. Furthermore, the NYTWA, which received assistance from a CLC, is a worker center that has become more like an unofficial union. Worker centers can also help overseas workers organize against US transnational corporations: organizations such as the Border Workers Regional Support Committee and the Coalition for Justice in the Maquiladoras have helped Mexican workers organize against foreign-owned firms.[42]

Worker centers are also often the breeding ground for innovating campaigns. These include local and national boycotts and forcing particular industries to raise wages for their workers. For example, in March 2005, the Coalition of Immokalee Workers (CIW) won a historic victory over Taco Bell. The CIW, along with student groups and community organizations, engaged in a boycott of Taco Bell. The CIW also engaged in three strikes, exposing human trafficking and slavery in the tomato fields, and even undertook a hunger strike in an attempt to improve the wages and working conditions of the tomato pickers. The use of the secondary boycott tactic by the CIW is very interesting. As I argued in chapter 2, secondary boycotts were a great tactic used by unions in the 1930s and 1940s that led to many victories. As a result, the Taft-Hartley Act disallowed them. However, as the ban on secondary boycotts applies only to unions, worker centers and other organizations are free to engage in such activity.

In a positive result for the CIW, the owner of Taco Bell—Yum Brands—agreed to buy tomatoes only from suppliers who paid the workers an extra penny per pound for the tomatoes they picked. While it may seem an insignificant amount, an extra penny per pound means that the workers wages were effectively doubled. Yum Brands also agreed to cooperate with the CIW to improve working conditions in all Florida tomato fields, and to work with the CIW and other groups in an attempt to get the state to implement new laws to protect all tomato farm workers.[43]

WORKER CENTERS' PROBLEMS AND SOLUTIONS

Unfortunately, as the Workplace Project in Hempstead, Long Island, demonstrates, in addition to solving problems that immigrants have with employers, immigrant workers use worker centers to solve problems they are having with their union. Eight percent of the Workplace Project's cases involve immigrant workers in dispute with their unions. One example involved undocumented Guatemalan candy-factory workers who were forced by their employer to change their names every six months. The employer did this because the union's contract with the employer allowed workers to join the union after six months of employment. The union accepted this because it did not want the workers as union members.[44]

The Workplace Project also assists workers to reform their unions through helping members who want to replace ineffectual or unresponsive shop stewards and union representatives. The project helped replace a SEIU business agent with an activist, bilingual Latino worker, and it helped workers at the Davis Vision Company elect a new shop steward (a member of the Workplace Project) after their union ignored workers' concerns that the company kept changing their contract.[45]

Another problem with potential union–worker center alliances is that as some unions are bureaucratic institutions, they are often very wary of worker centers. This is often because worker centers believe in bottom-up organizing, where members have an active role and there is no difference between them and the worker center staff. They believe that democracy and active involvement by its members is essential to organizing. In contrast, since the 1950s unions have generally relied on top-down organizing. This has led to alliances between worker centers and unions collapsing. The OTOC-UFCW alliance was very successful in organizing workers; 1,000 workers were organized in less than 2 years. The organizing drive was based on democratic principles and members being involved in determining strategies. However, the top-down approach of the UFCW dominated collective bargaining negotiations and the union structure. The union did not listen to its members, and as a result the contract it negotiated ignored workplace issues most important to workers as well as questions on immigration. This clash of cultures led to the alliance largely falling apart.[46]

Immigrants often greatly contribute in positively transforming unions, but that they go to worker centers to solve problems they are having with their unions, and that some unions are fearful of having alliances with worker centers, illustrates the long road ahead for any positive change in unions. Unfortunately, there is little in the way of worker center–union alliances. In 2003, only 15 percent of worker centers had formal alliances with unions, while 82 percent of centers had only occasional associations with unions.[47] This is nothing short of disappointing.

Funding is always a problem for worker centers; in this regard, unions should certainly help. Worker centers generally have small budgets and usually do not charge for their services. On average, the majority of worker centers operate on less than $250,000 per year, with only 9 percent of worker centers having a budget over $500,000. While a small budget does not mean a worker center cannot perform heroically (the NYTWA's operating budget is only $160,000, yet it is very successful, and the Chinese Worker Organizing Center in San Francisco helped 240 workers recover over $1 million in unpaid wages[48]), if it had a larger budget it could help more people. Unions should help cover the operating expenses of worker centers, and they should provide additional resources such as volunteers. By doing so, unions are not only helping workers—which should be the goal of unions, whether or not the worker is a union member—they are also forging ties with many potential new union members. Indeed, the successful organizing drive of black-car drivers in New York was partly due to the International Association of Machinists and Aerospace Workers willing to provide resources for an independent worker organizing effort.[49]

While it is unlikely that the workers will automatically become union members (in part because many are undocumented), unions will be building ties to the community and many potential future union members. Thus, it is a win-win situation for all concerned. Worker centers will have increased resources to help in their work, workers will have an additional body to help them and protect their rights, and unions will be helping many workers and will have access to a breeding ground of many future militant union members. In a positive development, the AFL-CIO reached an agreement with the National Day Laborer Organizing Network in August 2006 that allows worker centers to affiliate with state and local labor councils. It was this decree that allowed the NYTWA to join the local CLC. Gordon provides us with a good proposal on what unions should do to help build the partnership between unions and worker centers: "Unions must resist the temptation to borrow a center's cultural, linguistic, and local organizing expertise in the heat of a campaign, only to retreat when it is over. If a worker center helps to organize a winning union campaign, it should receive a share of the resulting dues collected through payroll deductions. A good relationship takes time as well as money. Only long-term work on issues of interest to the membership of both organizations will cement the partnership."[50] Following this advice would be a step in the right direction. Nonetheless, worker centers also have to understand that it is not always a union's fault when something goes wrong. Fine argues that worker centers have to accept that "unions often know more than they do about labor law and union organizing....Independent union organizing efforts [conducted by worker centers that fail]...reinforce a union perception that worker centers are sometimes overconfident about their ability to succeed where unions fail and insufficiently prepared for the level of opposition they encounter in organizing drives."[51] Worker centers and unions should learn from each other and work together for the benefit of all workers. Unions should view worker centers as Fine views them: the best way to understand worker centers is to view them as "preunions," that is, organizations that are building the foundations for future union organizing campaigns.[52]

Another major problem that must be overcome is that almost every worker centers defines itself by the ethnic origins of its constituents. This certainly creates unity among its members, but it can also create disunity among other ethnic groups if the members of a worker center want to join a union. However, this will be a problem only if people make it a problem. The union should welcome the new members regardless of whether they consist entirely of one ethnic group. Likewise, the worker center members should understand that there may be different cultures within the union that do things differently. In the end, no matter how many different ethnic groups are in a union, they are all fighting for the same rights and principles. There very well may be flare-ups and arguments, but these things are to be expected. What matters is how people respond to these challenges. There is absolutely no good reason why whites cannot work with African Americans, and African Americans cannot work with Latinos, and so on. It certainly may not be easy initially if a large number of immigrant workers join a union and they go from the majority grouping within a worker center to now being a minority, and it may not be easy for the union to adjust to a large minority grouping within the union. But through time, patience, and confronting any issue that arises due to the now-diverse union, this problem can be overcome. To suggest otherwise is foolish. The national organizer of the TDU said the following when discussing multiethnic unions: "The idea that white workers won't elect Latino or Black leaders is simply wrong....Whatever these white workers might think about race in some other context, in the union they understand the need for unity and representation....The union context brings the best out of people."[53]

Even if worker centers and unions do not forge close ties, it is undoubtedly true that worker centers help people who might otherwise not receive help. Moreover, worker centers empower people. Maria Aparicio, a member of the Workplace Project, stated, "I did not know what my labor rights were.

I would say that for many people who are outside...[worker centers]—they are the same as I was....When I began to join the Workplace Project I took the Workers Course. Before, they sometimes used to call me a fighter. Well, knowing my rights, I became more of a fighter still!" As another worker stated, "I was not a leader before coming to the Workplace Project. I was not, I did not have the capacity, I did not even dream of being a leader. I was not trained. Now, I feel more at liberty to express myself....Now that I am a leader, I would help others—we have to let other people know their rights, what they are due. If a person does not give, he cannot receive."[54] Irrespective of the potential for unions to organize new members, empowering people, especially marginalized and demoralized workers, is the worker centers' greatest achievement.

TRADE UNION EDUCATIONAL LEAGUE: LEARNING FROM THE PAST

Another tactic the labor movement should use in its attempted revitalization is a strategy that was used in the 1920s and 1930s, namely, the Trade Union Educational League (TUEL). The TUEL formed in 1920 following the breakup of the US Socialist Party. The TUEL advocated union democracy, racial equality, and the formation of a Labor Party; it led strikes and was involved in numerous rank-and-file movements. Its purpose was to push for more progressive politics and labor unity, help build unions in all industries, and even start unions from scratch. The TUEL mobilized many workers into struggle: it "linked the various rank and file opposition movements into a broad progressive current across the labor movement giving these efforts a class-wide framework, a shared vision of what unionism could be, and a common basic program."[55] The TUEL was instrumental in building some of the union powerhouses of the 1930s and 1940s. Unions started by the TUEL eventually transformed into the UE, the UAW, the Farm Equipment Workers, and the United Rubber Workers.

The "establishment of TUEL-affiliated local unions was very much an ebb-and-flow situation. When there were important workplace issues, the membership would swell, and battles for higher wages or better working conditions would erupt. In other times the membership would be reduced to the hard core of committed activists, usually those with working-class political views, socialists, communists, or anarchists. They provided the grounding and core that kept the unions alive."[56] The left-wing members helped the survival of the TUEL, just as they were instrumental in the organizing success of CIO unions in the 1930s and 1940s (see chapter 2).

How would a modern-day TUEL look and function? The international representative of the UE, David Cohen, and former UE president Judy Atkins argue that there should be national and local TUEL committees:

There would need to be some sort of national coordinating committee, not to issue directives and commands but to synthesize the different experiences and to try to draw some conclusions that would aid other workers in their efforts. We see TUEL committees functioning in their own workplaces but not separated from the rest of the labor movement. We would hope that in given geographical areas there would be regional meetings, to provide a larger base of support for the workers. There could be sectoral meetings on a national basis, workers in the same industry getting together to compare notes and plan campaigns. Tied in with these would be corporate meetings, i.e., workers who work for the same boss getting together. Some sort of newspaper or newsletter could link all these different workers together.[57]

The vision of a modern-day TUEL is similar to the vision of social justice unions. The TUEL would have alliances with the local community and with social movements, and it would engage in political struggles, such as the fight for national health insurance and saving Social Security. It would engage in all issues that affect workers. The TUEL would not just be a lapdog to the Democrats, but it would engage in independent political action. Moreover, it would form alliances with workers and unions worldwide on the basis of the UE's alliance with the Frente Autentico del Trabajo (Authentic Workers Front; FAT). The UE provides FAT with financial support, research capability, and rank-and-file involvement in the United States in support of Mexican organizing drives.[58] In return, FAT helps the UE in its organizing drives. For example, FAT "provided Mexican organizers, whose work with Mexican employees in a . . . virulently anti-union Milwaukee foundry was vital to the UE's successful unionisation drive there."[59] As part of the strategy to organize the foundry workers, the Mexican organizer distributed a leaflet to workers. It stated that the "UE and the FAT fight for the same ideals. . . . I feel proud to see my countrymen demanding their union rights. And it's moving to see workers of all races and nationalities joining forces. . . . Keep on, brothers and sisters. The way to the future is the union!"[60]

The main difference between social justice unions and the TUEL is that a local TUEL does not necessarily have to be a union. The National Labor Relations Act (NLRA) protects workers coming together for mutual aid or protection in a workplace. This means that a nonofficial union can engage in struggle at any business. A local TUEL at a business can fight for better wages and better working conditions, as well as trying to form an official union, all the while protected by labor law.[61] The formation of a TUEL or similar organization is by itself unlikely to lead to the labor movement's revitalization, but combined with social justice unions, CLCs, and worker centers, a TUEL can certainly be a great benefit.

While one may argue that such an organization will never happen or be successful, there are already instances of such groups succeeding. The Communication Workers of America (CWA) has formed versions of a TUEL or worker organizations at GE. The groups, known as Working at GE (WAGE), pay dues of only $10 per month and the members have full voting rights of the CWA. As members of the CWA, the WAGE workers are entitled to workplace accident insurance, low-cost mortgage rates, and thousands of dollars in union-family scholarships. WAGE has been successful in a number of situations across GE factories. Unfortunately, the attempt by WAGE at the Auburn plant to take the next step and become a majority union was a failure.[62]

A version of the TUEL could help organize workers at Wal-Mart. Wal-Mart's antiunion reputation is well known in America. However, in almost every other country where Wal-Mart has stores, the workers are unionized. Wal-Mart workers are unionized in Argentina, Canada (although Wal-Mart is doing whatever it can to de-unionize its Canadian workforce), Mexico, the United Kingdom, and even China. It is certainly unlikely that unionization efforts at Wal-Mart will succeed in America, at least in the short term. Even if there were a vast reversal of fortune and the UFCW (the main union trying to organize Wal-Mart) managed to organize 30 Wal-Mart stores a year (which is currently almost impossible due to labor law and Wal-Mart's strong dislike of unions), it would be well over 100 years before Wal-Mart was entirely unionized.[63] Thus, something like a TUEL could be an enormous benefit.

Along the lines outlined earlier, there could be Wal-Mart TUELs or worker organizations in as many stores as possible. These associations can be linked both regionally and nationally through regular meetings and informal get-togethers. Such an organization would push the idea that workers have rights that must be upheld. As Charles J. Morris argues,

> The emphasis will center on employees who desire to join a union and become union members, not the solicitation or authorization cards or the seeking of votes for a union election day. . . . [A]s soon as a cohesive group of union-minded employees can come together, they will organize themselves . . . into a functioning labor union. From then on, every one of these . . . members will be advised to channel all issues relating to job performance or compensation through their medium of their union.[64]

As Wade Rathke argues, by collecting nominal dues from members (Wal-Mart would not collect dues for the TUEL), there would be numerous face-to-face meetings, which are helpful in any organizing effort. If only 1 percent of Wal-Mart workers joined the TUEL, membership would be 13,000. Thus, recruiting even a small percentage of workers, the TUEL would have tens of thousands of members. The most obvious question is, will workers be fired for belonging to a Wal-Mart TUEL? The answer is that they very well could be, but Wal-Mart would be breaking the law. The workers are protected by labor law (as all versions of a TUEL would be). Section 7 of the NLRA states, "Employees shall have the right to self-organization, to form, to join, or assist labor organizations, to bargain collectively through representatives of their own choosing, and to engage in other concerted activities for the purposes of collective bargaining or other mutual aid or protection." This means that any group can form and fight for better wages, hours, and working conditions. The group does not have to be an official union or even a majority union. A workers association or TUEL just has to try to improve workers' lives and let their employer know of such a grouping to be protected by labor law.[65] Wal-Mart is still likely to do everything in its power to thwart the efforts of a TUEL, even disciplining or firing its members. Nevertheless, the rule of law protects the workers, and while this is no guarantee they will be protected, it is a good start.

A Wal-Mart TUEL should certainly not be left to fend for itself. Unions should do everything in their power to ensure the success of the TUEL. Likewise, Wal-Mart values its community reputations; thus, a Wal-Mart TUEL should reach out and form alliances with community groups and new social movements, many of which are already anti-Wal-Mart. A TUEL-community alliance already has Wal-Mart fearful. Wal-Mart CEO H. Lee Scott stated that "our critics seem to have a broader and, I believe, more troubling aim: to wrap the vital debate the country needs in the years ahead about the proper role of business and government in assuring that capitalism creates a decent society."[66] That the CEO of Wal-Mart seems to believe that ensuring that capitalism creates a decent society is a troubling aim speaks volumes about Wal-Mart.

CONCLUSION

Elly Leary sums up the importance of such organizations as CLCs, worker centers, and TUELs: "Non-union working-class organizations dealing with worker issues have a central place in the labor movement. Generally smaller in size than many union locals, workers' centers have the flexibility to experiment with different methods of engaging workers and training leaders. Furthermore, given the right's success in creating an anti-union climate (by popularizing the view that unions are obsolete), centers can appeal to broad sections of the working class that unions may have a difficult time reaching."[67] CLCs, worker centers, and TUELs are all important components in labor's revival. When you are battling for your future, every little bit helps. As we have seen, CLCs and worker centers are helping tens of thousands of workers and are invaluable components in the struggle for a decent society.

7

Conclusion: A Beginning

The previous chapters have outlined proposed strategies that will revive the fortunes of organized labor and workers. As I have demonstrated, some will greatly help labor, some will be of limited benefit, and others will quicken labor's decline. This chapter provides an overview of the issues analyzed previously, and it also looks at forces that may help or hamper labor's revival. Finally, I will argue that announcement of organized labor's death is very premature.

FACTORS AFFECTING THE LIKELIHOOD
OF UNION REVITALIZATION

Impact of Government Policies

While I have shown that social justice unions achieve better collective bargaining agreements and organize more new workers, and that CLCs and worker centers can help all, another theme was that government policies either helped or hindered unions. The then Canadian UAW benefited from government involvement in its 1979 collective bargaining negotiations with Chrysler. The Canadian government was an active participant in the negotiations and helped the union achieve job guarantees, increased investment in Canada, and no additional concessions. Likewise, TDU greatly profited from the American government's decision not to place the Teamsters in trusteeship, but to instead allow the rank and file to vote for the top union officials. This is not to argue that TDU had no role in the government's decision or that TDU would not have been able to reform the Teamsters without government help. As Lichtenstein states, "When the government finally moved to root out Teamster criminality, TDU influence helped shape the settlement, especially those provisions that opened up the Teamster election process to make possible a genuinely democratic contest."[1] However, the government's involvement greatly helped TDU, and it is likely that change occurred much faster than would have been achieved otherwise. The government's decision not to intervene in the 1997

UPS strike also benefited the Teamsters. This decision surprised UPS's leadership and was a great boost to striking UPS employees. Likewise, the great upsurge in unionism in the 1930s and 1940s was in part due to the changes in labor law.

While government decisions helped both the Canadian UAW and TDU, the opposite occurred for a vastly successful left-wing union like the UE. Government interference almost destroyed the union and greatly contributed to the UE's dramatic decline. Some of the decisions that had an adverse effect on the UE included a provision in the Taft-Hartley Act where union members had to sign affidavits stating they were not Communists, and the Atomic Energy Commission's decree to companies not to recognize unions that were labeled as security risks. These decisions resulted in the UE losing representation at many plants. Furthermore, the government scheduled House Committee on Un-American Activities sessions to correspond with NLRB certification elections, which further hampered the union's organizing efforts. Government repression was complemented by the actions of rival unions that raided the UE's membership. The International Union of Electrical Workers; the International Brotherhood of Electrical Workers; the UAW; the Teamsters; the AFL Jewelry Workers; the Glass, Ceramic and Silica Union; and the AFL Carpenters conducted over 500 raids on UE Locals. Both the government and rival unions, including nonbusiness unions (at that time) such as the UAW, attacked the UE. As Ian Robinson argues,

> The radical agenda of SMUs [social movement unions] means that government and employers often target them with higher levels of repression than rival union types. We have seen this dynamic recur in U.S. labor history, and the result was clear: SMUs were marginalized except during the great economic crises of the 1930s. The lesson, it seems, is that even with superior mobilization capacity, SMUs will be crushed by the superior power resources of the state, employers, and more conservative unions—if they are willing and able to cooperate. Less inclusive and radical forms of unionism will thus come to dominate unless such a coordinated repressive response proves impossible.[2]

However, the Canadian UAW and the Teamsters benefited from government involvement (or in the case of the UPS strike, noninvolvement). Thus, it is not necessarily the case that social justice unions face greater repression than other types of unions (which Robinson does note). Nevertheless, in the majority of situations, especially in this era of neoliberal globalization, governments and conservative unions will likely try to prevent any radical unions' agenda from succeeding. As J. M. Barbalet argues, "Every time that radical unionism has flourished in the USA, it has been destroyed or severely damaged by political repression. In addition, the 'mainstream' labour movement 'came under special attack when it showed signs of becoming radical'. In particular, state repression had the effect of totally removing the radical element from the labour movement, and of providing a strong incentive away from the radical end of the political and industrial organisational spectrum."[3]

IMPACT OF STRUCTURAL CONDITIONS AND DEMOGRAPHIC CHANGE

While more successful than business unions, social justice unionism, CLCs, worker centers, TUELs, or any other potential strategy (such as labor-community alliances) is unlikely to result in a dramatic revival of American unionism at this stage. Unions are relatively powerless compared to governments, and government policy has greatly contributed to unions' successes and failures. In this era of neoliberalism, governments are increasingly likely to attempt to undermine unions and their allies.

It is doubtful that the current conditions are conducive to progressive unionism becoming the dominant union ideology throughout America. The Teamsters (under Carey's leadership) were successful in achieving significant gains in wages and working conditions. Likewise, a union like the CAW has been successful in organizing the unorganized. In labor's past, the UE, which had all the hallmarks of a social justice union, was successful. The UE organized the unorganized, had alliances with community groups, believed in union democracy and rank-and-file involvement, and was at the forefront of fighting for all workers (including so-called minorities). UE membership grew from less than 50,000 in 1939 to 432,000 during the middle of World War II, and by VJ day, the UE had 750,000 members. The improvement in the economy helped the union's organizing efforts. Moreover, it was the UE's belief in the benefits of organizing the unorganized and its rank-and-file unionism that contributed to the remarkable gains in membership. The Report of the General Officers to the 8th UE Convention in 1942 argued that the UE should organize the unorganized.[4] Likewise, at the 1946 CIO convention, Matles stated, "All men are created equal—and we propose to fight for that principle....And if we continue to organize this movement of ours on that principle, then the overwhelming majority of the unorganized workers will rally to us. They will join us. And our ranks will be tremendously increased."[5] The only unions that achieved growth compared with the UEs during the war years were the UAW (165,000 to 1 million) and the United Steel Workers of America (USWA) (its membership increased threefold to 700,000). In 1946, the UE was successful in 84.1 percent of NLRB certification elections, which was the highest rate for any union. That year the CIO organized 350,000 workers, with 20 percent organized by the UE.[6] The UE's record in consistently winning pro-labor contracts matches its success in organizing workers. Stepan-Norris and Zeitlin, in their comprehensive study of CIO unions' contracts with employers from 1938 to 1955, argue that the UE contracts were more pro-labor than other unions.[7] For example, they concluded:

> An examination of the local agreements of each of these Big 3 Internationals [UE, UAW, USWA] reveals that those won by UE Locals were more systematically pro-labor...than were the UAW's; the USWA was a distant third in pro-labor provisions. The same pattern appears in these unions' national contracts...[T]he agreements between UE and General Electric over the years were consistently pro-labor; those between UAW and General Motors less so; and those between the USWA and Carnegie-Illinois (which became US Steel in late 1950) were the least pro-labor.[8]

They note that not one of the UE/GE national contracts "ceded management rights or prerogatives."[9] However, apart from a brief period when the UE was a major union in the 1940s with over 500,000 members and there were other militant left-wing unions (predominantly within the CIO), and the current success of the CAW, social justice unionism has not been the dominant union ideology in North America. Indeed, the UE never abandoned its social justice unionism ideology, but it was not enough to prevent its decline due to the massive attacks conducted by the government, as well as the betrayal from other unions.

Despite the downturn in unionism and the increased talk of change, it is difficult to envisage that there will be a major shift in union ideology in the near future. Nevertheless, one could have argued in the years preceding the fall of Communism in Eastern Europe that this system would be in place for the foreseeable future. In other words, it is very difficult to determine when a major change will occur. Halliday claims that "while revolutionaries and their opponents have long advocated a voluntaristic view, stressing the role of human will and organisation, few deny that such action cannot succeed except where objective factors enable them to do so."[10] As Marx argued, "Men make their own history, but they do not make it just as they please; they do not make it under circumstances chosen by themselves, but under circumstances directly found, given and transmitted from the past."[11] For a major change to occur, there is a need for both structural facilitators, such as an economic collapse, and people and/or organizations, such as unions, to be in a position to respond effectively.

Structural conditions contributed to the success (even if the success was brief) of social movement unionism, as well as other forms of progressive unionism in countries such as Brazil, South Korea, and South Africa in the 1980s and 1990s.[12] However, at the same time, social actors have contributed to the rise of progressive unionism outside America. For example, the Kilusang Msyo Uno (KMU) gained strength because of its nationalism and efforts to democratize the Philippines. As Lois A. West notes, "KMU members have rooted their critique of foreign and labor intervention in their conception of Philippine nationalism which they saw as culturally based."[13] A KMU leader claimed:

> Nationalism provides one with the cultural level. It's necessary to be able to integrate ourselves into a people, that is, you've got to integrate people with different histories....Everybody else has his own history, and it's not simply the history of the Tagalogs that is the history of the Philippines. You've got to bring this into a national culture and a nation state. The only thing that I'm clear in my mind is that you've got to create strong unions, strong people's organizations, build good bureaucrats, a strong civil service system, and rein in the military.[14]

West states that the KMU viewed the "nationalist agenda...as a primary organizing tool...as the national democratic movement continued to link the Philippines government to the Americans in what they called U.S.-Marcos, U.S.-Aquino, and...U.S.-Ramos regimes."[15] The nationalist movement in the Philippines greatly benefited the KMU.

The conditions in Brazil, South Korea, and South Africa that led to the rise of progressive unionism are not applicable to America. Nor are there any other similar conditions in the short term that will dramatically increase the chances that unions will become social justice unions and embrace CLCs, worker centers, and a TUEL, or at the very least, move away from business unionism.

There is evidence, however, that so-called minorities, such as women, African Americans, Latinos, and immigrants, can contribute to the revitalization of unions and lead them to adopt progressive agendas. For example, as previously noted, immigrant workers often have a significant role in the reintroduction of rank-and-file unionism and militancy in many unions. In addition, the growth of Latino members was intertwined with the growth of TDU and in other reform movements such as New Directions within the UAW and the New York Transit Authority workers within the Transport Workers Union. Immanuel Ness argues that immigrant workers in New York are "often *more* militant than its native-born workers. Immigrants in New York's unregulated sector frequently engage in walkouts and sit-down strikes for higher wages and union recognition in the apparel, food service, private transportation, and delivery industries."[16]

Likewise, Lichtenstein claims that women workers, combined with a sense of community, led to an increase in solidarity in America in the 1930s:

> Women workers were a key part in the labor upsurge when an organic element of that movement included rent strikes, soup kitchens, and neighborhood political mobilizations.... [W]omen made the union impulse present throughout the neighborhoods and communities. Labor-based tenant organizations, soup kitchens, food cooperatives, recreation halls, singing societies, and education programs drew women workers as well as the wives and daughters of male unionists into a dense, supportive social network that thickened the ties of solidarity inside and outside the factory.[17]

Moreover, as previously argued, the greater the number of women and/or African Americans, Latinos, and immigrants, the greater the likelihood of unions being successful in certification elections. Latinos and African Americans also want to join unions. In the 1994 National Representation and Participation Survey, 51 percent of Latinos who were not union members wanted to join a union, while 64 percent of African Americans would vote for a union in a certification election. In a 2001–2002 survey, 74 percent of nonunion African Americans in California would vote for a union, as would 67 percent of nonunion Latinos. In comparison, only 33 percent of whites would vote for a union.[18] These figures indicate that unions should be doing everything possible to organize African Americans and Latinos.

There has been a rise in the number of so-called minorities joining unions, but the majority of unions are still firmly under the grip of business unionism. Thus, it is doubtful that this by itself will lead to social justice unionism becoming more popular. It is also unlikely that the conditions that resulted in the rise of progressive unionism in Brazil, South Korea, and South Africa will manifest in America. Nevertheless, it is possible that a number of factors combined could lead to the revival of organized labor.

Related to the preference of minorities to join unions is that union leaders with previous experience of being involved in community organizations and new social movements play an important role in what Voss and Sherman label as "revitalized" union Locals. These Locals "shifted away from servicing current union members to organizing the unorganized and...used unconventional disruptive tactics in...organizing campaigns."[19] These leaders think differently from the traditional union movement and are willing to do things differently to get results. These types of leaders usually are minorities themselves or they have long been involved with minority groups. A HERE leader capitulates the different thinking of people brought in from the outside:

> [We] don't have a world vision that everything's okay. We haven't been encapsulated in the rather safe union world, we've been out in the rest of the completely nonunionized world. And bringing in people I think with that kind of vision and energy has really driven some of our [growth]....[For example, one organizer] is really driven to organize, and it's not because he was a bellman or a dishwasher somewhere, he just got a certain worldview of poverty and power, and he worked for [a community organizing group], I mean, he has not been out talking to unionized workers! He's out talking to people on the threshold of total disaster. So his world vision is really different than a UFCW retail clerk investing in his vacation home for 15 years....And that's how he came into this and said "We gotta organize, man. I like what unions have, I've never had it, I've been talking to people that don't have anything."[20]

It is these types of leaders that unions need: leaders who do not just care about servicing union members, but care about all people and the lives they lead. Likewise, it is important for union leaders not to get caught up in the traditional way of doing things. A labor lawyer who was involved in the Vietnam anti-war movement explained the importance of thinking outside the box:

> The entire labor movement was like that, it followed proper channels. Just exactly what we learned during the Vietnam war does not work. That the proper channels are laid down to defuse energy that's directed at the ruling class, not to impair that class's interests. And that's one of the ways that working in the antiwar movement was so helpful to me, because I realized as a result of the experiences there that reason and proper channels are only for defusing energy, not for channeling it. And you have to act outside those structures if you intend to get anything done.[21]

In addition to changing the union culture and the importance of social actors, neoliberal restructuring does offer a potential structural transformation that could lead to more American unions embracing social justice unionism. Robinson argues that neoliberal restructuring can promote social movement unionism in the developed world (specifically, Canada and the United States). In a far-reaching study, he concluded that neoliberal restructuring (NLR)

> has changed the conditions in which U.S. unions operate in ways that have promoted a shift away from the long dominant business unionism

toward SMU [social movement unionism]. NLR is not the only factor responsible for this shift; the changing demographics of the workforce [increasing number of women and people of color, especially Latino immigrants] are also very important, and these are only partly determined by NLR. Nor do structural changes dictate any particular response from unions. The business union culture remains strong within some unions and may continue to do so whether or not it "works" as measured by union membership growth or power. For some leaders, any other orientation is unacceptable, even if the failure to change seems likely to doom the organization to decline or even obliteration.

For this reason, the shift toward SMU, in the United States as in Canada, is likely to be both less universal and less rapid than many who favor SMU would hope.[22]

As Robinson correctly argues, there is no guarantee that neoliberal restructuring will lead to social movement unionism becoming the dominant union practice. Nevertheless, the rise of neoliberalism does offer American unions the chance to embrace change. However, economic conditions by themselves are unlikely to lead unions toward making positive changes. History has shown that a decline in economic conditions can lead to the Far Right gaining power: "Past and present evidence suggests that economic and political crisis can also lead to mass fascism (Hitler's Germany and Mussolini's Italy), religious fundamentalism (North Africa), ethnic chauvinism (Yugoslavia), exhaustion and disorientation (Poland), terroristic communism (Khmer Rouge, Shining Path) and neocorporatism ('social concentration' strategies in Latin America?)."[23]

Another strategy that can help unions make changes is worker education programs. Programs implemented by the Brazilian labor federation Central Única dos Trabalhadores (CUT) have led to an increase in worker participation. Mark Langevin argues: "While current data does not allow for conclusions, clearly the growth of CUT and its educational project since 1990 would indicate a steady trend toward a greater number of unions providing labor education to their directors, union employees, and the rank and file. Because of the new directions in labor education, more workers and unionists have the opportunity to participate in their labor organizations and the social movement which attempts to advance their collective interests."[24]

Likewise, the education programs of the CAW have helped in its goal of being a social justice union. The CAW's Education Department is an important facet in the union's goal of continued rank-and-file involvement and for it to be a social justice union. While many unions have education departments, the key issue is what unions do with them and what they teach. Half-hearted programs or programs that demonstrate the "benefits" of unions concentrating only on bread-and-butter issues through a top-down approach are not going to help organized labor regain its strength and, more importantly, help workers.

The CAW claims the goal of the Education Department is to "create the programs and material to help activists get a handle on what is happening in the world, put it into the context of our history and philosophy and move ahead towards social unionism."[25] As Reuben Roth notes, the "theme of 'social change' is often repeated in CAW literature.... The goal of politicizing trade union activists and raising working class consciousness is not a subterfuge, but an implicitly stated, hoped-for outcome of their educational programs."[26] The Paid Education Leave Program is one of the most important programs in the CAW Education Department. The program is a four-week course that covers such topics as labor history, sociology, political science, and economics. Over 5,500 CAW members have completed the course since its inception, with a majority now occupying leadership positions in the union.[27] Gindin argues that "within the CAW a group of staffers working in research and education have been trying to flesh out an alternative direction." The key was "moving beyond questions of distribution, and working through the implications of shifting capitalism's focus on the accumulation of capital and control over labour power, to socialists' concern with the accumulation of capacities and democratic intervention."[28] The CAW's education programs have led to a change in workers' attitudes. Workers emerged from the programs "affected by the general orientation towards an independent working class perspective, the emphasis on thinking about capacities, the broadening of the theme of democracy and a new self-consciousness of their history." In addition, the people who taught the programs have become activists.[29]

D. W. Livingstone and Reuben Roth agree with these conclusions. They analyzed the organized and informal learning methods of CAW members in relation to economic justice issues at the GM plant at Oshawa, Canada. As part of their study, they conducted interviews with workers at the plant who completed the Paid Education Leave Program. One worker stated that while he could not remember the actual specifics of an antiracist and anti-capitalism education course, he "came back into the plant with an immense socialist vigour especially against racism." Another worker felt empathy for laid-off workers in a nearby plant. He claimed that the workers had "been jerked around by a corporation that's making a lot of money and there's no reason for it."[30] The workers' responses supported Gindin's findings that the CAW's Education Department is changing workers' attitudes. The CAW and CUT education programs demonstrate that adopting such programs will help facilitate the spread of social justice unionism and other positive strategies.[31]

Worker education programs—in addition to the changing workforce demography, the rise of new social movements (which accompanied the ascent of social movement unionism in Brazil and South Africa, and an increase in public sector unionism in the United States), with union leaders being drawn from the ranks of such movements, and a decline in workers' economic conditions (possibly as a result of neoliberal restructuring)—potentially offer the best hope for a radical change in union culture. However, the revitalization of organized labor is far from certain.

Nevertheless, by unions sticking their heads in the sand for decades, this has led to organized labor's current predicament. Doing nothing or only making minor changes will not prevent the death of unionism in America, and, more importantly, it will not help workers, both in America and worldwide. The do-nothing strategy has certainly not helped unions and workers in the last 30 years. Unions, leaders, and rank-and-file workers who are prepared to take risks and implement major changes are what is needed. While I have reservations about the SEIU and Change to Win, they at least are willing to make changes and not rest on tradition. Labor needs more efforts like these, with one difference, namely, engaging in strategies that will have an undoubted benefit to unions and workers, such as social justice unionism. Both the SEIU and Change to Win have good strategies, such as their efforts to organize the unorganized. However, their belief in labor-management partnerships, their indifference to union democracy, and their top-down approach are unlikely to help unions and workers. These strategies can work in particular campaigns or, in the case of the SEIU, a particular union. However, part of the reason why labor got into the mess it finds itself in is because it did not care about union democracy and it foolishly believed that it had a partnership with business and government, a partnership that was annulled with prejudice by labor's "partners." Business does not want to have a partnership with labor, as it is openly hostile to what it calls "big labor." While some businesses welcome a partnership with labor, they are in a very small minority.

The same commitment by all aspects of unions to embrace social justice unionism, CLCs, worker centers, and a revived TUEL would have much more positive results. This change is not going to come without a commitment from all sectors of organized labor: the AFL-CIO, Change to Win, national unions, local unions, leaders at all levels, and the rank and file. Where the change comes from is irrelevant. However, any strategy must embrace ordinary workers. It is highly unlikely that major change will happen without the rank and file on board, because, after all, the purpose of unions is to protect and help such workers.

A BEGINNING

While social justice unionism is not currently widely practiced in America, it has been successful in a number of situations throughout the world. In America, by fighting for workplace (such as higher wages) *and* nonworkplace issues (such as adequate childcare or the fight against racism), social justice unions have improved society for all. On purely bread-and-butter issues, social justice unions have achieved better collective bargaining agreements than their rival business unions, as well as organized more new workers per capita. Likewise, CLCs and worker centers have been successful in helping to organize workers, as well as helping workers in a variety of ways. Therefore, if unions embrace social justice unionism, help CLCs and worker centers, and embrace alternative strategies such as a revived TUEL, this will result in the union movement regaining some of the strength that has been lost through decades of business unionism. How much strength is uncertain, but it is *a* beginning.

NOTES

CHAPTER 1

1. Rick Fantasia and Kim Voss, *Hard Work* (Berkeley: University of California Press, 2004), 15.

2. Chris Zappone, "Congress Oks Minimum Wage Boost," CNN Web site, http://money.cnn.com/2007/05/24/news/economy/minimum_wage/index.htm?postversion=2007052422.

3. Fantasia and Voss, *Hard Work*, 15–16; "Working Poor," *Monthly Labor Review* 129, no. 7 (July 2006): 2.

4. Jeff Madrick, "Goodbye, Horatio Alger," *The Nation*, February 5, 2007, 20–24.

5. Service Employees International Union (SEIU), SEIU Web site, http://www.seiu.org/faqs/faq_howcanaunionhelp.cfm.

6. R. Cohen, "Transnational Social Movements: An Assessment" (paper to the Transnational Communities Program, June 19, 1998), posted at www.transcomm.ox.ac.uk/working%20papers/cohen.pdf4.

7. Boris Frankel, *The Post-Industrial Utopians* (Oxford, UK: Polity Press, 1987), 238.

8. Francis Mulhern, "Towards 2000, or News from You-Know-Where," *New Left Review* 148 (November–December 1984): 22 (emphasis in original).

9. Frankel, *Post-Industrial Utopians*, 238; see, for example, Robert Gibb, "Leadership, Political Opportunities and Organisational Identity in the French Anti-racist Movement," in *Leadership and Social Movements*, ed. Colin Barker, Alan Johnson, and Michael Lavalette (Manchester, UK: Manchester University Press, 2001) for tension between the leadership and grassroots members in the French antiracist movement; and Carol Hanisch, "Struggles over Leadership in the Women's Liberation Movement," in *Leadership and Social Movements*, ed. Colin Barker, Alan Johnson, and Michael Lavalette (Manchester, UK: Manchester University Press, 2001) for examples of new social movements being plagued by old politics.

10. Verity Burgmann, *Power and Protest* (Sydney, Australia: Allen & Unwin, 1993), 264; see Gibb, "Leadership, Political Opportunities and Organisational Identity in the French Anti-Racist Movement" for analysis on the French antiracist movement.

11. Stephanie Ross, "Is This What Democracy Looks Like? The Politics of the Anti-Globalization Movement in North America," in *Socialist Register 2003*, ed. Leo Panitch and Colin Leys (London: Merlin Press, 2002), 283; Claus Offe, "Reflections on the Institutional Self-Transformation of Movement Politics: A Tentative Stage Mode," in

Challenging the Political Order, ed. Russell J. Dalton and Manfred Kuechler (New York: Oxford University Press, 1990), 238–39.

12. Barbara Epstein, "Anarchism and the Anti-Globalization Movement," *Monthly Review,* September 2001, 8–9.

13. Hanisch, "Struggles over Leadership," 93.

14. See, for example, Peter Waterman, "Whatever Happened to the 'New Social Unionism'?" (paper for workshop on "International Trade Unionism in a Network Society: What's New about the 'New Labour Internationalism'?," organized by the Leeds Working Group on International Labour Networking and hosted by Leeds Metropolitan University, Leeds, UK, May 2–3, 2003), 7.

15. Ross, "Is This What Democracy Looks Like," 292 (emphasis in original).

16. Burgmann, *Power and Protest,* 264. Burgmann analyzed the aborigine movement, the women's movement, gay liberation, and the peace and green movements.

17. Gail Omvedt, *Reinventing Revolution: New Socialist Movements and Traditions in India* (Armonk, NY: M. E. Sharpe, 1993).

18. Burgmann, *Power and Protest,* 266–67.

19. Jan Art Scholte, "Global Civil Society: Changing the World?" CSGR Working Paper 31/99, University of Warwick, May 1999, 4; "Citizens' Groups: The Nongovernmental Order—Will NGOs Democratise, or Merely Disrupt, Global Governance," *The Economist,* December 11, 1999, 20; Alex Demirovic, "NGOs and Social Movements: A Study in Contrasts," *Capitalism, Nature, Socialism* 11, no. 4 (December 2000): 134.

20. Nezavisimaya Gazeta, quoted in Boris Kagarlitsky, *The Return of Radicalism: Reshaping the Left Institutions* (London: Pluto Press, 2000), 90.

21. See, for example, James Petras, "NGOs: In the Service of Imperialism," *Journal of Contemporary Asia* 29, no. 4 (October 1999); P. J. Simmons, "Learning to Live with NGOs," *Foreign Policy* 112 (Fall 1998): 82; Scholte, "Global Civil Society," 30.

22. David Hulme and Michael Edwards, "NGOs, States and Donors: An Overview," in *NGOs, States and Donors: Too Close for Comfort?* ed. David Hulme and Michael Edwards (New York: St. Martin's Press, 1997), 7.

23. Michael Edwards and David Hulme, "Introduction: NGO Performance and Accountability," in *Beyond the Magic Bullet: NGO Performance and Accountability in the Post-Cold War World,* ed. Michael Edwards and David Hulme (Bloomfield, CT: Kumarian Press, 1996), 3, 7; David Hulme and Michael Edwards, "Conclusion: Too Close to the Powerful, Too Far from the Powerless?" in *NGOs, States and Donors: Too Close for Comfort?* ed. David Hulme and Michael Edwards (New York: St. Martin's Press, 1997), 277.

24. James Petras, "Imperialism and NGOs in Latin America," *Monthly Review* 49, no. 7 (December 1997): 18–20. For other examples of NGOs being willing participants in the spread of neoliberalism in Latin America see Petras, "Imperialism and NGOs in Latin America."

25. "Citizens' Groups: The Non-governmental Order," 20; Harry Cleaver, "Computer-Linked Social Movements and the Global Threat to Capitalism," Global Solidarity Dialogue, http://www.antenna.nl/~waterman/cleaver2.html.

CHAPTER 2

1. Michael Eisenscher, "Is the Secret to Labor's Future in Its Past?" *WorkingUSA* 5, no. 4 (2002): 99.

2. Woodrow Wilson, quoted in Nelson Lichtenstein, *State of the Union: A Century of American Labor* (Princeton, NJ: Princeton University Press, 2002), 4.

3. The quote is from Eisenscher, "Is the Secret," 99; Lichtenstein, *State of the Union*, 23. The American plan was a campaign by employers to destroy independent unions.

4. Richard W. Hurd, "Contesting the Dinosaur Image: The Labor Movement's Search for a Future," *Labor Studies Journal* 22, no. 4 (Winter 1998), 7.

5. Lichtenstein, *State of the Union*, 37.

6. Franklin Roosevelt, quoted in Lichtenstein, *State of the Union*, 30.

7. *New York Times Magazine* quoted in Russell B. Porter, "The C.I.O.," in *American Labor since the New Deal*, ed. Melvyn Dubofsky (Chicago: Quadrangle Books, 1971), 99–101.

8. David Wellman, *The Union Makes Us Strong* (Cambridge and New York: Cambridge University Press, 1995), 41; Ronald L. Filippelli and Mark D. McColloch, *Cold War in the Working Class: The Rise and Decline of the United Electrical Workers* (New York: State University of New York, 1995), 35–46; Ronald Schatz, "The End of Corporate Liberalism: Class Struggle in the Electrical Manufacturing Industry, 1933–1950," *Radical America* 9 (July–August 1975): 192; "Union Files NLRB Charges Against Westinghouse Co," *UE News*, April 8, 1939, 1; "W'House Must Sign, NLRB Declares in Proposed Order," *UE News*, February 17, 1940, 1; "Westinghouse Must Sign," *UE News*, April 6, 1940, 1; "Westinghouse to Negotiate on Nat. Basis," *UE News*, April 5, 1941, 1.

9. Zieger, quoted in Wellman, *The Union Makes Us Strong*, 40.

10. Lichtenstein, *State of the Union*, 78, 45.

11. James J. Matles and James Higgins, *Them and Us: Struggles of a Rank-and-File Union* (Upper Saddle River, NJ: Prentice-Hall, 1995), 138–39; Filippelli and McColloch, *Cold War in the Working Class*, 84; "Westinghouse Locks Out 36,000 in Lowpay Drive," *UE News*, September 22, 1945, 1, 3; "38,000 Back at W'House As Co. Union Drops Strike," *UE News*, October 6, 1945, 1.

12. "Huge 'Yes' Vote Sweeps GE, W'House, GM Plants," *UE News*, December 22, 1945, 1, 5.

13. Matles and Higgins, *Them and Us*, 141–42; Filippelli and McColloch, *Cold War in the Working Class*, 86–87; "UE Membership in GM Rejects 13½¢ Offer," *UE News*, December 15, 1945, 6; Schatz, "The End of Corporate Liberalism," 199.

14. Matles and Higgins, *Them and Us*, 145–47; Filippelli and McColloch, *Cold War in the Working Class*, 87–88; Ronald L. Filippelli, "UE: An Uncertain Legacy," *Political Power and Social Theory* 4 (1984): 228–29; Robert H. Zieger, *The CIO 1935–1955* (Chapel Hill and London: The University of North Carolina Press, 1995), 220–24; "Workers Hail Victory at GM," *UE News*, February 16, 1946, 1, 3; "GE Settles for 18½; W'House Offers 9.7," *UE News*, March 23, 1946, 1, 3; "Organizational Report by Director of Organization for the Months of November, December 1945 and January 1946," 1946, 2, United Electrical, Radio and Machine Workers of America Archive [UEA], University of Pittsburgh, Box 1523; "To All UE Westinghouse Members," May 7, 1946, UEA, Box 1431, FF 139; "Westinghouse Agrees to 18 Plus 1, Union Security, and Full Contract," *UE News*, May 11, 1946, 5.

15. Matles and Higgins, *Them and Us*, 147; James Matles, quoted in Ruth Milkman, "Female Factory Labor and Industrial Structure: Control and Conflict over 'Women's Place' in Auto and Electrical Manufacturing," *Politics & Society* 12, no. 2 (1983): 184–85.

16. Milkman, "Female Factory Labor," 185; "Organizational Report by Director of Organization for the Months of May, June and July 1946," 1946, 4, UEA, Box 1523.

17. Steven Henry Lopez, *Reorganizing the Rust Belt* (Berkeley, Los Angeles, and London: University of California Press, 2004), 20.

18. Hurd, "Contesting the Dinosaur Image," 7

19. AFL-CIO, "Right to Work for Less," http://www.aflcio.org/issues/legislativealert/stateissues/work.

20. Fantasia and Voss, *Hard Work*, 50–52.

21. Lichtenstein, *State of the Union,* 116.

22. Stepan-Norris and Zeitlin determine whether a contract is pro-labor in the following areas: management prerogatives, the right to strike, contract term, trade-off provisions, and grievance procedure; see Judith Stepan-Norris and Maurice Zeitlin, "Union Democracy, Radical Leadership, and the Hegemony of Capital," *American Sociological Review* 60, no. 6 (December 1995): 839–40, 845–46.

23. Ellen Schrecker, "McCarthyism and Organized Labor," *WorkingUSA* 3, no. 5 (January/February 2000): 96–97.

24. Ibid., 96.

25. Quote from David Oshinsky, "Labor's Cold War: The CIO and the Communists," in *Major Problems in the History of American Workers: Documents and Essays,* ed. Eileen Boris and Nelson Lichtenstein (Lexington, Massachusetts: D.C. Heath and Company 1991), 519; Matles and Higgins, *Them and Us,* 201–2, 210–14; Stepan-Norris and Zeitlin, *Left Out,* 282.

26. *UE News,* October 5, 1953, 2; James J. Matles, quoted in *UE News,* November 30, 1953, 1.

27. *UE* News, March 27, 1948, 3, 7; Matles and Higgins, *Them and Us,* 192–94; Filippelli and McColloch, *Cold War in the Working Class,* 119–21, 157. Quote from Filippelli and McColloch, 133–34.

28. Fantasia and Voss, *Hard Work,* 54–55.

29. Lichtenstein, *State of the Union,* 147.

30. Robert Hoxie, *Trade Unionism in the United States,* 2nd ed. (New York: Appleton, Century, Crofts, 1966), 62.

31. Dan Swinney, "Strategic Lessons for Labor from Candyland," *New Labor Forum* 55 (Fall/Winter 1999).

32. Khalil Hassan, "The Future of the Labor Left," *Monthly Review,* July–August 2000, 67. However, it is important to note that not all business unions are undemocratic with any rank-and-file involvement, but the majority of them are.

33. Kim Moody, *An Injury to All: The Decline of American Unionism* (London: Verso, 1988): 65.

34. Meany, quoted in ibid., 125.

35. Jane Bayes, "Globalization from Below: U.S. Labor and Social Movement Unionism" (paper presented to the Western Political Science Association Meetings, Las Vegas, NV, March 15–17, 2001), 21.

36. Michael Eisenscher, "Labor: Turning the Corner Will Take More Than Mobilization," in *The Transformation of US Unions: Voices, Visions, and Strategies from the Grassroots,* ed. Ray M. Tillman and Michael S. Cummings (London: Lynne Rienner Publishers, 1999), 62.

37. Dan Clawson, *The Next Upsurge* (Ithaca, NY, and London: ILR Press, 2003), 32.

38. Hurd, "Contesting the Dinosaur Image," 9.

39. All figures are in US dollars unless otherwise indicated.

40. John Holmes and A. Rusonik, "The Break-Up of an International Labour Union: Uneven Development in the North American Auto Industry and the Schism in the UAW," *Environment and Planning A* 23 (1991): 20–21; Charlotte Yates, *From Plant to Politics: The Autoworkers Union in Postwar Canada* (Philadelphia: Temple University Press, 1993), 195.

41. Holmes and Rusonik, "The Break-Up of an International Labour Union," 21.

42. Ibid.

43. Yates, *From Plant to Politics,* 196.

44. Ibid., 197.

45. Lichtenstein, *State of the Union,* 234.

46. Fantasia and Voss, *Hard Work,* 65.

47. Hurd, "Contesting the Dinosaur Image," 11.

48. R. W. McChesney, introduction to *Profit over People: Neoliberalism and the Global Order,* by Noam Chomsky (New York: Seven Stories Press, 1999), 7.

49. Eric Helleiner, "Freeing Money: Why Have Some States Been More Willing to Liberalize Capital Controls than Trade Barriers," *Policy Sciences* 27, no. 4 (1994): 306. See pp. 307–8 for US policy in regard to liberalizing the financial markets in the 1960s and 1970s.

50. Ibid.

51. Epstein, "Anarchism and the Anti-Globalization Movement," 381.

52. Helleiner, "Freeing Money," 301.

53. Hurd, "Contesting the Dinosaur Image," 9–10.

54. John Cassidy, "Why Karl Marx Was Right," *The New Yorker,* October 27, 1997, 254; John Gray, *False Dawn* (London: Granta Books, 1998), 114; Fantasia and Voss, *Hard Work,* 11.

CHAPTER 3

1. Economic Policy Council, quoted in David Brody, *Workers in Industrial America: Essays on the Twentieth Century Struggle,* 2nd ed. (Oxford: Oxford University Press, 1993), 256.

2. Bruce Nissen, "What Are Scholars Telling the U.S. Labor Movement to Do?" *Labor History* 44, no. 2 (2003): 157.

3. Anil Verma and Joel Cutcher-Gershenfeld, "Joint Governance in the Workplace: Beyond Union-Management Cooperation and Worker Participation," in *Employee Representation: Alternatives and Future Directions,* ed. Bruce E. Kaufman and Morris M. Kleiner (Madison, WI: Industrial Relations Research Association, 1993), 200 (emphasis in original).

4. Bruce Nissen, "Alternative Strategic Directions for the U.S. Labor Movement: Recent Scholarship," *Labor Studies Journal* 28, no. 1 (Spring 2003): 144–45.

5. For an overview of the relationship among Harley-Davidson, the International Association of Machinists, and the Paperworkers, Allied and Chemical Employees, see Nissen, "What Are Scholars Telling the U.S. Labor Movement to Do?" 158–59; for an overview of Shell (Sarina Plant) and the Energy and Chemical Workers' Union, see Verma and Cutcher-Gershenfeld, "Joint Governance in the Workplace," 210–11; for an overview of Xerox Corporation and UNITE, see Verma and Cutcher-Gershenfeld, "Joint Governance in the Workplace," 211–12. For an overview of Saturn, see Saul A. Rubinstein and Thomas A. Kochan, *Learning from Saturn: Possibilities for Corporate Governance and Employee Relations* (Ithaca, NY, and London: ILR Press, 2001); Saul Rubinstein, Michael Bennet, and Thomas Kochan, "The Saturn Partnership: Co-Management and the Reinvention of the Local Union," in *Employee Representation: Alternatives and Future Directions,* ed. Bruce E. Kaufman and Morris M. Kleiner (Madison, WI: Industrial Relations Research Association, 1993).

6. Nissen, "Alternative Strategic Directions for the U.S. Labor Movement," 137.

7. Rubinstein and Kochan, *Learning from Saturn,* 41–42, 25.

8. Nissen, "Alternative Strategic Directions for the U.S. Labor Movement," 137.

9. Clawson, *The Next Upsurge,* 20.

10. Brody, *Workers in Industrial America,* 263.

11. Kim Moody, *Workers in a Lean World* (London: Verso, 1997), 277, 292.

12. C. Wright Mills, quoted in Judith Stepan-Norris and Maurice Zeitlin, *Left Out: Reds and America's Industrial Unions* (Cambridge: Cambridge University Press, 2003), 162.

13. Ibid., 187.

14. For a good, concise overview of the rank-and-file involvement in the Knights of Labor and the Industrial Workers of the World, see Peter Rachleff, "Why Participation? Lessons from the Past for the Future: A Response to Charles Hecksher's Article 'Participatory Unionism,'" *Labor Studies Journal* 25, no. 4 (2001): 22–23.

15. Wellman, *The Union Makes Us Strong,* 308.

16. Eve S. Weinbaum and Gordon Lafer, "Outside Agitators and Other Red Herrings: Getting Past the 'Top-Down/Bottom-Up' Debate," *New Labor Forum* 10 (Spring–Summer 2002), 28.

17. Ibid., 34

18. Ibid, 34.

19. Kim Voss and Rachel Sherman, "Breaking the Iron Law of Oligarchy: Union Revitalization in the American Labor Movement," *American Journal of Sociology* 106, no. 2 (September 2000): 325.

20. Ibid., 337–38.

21. John Kelly, *Trade Unions and Socialist Politics* (London and New York: Verso, 1988), 182.

22. Ibid., 156–61.

23. Filippelli and McColloch, *Cold War in the Working Class,* 173; Matles and Higgins, *Them and Us,* 286; "Strike on as GE Refuses to Budge," *UE News,* November 3, 1969, 1, 9; quote from Matles and Higgins, *Them and Us,* 286–87.

24. Ruth Milkman, *L.A. Story* (New York: Russell Sage Foundation, 2006), 185.

25. Richard Hyman, *Marxism and the Sociology of Trade Unionism* (London: Pluto Press, 1971), 15; Voss and Sherman, "Breaking the Iron Law of Oligarchy," 305; Robert Michels, *Political Parties* (New York: Dover Publications, 1959), 144–45.

26. Michels, *Political Parties,* 305.

27. Moody, *Workers in a Lean World,* 297–98.

28. Alvin W. Gouldner, "Metaphysical Pathos and the Theory of Bureaucracy," *American Political Science Review* 49, no. 2 (June 1955): 506.

29. Stepan-Norris and Zeitlin, *Left Out,* 94.

30. Voss and Sherman, "Breaking the Iron Law of Oligarchy," 343.

31. Michael D. Yates, "Does the U.S. Labor Movement Have a Future?" *Monthly Review* 48, no. 9 (February 1997): 4–5.

32. Jeremy Brecher and Tim Costello, "Concluding Essay: Labor-Community Coalitions and the Restructuring of Power," in *Building Bridges: The Emerging Grassroots Coalition of Labor and Community,* ed. Jeremy Brecher and Tim Costello (New York: Monthly Review Press, 1990), 335.

33. Quote from Linda Chavez-Thompson, "Communities at Work: How New Alliances are Restoring our Right to Organize," *New Labor Forum,* 3, Fall/Winter 1998, http://qcpages.qc.edu/newlaborforum/html/3_article.html. For examples of labor-community alliances see, Bruce Nissen and Seth Rosen, "Community-Based Organizing: Transforming Union Organizing Programs from the Bottom Up," in *Which Direction for Organized Labor?* ed. Bruce Nissen (Detroit, MI: Wayne State University Press, 1999); Linda Chavez-Thompson, "Communities at Work: How New Alliances Are Restoring Our Right to Organize," *New Labor Forum* 3 (Fall/Winter 1998), http://qcpages.qc.cuny.edu/newlaborforum/old/html/3_article.html.

34. Brecher and Costello, "Concluding Essay," 340.

35. Gay W. Seidman, *Manufacturing Militance: Workers' Movements in Brazil and South Africa, 1970–1985* (Berkeley: University of California Press, 1993), 208–9.

36. Ibid., 220–21.

37. Phillip Hirschsohn, "From Grassroots Democracy to National Mobilization: COSATU as a Model of Social Movement Unionism," *Economic and Industrial Democracy* 19 (1998): 643.

38. Ibid.

39. Glenn Adler, Judy Maller, and Eddie Webster, "Unions, Direct Action and Transition in South Africa," in *Peace, Politics and Violence in the New South Africa,* ed. Norman Etherington (London: Hans Zell Publishers, 1992), 318; Eddie Webster, "The Rise of Social-Movement Unionism: The Two Faces of the Black Trade Union Movement in South Africa," in *State, Resistance and Change in South Africa,* ed. Philip Frankel, Noam Pines, and Mark Swilling (New York: Croom Helm, 1988), 190.

40. Stanley Aronowitz, *From the Ashes of the Old: American Labor and America's Future* (Boston: Houghton Mifflin, 1998), 634, 72–73.

41. Voss and Sherman, "Breaking the Iron Law of Oligarchy," 328.

42. Marshal Ganz, Kim Voss, Teresa Sharpe, Carl Somers, and George Strauss, "Against the Tide: Projects and Pathways of the New Generation of Union Leaders, 1984–2001," in *Rebuilding Labor: Organizing and Organizers in the New Union Movement,* ed. Ruth Milkman and Kim Voss (Ithaca, NY, and London: Cornell University Press, 2004), 158, 191.

43. Clawson, *The Next Upsurge,* 110–13.

44. Janice Fine, "Building Community Unions," *The Nation,* January 1, 2001, 20.

45. Clawson, *The Next Upsurge,* 117.

46. For an example of the UAW benefiting during collective bargaining because of its work in the Stamford Organizing Project, see Fine, "Building Community Unions," 20–21.

47. Rosemary Feurer, "William Sentner, the UE, and Civic Unionism in St. Louis," in *The CIO's Left-Led Union,* ed. Steve Rosswurm (New Brunswick, NJ: Rutgers University Press, 1992), 101.

48. *St. Louis Star-Times* quoted in "How a Union Saved 1500 Jobs, a $2,000,000 Payroll and the Business They Create for St. Louis," March 1940, 5–6, UEA, Box 1430, FF6.

49. Feurer, "William Sentner," 108–12; Tom Wright, "St. Louis Community Leaders Join UE in Reconversion Conference," *UE News,* August 5, 1944, 6–7.

50. Andrew E. G. Jonas, "Investigating the Local-Global Paradox," in *Organizing the Landscape: Geographical Perspectives on Labor Unionism,* ed. Andrew Herod (London: University of Minnesota Press, 1998), 333, 337; Andrew E. G. Jonas, "Labor and Community in the Deindustrialization of Urban America," *Journal of Urban Affairs* 17, no. 2 (1995): 189; Reverend Jesse Jackson, quoted in *UE News,* December 11, 1987, 3.

51. Frederick H. Lowe, "Stewart-Warner Sending 400 Chicago Jobs to Tennessee," *Chicago Sun-Times,* December 19, 1987, 40; Frederick H. Lowe, "Stewart-Warner Plant in Question," *Chicago Sun-Times,* June 28, 1989, 55.

52. Jonas, "Investigating the Local-Global Paradox," 345.

53. Frederick H. Lowe, "Stewart-Warner Rejects Workers' Wage-cut Offer," *Chicago Sun-Times,* October 24, 1989, 51; Frederick H. Lowe, "Stewart-Warner Will Announce Plant Fate," *Chicago Sun-Times,* November 3, 1989, 52.

54. Frederick H. Lowe, "Moving Work Here to Mexico//Stewart-Warner Shutting Down," *Chicago Sun-Times,* November 4, 1989, 31; "Local 1155 Gets Extension of Stewart-Warner Contract," *UE News,* January 15, 1993, 4; *UE News,* February 4, 1994, 2.

55. Katherine Sciacchitano, "Finding the Community in the Union and the Union in the Community: The First-Contract Campaign at Steeltech," in *Organizing to Win,* ed. Kate Bronfenbrenner et al. (Ithaca, NY: ILR Press, 1998), 151–52; Erik Gunn, "Steeltech Manufacturing Faces Unionizing Drive By Its Workers," *The Milwaukee Journal Sentinel,* November 2, 1993, C5; Erik Gunn, "Unionization Loses in Vote at Steeltech," *The Milwaukee Journal Sentinel,* December 20, 1993, 8; Mark Savage, "Steeltech Workers Endorse Union Electrical Workers Triumph By 5-Vote Margin in Second Balloting," *The Milwaukee Journal Sentinel,* November 5, 1994, 1D; *UE News,* November 18, 1994, 3.

56. Quoted in Erik Gunn and Jack Norman, "Union Activists Disrupt Steeltech Meeting," *The Milwaukee Journal Sentinel,* February 10, 1995, 1A; *UE News,* July 21, 1995, 3.

57. Sciacchitano, "Finding the Community," 161.

58. Tannette Johnson-Elle, "Cash Tight At Steeltech Suppliers, Unpaid Workers Laid Off Because of Delays on Federal Contract," *The Milwaukee Journal Sentinel,* February 17, 1996, 1; Barnaby J. Feder, "Some Dreams Come True, but Company Fights for Life," *The New York Times,* July 10, 1998, 1; *UE News,* August 23, 1998, 9; Lee Hawkins Jr, "Steeltech Workers Labor on Without Pay Some Hope For Back Pay, Others Just Want Health Coverage," *The Milwaukee Journal Sentinel,* July 17, 1999, 1; Lee Hawkins Jr, "Steeltech Creditors to Go Unpaid, Debt Far Exceeds Assets; Union May File Suit for Members' Back Wages," *The Milwaukee Journal Sentinel,* November 10, 1999, 1; Lee Hawkins Jr, "Workers out of Options to Get Their Back Pay from Steeltech," *The Milwaukee Journal Sentinel,* June 1, 2000, 015D.

59. "3,500 Strike to Brake WABCO Takeaways," *UE News,* November 9, 1981, 3; "Strong Community Support for 170-Day Strike at WABCO," *UE News,* April 19, 1982, 3; "Cutting Tool Unions Support Local 277 Strikes at Morse," *UE News,* June 7, 1982, 6–7; "Local 610 in Fight to Protect 1800 Jobs," *UE News,* September 16, 1985, 4; "Local 610 Campaigns to Build Jobs Fight," *UE News,* December 30, 1985, 3.

60. "Conglomerate Milked Morse Tools; Wants Pay Cuts," *UE News,* June 21, 1982, 4; "Morse Strike Settled; No Cuts in Pay or Benefits," *UE News,* August 23, 1982, 3; *UE News,* July 20, 1987, 6–7; *UE News,* August 10, 1987, 6.

61. See, for example, Kate Bronfenbrenner, "Changing to Organize," *The Nation,* September 3, 2001; Kate Bronfenbrenner and Tom Juravich, "It Takes More Than House Calls: Organizing to Win with a Comprehensive Union-Building Strategy," in *Organizing to Win,* ed. Kate Bronfenbrenner et al. (Ithaca, NY: ILR Press, 1998); Steve Early, "Membership-Based Organizing," in *A New Labor Movement for the New Century,* ed. Gregory Mantsios (New York: Garland Publishing, 1998); Stephen Lerner, "Taking the Offensive, Turning the Tide," in *A New Labor Movement for the New Century,* ed. Gregory Mantsios (New York: Garland Publishing, 1998).

62. Michael Goldfield, "Race and Labor Organization in the United States," in *Rising from the Ashes? Labor in the Age of "Global" Capital,* ed. Ellen Meiksins Wood, Peter Meiksins, and Michael Yates (New York: Monthly Review Press, 1998), 96–97.

63. Hassan, "The Future of the Labor Left," 67 (emphasis in original).

64. Hurd, "Contesting the Dinosaur Image," 25.

65. Bronfenbrenner and Juravich, "It Takes More Than House Calls," 33.

66. See, for example, David Bacon, "Globalization: Two Faces, Both Ugly," *Dollars and Sense,* March/April 2000; Andreas Breitenfellner, "Global Unionism: A Potential Player," *International Labour Review* 136, no. 4 (Winter 1997); Pharis Harvey, "Buying Time or Building a Future: Labor Strategies for a Global Economy," *Labor Research Review* 23 (1995); Jay Mazur, "Labour's New Internationalism," *Foreign Affairs* 79, no. 1 (January–February 2000); Robert O'Brien, "The Agency of Labour in a Changing Global Order," in *Political Economy and the Changing Global Order,* 3rd edition, ed. Richard Stubbs and Geoffrey R. D. Underhill (Oxford and New York: Oxford University Press, 2006); Robert O'Brien, "Workers and World Order: The Tentative Transformation of the International Union Movement," *Review of International Studies* 26 (2000).

67. Michael Yates, "'Workers of All Countries Unite': Will This Include the U.S. Labor Movement?" *Monthly Review* 52, no. 3 (July–August 2000): 47–48.

68. O'Brien, "Workers and World Order," 538.

69. Fred Halliday, *Revolution and World Politics* (London: MacMillan Press, 1999), 59–60, 62, 63–64.

70. Duncan Campbell, "Foreign Investment, Labour Mobility and the Quality of Employment," *International Labour Review* 133, no. 2 (1994): 187.

71. Moody, *Workers in a Lean World,* 7.

72. Ibid., 135–37.

73. Ibid., 274.

74. Halliday, *Revolution and World Politics*, 80; Karl Marx and Frederick Engels, *The Communist Manifesto* [1848] (London: Penguin Books, 1967), 92–93 (emphasis added).

75. Halliday, *Revolution and World Politics*, 80 (emphasis in original).

76. Susan Strange, "The Defective State," *Daedalus* 124, no. 2 (1995): 59; Paul Hirst, "The Global Economy—Myths and Realities," *International Affairs* 73, no. 3 (1997): 417; James Petras, "Globalization: A Critical Analysis," *Journal of Contemporary Asia* 29, no. 1 (1999): 18.

77. Hirst, "The Global Economy," 417.

78. Peter Gwynne, "The Myth of Globalization?" *MIT Sloan Management Review* 44, no. 2 (Winter 2003): 11.

79. Strange, "The Defective State," 60.

80. Linda Weiss, "Globalization and the Myth of the Powerless State," *New Left Review* 225 (September/October 1997): 10.

81. "Business: The Strange Life of Low-Tech America," *The Economist*, October 17, 1998, 73.

82. Hirst, "The Global Economy," 419.

83. "Business: The Strange Life of Low-Tech America," 73.

84. Winfried Ruigrok, "Why Nationality Is Still Important," *Financial Times*, January 5, 1996, 12.

85. Robert Wade, "Globalization and Its Limits: Reports of the Death of the National Economy Are Greatly Exaggerated," in *National Diversity and Global Capitalism*, ed. Suzanne Berger and Ronald Dore (Ithaca, NY, and London: Cornell University Press, 1996), 80–81 (emphasis in original).

86. Winfried Ruigrok, "Multinational Corporations in the Global Economy," in *Political Economy and the Changing Global Order*, 3rd ed., ed. Richard Stubbs and Geoffrey R. D. Underhill (Oxford and New York: Oxford University Press, 2006), 205.

87. UNCTAD, *World Investment Report, 2006* (New York and Geneva, Switzerland: United Nations, 2006), 33–35; "Average of the four shares: FDI inflows as a percentage of gross fixed capital formation for the past three years 2001–2003; FDI inward stocks as a percentage of GDP in 2003; value added of foreign affiliates as a percentage of GDP in 2003; and employment of foreign affiliates as a percentage of total employment in 2003" (ibid., 11).

88. Moody, *Workers in a Lean World*, 280.

89. Kim Moody and Mary McGinn, *Unions and Free Trade: Solidarity vs. Competition* (Detroit, MI: A Labor Notes Book, 1992), 55.

90. Noel Castree, "Geographic Scale and Grass-Roots Internationalism: The Liverpool Dock Dispute, 1995–1998," *Economic Geography* 76, no. 3 (July 2000): 284.

91. Clawson, *The Next Upsurge*, 143. The largest job growth industries as listed by Clawson (see p. 143) are "cashiers, registered nurses, retail salespersons, truck drivers, home health aides, teacher aides and educational assistants, nursing aides, receptionists and information clerks, secondary-school teachers, child care workers, clerical supervisors and managers, marketing and sales supervisors, maintenance repairers, food counter and fountain workers, special education teachers, food preparation workers, guards, general office clerks, waiters and waitresses, social workers, adjustment clerks, short-order and fast food cooks, personal and homecare aides, food service and lodging managers, and medical assistants."

92. Ibid., 142–44.

93. Moody and McGinn, *Unions and Free Trade*, 52–56.

94. David Bacon, "World Labor Needs Independence and Solidarity," *Monthly Review* 52, no. 3 (July–August 2000): 89.

95. David Bacon, "Unions without Borders: A New Kind of Internationalism Is Challenging Neoliberal Globalism," *The Nation,* January 22, 2001, 24.

96. Nissen, "Alternative Strategic Directions for the U.S. Labor Movement," 142–44; Bronfenbrenner and Juravich, "It Takes More Than House Calls," 21–25, 29–33.

97. Moody, *Workers in a Lean World,* 276–77; Christopher Schenk, "Social Movement Unionism: Beyond the Organizing Model," in *Trade Unions in Renewal: A Comparative Study,* ed. Peter Fairbrother and Charlotte A. B. Yates (London and New York: Continuum, 2003), 250.

98. Gregory Mantsios, "What Does Labor Stand For?" in *A New Labor Movement for the New Century,* ed. Gregory Mantsios (New York: Garland Publishing, 1998), 60–63; Bacon, "World Labor Needs Independence and Solidarity," 97–98.

99. Bruce Nissen, "Alliances across the Border: U.S. Labor in the Era of Globalization," *Working USA* 3, no. 1 (1999): 43–55.

100. Greg Smithsimon, "Transnational Labor Organizing," *Socialist Review* 27, no. 3–4 (1999): 73; Kim Scipes, "AFL-CIO in Venezuela: Déjà Vu All Over Again," *Labor Notes,* April 2003.

CHAPTER 4

1. Lopez, *Reorganizing the Rust Belt,* 9.

2. SEIU, "About SEIU," http://www.seiu.org/about/index.cfm.

3. Roger Waldinger, Chris Erickson, Ruth Milkman, Daniel J. B. Mitchell, Abel Valenzuela, Kent Wong, and Maurice Zeitlin, "Justice for Janitors: Organizing in Difficult Times," *Dissent* 44, no. 1 (Winter 1997): 38.

4. Carter Wright, "A Clean Sweep: Justice for Janitors," *Multinational Monitor,* January/February 2001, 13.

5. Quote from Jose La Luz and Paula Finn, "Getting Serious about Inclusion: A Comprehensive Approach," in *A New Labor Movement for the New Century,* ed. Gregory Mantsios (New York: Garland Publishing, 1998), 203; David Bacon, "West Coast Janitors Get Ready to Fight," *Z Magazine,* April 1997, www.zmag.org/ZMag/articles/apr97bacon.html.

6. David Bacon, "West Coast Janitors Get Ready to Fight."

7. Clawson, *The Next Upsurge,* 101.

8. Luz and Finn, "Getting Serious about Inclusion," 203; Wright, "A Clean Sweep"; Jane Williams, "Restructuring Labor's Identity: The Justice for Janitors Campaign in Washington, D.C.," in *The Transformation of US Unions: Voices, Visions, and Strategies from the Grassroots,* ed. Ray M. Tillman and Michael S. Cummings (London: Lynne Rienner Publishers, 1999).

9. SEIU, "Janitors' Victory in Houston Sparks Hope for New Era of Economic Gains for Families in America," http://seiu.org/media/pressreleases.cfm?pr_id=1354.

10. Sue Kirchhoff, "Labor Leaders Hope Higher Minimum Wage is just the Beginning," *USA Today,* January 10, 2007, 3B. The Employee Free Choice Act did not pass though the Senate after already passing through the House. Under the act, if a majority of workers sign a form stating that they want to join a union, the employer must agree to the workers' wishes. This would obviously be beneficial for unions and workers alike. If the Democrats gain the presidency, it will be interesting to see what happens, because as I argue later, the Democrats generally promise the labor movement the world and deliver very little.

11. Moody, *An Injury to All,* 257, 285–87.

12. Goldfield, "Race and Labor Organization," 97.

13. Kate Bronfenbrenner and Robert Hickey, "Changing to Organize: A National Assessment of Union Strategies," in *Rebuilding Labor: Organizing and Organizers in the New Union Movement,* ed. Ruth Milkman and Kim Voss (Ithaca, NY: Cornell University Press, 2004), 37.

14. Christopher L. Erickson, Catherine L. Fisk, Ruth Milkman, Daniel J. B. Mitchell, and Kent Wong, "Justice for Janitors in Los Angeles: Lessons from Three Rounds of Negotiations," *British Journal of Industrial Relations* 40, no. 3 (2002): 556–57.

15. Kim Moody, "American Labor: A Movement Again?" in *Rising from the Ashes? Labor in the Age of "Global" Capital,* ed. Ellen Meiksins Wood, Peter Meiksins, and Michael Yates (New York: Monthly Review Press, 1998), 65; Mike Parker and Martha Gruelle, *Democracy Is Power: Rebuilding Unions from the Bottom Up* (Detroit, MI: Labor Notes, 1999), 28; Lydia Savage, "Justice for Janitors: Scales of Organizing and Representing Workers," *Antipode* 38, no. 3 (June 2006): 655.

16. Vanessa Tait, *Poor Workers' Unions* (Cambridge, MA: South End Press, 2005), 201–2.

17. Fred Wulkan, "Facing Movement for Democracy, SEIU Gives Massachusetts Members to Teachers Union," *Labor Notes,* February 2006, 3–4.

18. Ian Greer, "Business Union vs Business Union? Understanding the Split in the US Labour Movement," *Capital & Class,* Autumn 2006, 4.

19. AFL-CIO, "What's the Difference," http://www.aflcio.org/aboutus/difference.cfm.

20. Stern, quoted in Richard Hurd, "The Failure of Organizing, the New Unity Partnership, and the Future of the Labor Movement," *WorkingUSA* 8 (September 2004): 15.

21. Lerner, quoted in Jeff Crosby, "Democracy, Density, and Transformation: We Need Them All," *WorkingUSA* v. 8 (2005): 741.

22. Stern, quoted in Harold Meyerson, "Labor's Civil War," *American Prospect,* June 2005, http://www.prospect.org/web/page.ww?section=root&name=ViewWeb&articleId=9771.

23. Press release, quoted in Marick F. Masters, Ray Gibney, and Tom Zagenczyk, "The AFL-CIO v. CTW: The Competing Visions, Strategies, and Structures," *Journal of Labor Research* 27, no. 4 (Fall 2006): 488–89.

24. Chris Kutalik, "What Does the AFL-CIO Split Mean?" *Labor Notes,* September 2005, 7.

25. International Brotherhood of Teamsters, "Letter to John Sweeney," July 25, 2005, http://www.rtands.com/breaking_news_archive.shtml; SEIU, press release, July 25, 2005, http://www.seiu.org/media/pressreleases.cfm?pr_id=1237.

26. Masters et al., "The AFL-CIO v. CTW," 491.

27. Meyerson, "Labor's Civil War"; Masters et al., "The AFL-CIO v. CTW," 496; AFL-CIO, "What's the Difference."

28. Samuel Estreicher, "Disunity with the House of Labor: Change to Win or to Stay the Course?" *Journal of Labor Research* 27, no. 4 (Fall 2006): 506.

29. Masters et al., "The AFL-CIO v. CTW," 497.

30. Quote and information from Hurd, "The Failure of Organizing," 16–17.

31. Stern, quoted in Masters et al., "The AFL-CIO v. CTW," 495.

32. Stern, quoted in Jeff Crosby, "Can Anything Good Come from This?" *New Labor Forum* 15, no. 1 (Spring 2006): 35.

33. Quote and information from William Johnson, "Labor-Management Partnership as Part of Service Employees Vision for Power," *Labor Notes,* July 2005, 9–10.

34. Quote from Marc Cooper, "Say It. Ain't So, Miguel," *L.A. Weekly,* July 2002, posted at http://www.consumerwatchdog.org/healthcare/nw/?postId=560; Kay McVay, "Undemocratic Moves," *California Nurse,* August 2002, 3.

35. Quoted in David Bacon, "Partnership in a War Zone," http://dbacon.igc.org/Unions/07kaiser.htm; Nick Schou, "Nursing a Grudge," *OC Weekly,* May 16, 2003, http://www.consumerwatchdog.org/nw/?postId=661&pageTitle=Nursing+A+Grudge.

36. Ralph Thomas, "Union, Nursing Home Alliance Team Up," *Seattle Times,* March 5, 2007.

37. Rose Ann Demoro, "Turmoil in the AFL-CIO: A Dollars & Sense Roundtable (Service Employees International Union and International Brotherhood of Teamsters withdraw from AFL-CIO)," *Dollars & Sense,* September 1, 2005, http://www.dollarsandsense.org/archives/2005/0905demoro.html.

38. Quoted in Chris Kutalik, "A Play for Power?" *Labor Notes,* September 2005, 9.

39. Hurd, "The Failure of Organizing," 19.

40. Stepan-Norris and Zeitlin, *Left Out,* 162–63.

41. Ibid., 187.

42. Herman Benson, "AFL-CIO Split Poses the Question: Must Labor Bureaucratize to Organize?" *Union Democracy Review* 157 (2005), http://bensonsudblog.blogspot.com/2005_08_01_archive.html.

43. Change to Win, *Constitution,* 2005, 15.

44. Masters et al., "The AFL-CIO v. CTW," 493.

45. Benson, "AFL-CIO Split Poses the Question"; Janice Fine, "Debating Labor's Future," *The Nation,* August 1, 2005, http://www.thenation.com/doc/20050801/fine.

46. Crosby, "Democracy, Density, and Transformation," 738.

47. David Moberg, "Reforming the Teamsters," *The Nation,* September 2–9, 2002, 30; Quote from Jim Larkin, "Which Way for the Teamsters?" *The Nation,* October 8, 2001, 21.

48. Steve Early, "Turmoil in the AFL-CIO: A Dollars & Sense Roundtable (Service Employees International Union and International Brotherhood of Teamsters withdraw from AFL-CIO)," *Dollars & Sense,* September 1, 2005, http://www.dollarsandsense.org/archives/2005/0905early.html.

49. Ibid.; Tait, *Poor Workers' Unions,* 208–9.

50. Stern, quoted in Steve Early, "Book Review: A Country That Works: Getting America Back on Track—By Stern, Andy America Needs a Raise: Fighting for Economic Security and Social Justice—By Sweeney, John," *WorkingUSA* 10, no. 1 (2007): 146.

CHAPTER 5

1. Ian Robinson, "Neoliberal Restructuring and U.S. Unions: Toward Social Movement Unionism?" *Critical Sociology* 26, no. 1–2 (2000): 109.

2. See, for example, Bayes, "Globalization from Below"; Stuart Eimer, "From Business Unionism to 'Social Movement Unionism': The Case of AFL-CIO, Milwaukee County Labor Council," *Labor Studies Journal* 24, no. 2 (Summer 1999); Fantasia and Voss, *Hard Work*; Hassan, "The Future of the Labor Left;" Sonya Huber and Stephanie Luce, "Jobs with Justice at 14: Building Social Movement Unionism," *Labor Notes,* October 2001; Lopez, *Reorganizing the Rust Belt*; Nissen, "Alternative Strategic Directions"; Ian Robinson, "Does Neoliberal Restructuring Promote Social Movement Unionism? U.S. Developments in Comparative Perspective," in *Unions in a Globalized Environment,* ed. Bruce Nissen (Armonk, NY: M. E. Sharpe, 2002); Schenk, "Social Movement Unionism"; Lowell Turner and Richard W. Hurd, "Building Social Movement Unionism," in *Rekindling the Movement: Labor's Quest for Relevance in the Twenty-First Century,* ed. Lowell Turner, Harry C. Katz, and Richard W. Hurd (Ithaca, NY, and London: Cornell University Press, 2001).

3. Moody, *Workers in a Lean World,* 4–5.

4. Dan La Botz, "The Fight at UPS: The Teamsters' Victory and the Future of the 'New Labor Movement,'" *Solidarity Website,* http://www.solidarity-us.org/ups.

5. Ibid.; Dan La Botz, *Rank-and-File Rebellion: Teamsters for a Democratic Union* (London: Verso, 1990), 115–18; Aaron Brenner, "Rank-and-File Teamster Movements in Comparative Perspective," in *Trade Union Politics: American Unions and Economic Change, 1960–1990s,* ed. Glenn Perusek and Kent Worcester (Atlantic Highlands, NJ: Humanities Press, 1995), 118.

6. David Beck, quoted in La Botz, *Rank-and-File Rebellion,* 121.

7. La Botz, *Rank-and-File Rebellion,* 123–25; Michael H. Belzer and Richard Hurd, "Government Oversight, Union Democracy, and Labor Racketeering: Lessons from the Teamsters Experience," *Journal of Labor Research* 20, no. 3 (Summer 1999): 344; David Witwer, *Corruption and Reform in the Teamsters Union* (Urbana and Chicago: University of Illinois Press, 2003), 160.

8. La Botz, *The Fight at UPS.* For an excellent overview of corruption in the Teamsters, see Witwer, *Corruption and Reform in the Teamsters Union;* La Botz, *Rank-and-File Rebellion,* 131–32; Belzer and Hurd, "Government Oversight," 345.

9. La Botz, *Rank-and-File Rebellion,* 138.

10. Industrial report, September 27, 28 (no year recorded), p. 3, International Socialists Archive, Tamiment Library, New York University, collection 88, box 1, folder 2.

11. Milton Fisk, *Socialism from Below in the United States* (Ohio: Herra Press, 1977); Brenner, "Rank-and-File Teamster Movements," 126–27.

12. Brenner, "Rank-and-File Teamster Movements," 126–27.

13. Ibid., 129.

14. Kim Moody, "Who Reformed the Teamsters?" *Against the Current* 7, no. 1 (new series, March–April 1992): 24; Ray M. Tillman, "Reform Movement in the Teamsters and United Auto Workers," in *The Transformation of US Unions: Voices, Visions, and Strategies from the Grassroots,* ed. Ray M. Tillman and Michael S. Cummings (London: Lynne Rienner Publishers, 1999), 141.

15. *Convoy Dispatch,* no. 71, June–July 1987, 1.

16. Kenneth C. Crowe, *Collision: How the Rank and File Took Back the Teamsters* (New York: Charles Scribner's Sons, 1993), 39; La Botz, *Rank-and-File Rebellion,* 286; La Botz, *The Fight at UPS;* Moody, "Who Reformed the Teamsters?" 25.

17. Tillman, "Reform Movement," 142.

18. *Convoy Dispatch,* no. 92, December 1989, 1; Ken Paff, quoted in Tillman, "Reform Movement," 142.

19. La Botz, *The Fight at UPS;* Tillman, "Reform Movement," 142; *The International Teamster,* February 1992, 13; Dianne Feeley, "Teamster Trouble II," *International Viewpoint* 297 (February 1998): 18; Phill Kwik, "It's a New Day in the Teamsters," *Labor Notes,* August 1991, 10.

20. Quote from Dan La Botz, "Rank and File Teamsters Fight for Labor's Future," *Dollars and Sense,* September/October, 1998, 17; La Botz, *The Fight at UPS.*

21. La Botz, *The Fight at UPS.*

22. *Convoy Dispatch,* no. 158, March 1997, 4.

23. Matt Witt and Rand Wilson, "The Teamsters' UPS Strike of 1997: Building a New Labor Movement," *Labor Studies Journal* 24, no. 1 (Spring 1999) accessed via Expanded Academic ASAP; La Botz, *The Fight at UPS;* David Moberg, "The UPS Strike: Lessons for Labor," *WorkingUSA,* 1 (3) September/October (1997): 13.

24. Witt and Wilson, "The Teamsters' UPS Strike of 1997," 63

25. Ibid., 63

26. *Associated Press Newswires,* August 7, 1997; Alexander Cockburn, "Counterpoint: 'Dear Jim': What Ron Carey Should Tell the Boss of UPS," *The Wall Street Journal,*

August 14, 1997, A13; Richard Rothstein, "Union Strength in the United States: Lessons from the UPS Strike," *International Labour Review* 136, no. 4 (Winter 1997): 477.

27. *Associated Press Newswires,* August 7, 1997.

28. Moberg, "The UPS Strike," 13; La Botz, *The Fight at UPS.*

29. Jane Slaughter, "UPS and Detroit Newspaper Strikes," *Monthly Review,* January 1998, 55.

30. Witt and Wilson, "The Teamsters' UPS Strike of 1997," 64–65; Moberg, "The UPS Strike," 14.

31. *Associated Press Newswires,* July 31, 1997; *The Wall Street Journal,* August 21, 1997.

32. Matt Witt and Rand Wilson, "Part-Time America Won't Work," in *Not Your Father's Union Movement: Inside the AFL-CIO,* ed. Jo-Ann Mort (London: Verso, 1998), 184; John Alden, quoted in Witt and Wilson, "The Teamsters' UPS Strike of 1997," 66.

33. Rothstein, "Union Strength in the United States," 473.

34. Witt and Wilson, "Part-Time America Won't Work," 182; Witt and Wilson, "The Teamsters' UPS Strike of 1997."

35. Witt and Wilson, "The Teamsters' UPS Strike of 1997," 65

36. Moberg, "The UPS Strike," 15.

37. *Associated Press Newswires,* August 20, 1997; Ron Carey, quoted in Rothstein, "Union Strength in the United States," 473.

38. Andy Dworkin, "Teamsters Union Protests Lack of New Full-time Jobs at United Parcel Service," *Knight-Ridder Tribune Business News,* July 11, 1998; Douglas A. Blackmon, "UPS Nullifies Part of Teamsters Contract—Package Firm Won't Create 2,000 Full-time Jobs Under 1997 Strike Pact" *The Wall Street Journal,* July 10, 1998, A3; "UPS Agrees to Create Another 2,000 Jobs under Teamsters Pact," *The Wall Street Journal,* March 31, 2000, A8; "After Losing Arbitration, UPS To Hire 2000 Full-Time Employees By June 10," *Dow Jones Business News,* March 30, 2000.

39. Rothstein, "Union Strength in the United States," 478–79.

40. Dan La Botz, "Why Is It So Hard to Reform the Teamsters?" *Dollars and Sense,* November/December 1998, 26; Jim Larkin, "Teamster Tragedy," *The Progressive,* January 1998, 22.

41. Teamsters for a Democratic Union, "UPS Rank & File Network Contract Bulletin," http://www.tdu.org/UPS_Bulletin_3.pdf; "UPS Posts Solid 1st Quarter Earnings," *Business Wire,* April 18, 2002; "UPDATE 2-UPS Quarterly Profit Drops 3.3 Percent," *Reuters News,* April 18, 2002; Teamsters for a Democratic Union, "Best Contract Ever," http://www.tdu.org/UPS/Best_Contract_Ever.pdf.

42. Michael Eskew, quoted in "UPS Chairman: 'Getting Close' to Teamster Deal," *Dow Jones News Service,* June 11, 2002.

43. Jimmy Hoffa Jr., quoted in Paul Miller, "UPS Strike Watch Is On," *Catalog Age* 19, no. 5 (April 1, 2002): 16; Hoffa Jr., quoted in Nancy Cleeland, "UPS Talks to Present Hoffa with Key Test," *Los Angeles Times,* March 10, 2002, C1; International Brotherhood of Teamsters, *Union Negotiating Proposals National Master United Parcel Service Agreement,* Article 22, Section 3 (2002).

44. International Brotherhood of Teamsters, "UPS Contract Campaign Update: Whatever It Takes," October 1, 2001, http://www.teamster.org/01newsb/hn_011001_4.htm.

45. Jimmy Hoffa Jr., quoted in "4,000 Teamster Rally in NY for Strong Contract at UPS," *PR Newswire,* June 23, 2002.

46. Teamsters for a Democratic Union, "Contract Bulletin 8," http://www.tdu.org/UPSBulletin8.pdf.

47. "UPS' Latest Offer Fails to Address Issues Important to Teamster Members," *PR Newswire,* June 27, 2002.

48. "Teamsters, UPS Reach 6-Year Deal," *AP Online,* July 16, 2002.

49. "Teamsters Sign 6-Year Deal with UPS," *Dow Jones News Service,* July 16, 2002; "Teamsters, UPS Reach 6-Year Deal."

50. International Brotherhood of Teamsters, "Highlights of the Tentative UPS National Agreement," http://www.trakups.org/materials/upshighlights.pdf; Teamsters for a Democratic Union, "Contract Bulletin, 14," http://www.tdu.org/UPSBulletin14.pdf; Teamsters for a Democratic Union, "Hoffa Uses 'Mystery Math' to Sell Agreement," http://www.tdu.org/UPS/UPS_Contract_411/UPS_Mystery_Math/ups_mystery_math. html; Teamsters for a Democratic Union, "Central States Pension Fund: No Pension Increase—Members Fight Back," http://www.tdu.org/Convoy/CSPF_Anger/CSPF_ Freeze/cspf_freeze.html; *National Master United Parcel Service Agreement for the Period: August 1, 2002 through July 21, 2008* (2002), 69–70.

51. National Master United Parcel Service Agreement, 31 (emphasis added).

52. "Inside Track—How UPS Delivered a New Deal—Labour Relations," *Financial Times,* August 1, 2002, 10.

53. International Brotherhood of Teamsters, "Teamsters Overwhelmingly Ratify Contract with UPS," http://www.trakups.org/News/nr_020829_1.htm (2002); Teamsters for a Democratic Union, "UPS Contact Vote Update," e-mail sent to author, September 5, 2002.

54. Teamsters for a Democratic Union, "Detroit Area UPSers Vote No; Hoffa Says Yes," http://www.tdu.org/UPS/UPS_Contract_411/UPS_Detroit_rider/ups_detroit_rider. html.

55. Teamsters for a Democratic Union, "Survey Results: UPS Teamsters Say Conditions Are Worse Today Than at Start of Contract," http://www.tdu.org/UPS/upssurvey results/upssurveyresults.html.

56. CAW, "Statement of Principles," http://www.caw.ca/whoweare/CAWpoliciesand statements/policystatements/cawprin_index.asp.

57. Ann C. Frost, "Union Involvement in Workplace Decision Making: Implications for Union Democracy," *Journal of Labor Research* 21, no. 2 (Spring 2000): 277.

58. Ibid., 279–80.

59. Sam Gindin, "Breaking Away: The Formation of the Canadian Auto Workers," *Studies in Political Economy* 29 (Summer 1989): 83; Frost, "Union Involvement in Workplace Decision Making," 277; CAW, "The CAW Constitution: Your Democratic Rights Guaranteed," http://www.caw.ca/jointhecaw/organizinglaws/canada/fact11.asp.

60. Stephen Herzenberg, "Whither Social Unionism? Labor and Restructuring in the US Auto Industry," in *The Challenge of Restructuring: North American Labor Movements Respond,* ed. Jane Jenson and Rianne Mahon (Philadelphia: Temple University Press, 1993), 322; Quote from Peter Downs, "Unsung Heroes of Union Democracy: Rank-and-File Organizers," in *The Transformation of US Unions: Voices, Visions, and Strategies from the Grassroots,* ed. Ray M. Tillman and Michael S. Cummings (London: Lynne Rienner Publishers, 1999), 127; Jane Slaughter, "Shrinking Auto Union Beats Back Reformers," *Labor Notes,* July 1992, 3, 15.

61. Buzz Hargrove, CAW Education Department, *Paid Education Leave Program [training manuals],* v. IV, CAW Canada, Willowdale quoted in D. W. Livingstone and Reuben Roth, "Workplace Communities and Transformative Learning: Oshawa Auto workers and the CAW," *Convergence,* v. XXX1, (3), 1998, p.13; CAW, "CAW National Executive Board Statement on the Crisis of Homelessness," http://www.caw.ca/ campaigns&issues/ongoingcampaigns/homelessness/nebstatementcrisis.asp.

62. Ibid.

63. CAW, "CAW Covering Letter on the Campaign against Ontario Child Care Cuts," http://www.caw.ca/campaigns&issues/ongoingcampaigns/carecuts/coverletter.asp.

64. CAW, "The CAW: A Dynamic Union"; CAW, "Membership Overview," http://www.caw.ca/whatwedo/bargaining/cbpac/2002program/chapter1.asp; SamGindin, "The CAW: The Birth and Transformation of a Union," CAW, http://www.caw.ca/whoweare/ourhistory/cawhistory/ch9/p4c9_2.html; UAW, Departmental Reports (33rd Constitutional Convention, Las Vegas, June 3–6, 2002), http://www.local2209.org/pdf/01977.pdf; UAW, "Who We Are," http://www.uaw.org/about/uawmembership.html.

65. Charlotte Yates, "Unity and Diversity: Challenges to an Expanding Canadian Auto workers' Union," *The Canadian Review of Sociology and Anthropology* 35, no. 1 (1998): 96.

66. Ibid.; Gindin, "The CAW."

67. Gindin, "The CAW"; However, this is not to argue that the mergers have not brought tensions within the CAW. For more on the problems that the CAW faces because of union mergers, see Yates, "Unity and Diversity."

68. Moody, *Workers in a Lean World,* 242.

69. Robin Alexander and Peter Gilmore, "The Emergence of Cross-Border Labor Solidarity," *NACLA Report on the Americas* 28, no. 1 (July/August 1994): 47, 51. The armed CTM (the dominant Mexican trade union) goons who were "clad in Ford uniforms, were allowed in the [Ford] factory where they shot and killed one worker and wounded eight others" (ibid., 51).

70. Steve Babson, "Cross-Border Trade with Mexico and the Prospect for Worker Solidarity: The Case of Mexico," *Critical Sociology* 26, no. 1–2 (2000): 29.

71. See, for example, Donald M. Wells, "When Push Comes to Shove: Competitiveness, Job Insecurity and Labour-Management Cooperation in Canada," *Economic and Industrial Democracy* 18, no. 2 (1997); Thomas Hyclak and Michael G. Kolchin, "The Drive for Autonomy by Canadian Auto Workers," in *Industrial Relations Research Association Series,* ed. Barbara D. Dennis, Proceedings of the Forty-First Annual Meeting, New York, December 28–30 (Madison, WI: The Association, 1988).

72. OECD, "Canada," *OECD Economic Outlook,* June 1997, 73; OECD, "United States," *OECD Economic Outlook,* June 1997, 43.

73. Nichole M. Christian, Rebecca Blumenstein, and Angelo B. Henderson, "Ford and UAW Reach Tentative Accord That Will Guarantee 95% of Union Jobs—Pact Could Spur Showdown With GM, Which Faces Pressure for Cutbacks," *The Wall Street Journal,* September 17, 1996, A3; Brian S. Akre, "UAW, Chrysler agree // Two Down, Talks Now Shift to GM," *Chicago Sun-Times,* September 30, 1996, 22; *Los Angeles Times,* September 17, 1996; "Ford's Job Guarantee puts GM in a Bind," *The Wall Street Journal Europe,* September 18, 1996, 2; Frank Swoboda, "UAW Strikes Put Pressure on GM; Union Wants Carmaker to Accept Pattern Pact," *The Washington Post,* October 31, 1996, E03; Rebecca Blumenstein, Nichole M. Christian, and Gabriella Stern, "UAW and GM Forge a Contract Allowing up to 30,000 Job Cuts," *The Wall Street Journal,* November 4, 1996, A3.

74. Rebecca Blumenstein, UAW Delegates Endorse Pact with GM—Three-Year Labor Accord that Slows Outsourcing Goes to Rank and File," *The Wall Street Journal,* November 7, 1996, A2.

75. Moody, *Workers in a Lean World,* 108.

76. "UAW and GM Forge a Contract Allowing Up to 30,000 Job Cuts," *The Wall Street Journal,* November 4, 1996; *Chicago Tribune,* November 5, 1996.

77. Tom Fennell, "Upbeat on the Line," *MacLean's,* October 28, 1996, 36; Susan Bourette, "Outsourcing Tops CAW Agenda Union Aims to Limit Contracting-out By GM in Negotiations with Big Three Auto Makers," *The Globe and Mail,* July 15, 1996, B1; Susan Bourette and Patrick Brethour, "Auto Workers Eyeing GM as Next Target After Chrysler Deal, Union Girds for Potentially Tougher Talks," *The Globe and Mail,* September 19, 1996, B1; Ian Jack, "GM has War Chest and Will to Fight CAW, Analysts Say," *The Financial Post,* October 5, 1996, 5; Nicolaas van Rijn, "Big Three Auto Firms Hit

by Vote for Strike Fall Walkout Gets Massive Majority, Union Says," *The Toronto Star,* August 26, 1996, A3.

78. Ian Jack, "GM and CAW Set for Tough Round of Talks," *The Financial Post,* October 19, 1996, 9; Nichole M. Christian, "GM and Canadian Union are Pushing to Settle 18-day Strike by Noon Today," *The Wall Street Journal,* October 21, 1996, A3.

79. Dave Robertson, quoted in Moody, *Workers in a Lean World,* 278.

80. Donovan Vincent, "It's a Deal! GM Workers Expected Back on Job Tonight," *The Toronto Star,* October 23, 1996, A1; *Los Angeles Times,* October 23, 1996.

81. *Los Angeles Times,* October 23, 1996; Quote from "GM Canadian Workers Ratify Contract Agreement Includes First: Health-care Benefits for Gay, Lesbian Partners," *The Dallas Morning News,* October 24, 1996, 1B.

82. Moody, *Workers in a Lean World,* 108.

83. Gindin, "The CAW."

84. See Michael Schiavone, "Social Movement Unionism in North America: An Evaluation of Kim Moody's Account" (PhD diss., Australian National University, 2004) for more examples of the success of social justice unionism.

CHAPTER 6

1. Kim Moody, "Immigrant Workers and Labor/Community Organization in the United States," *Union Ideas Network,* (2006), 1–4, http://uin.org.uk/content/view/186/66/.

2. Ibid., 12.

3. Ibid., 14.

4. *New York Times,* April 12, 2006, A16.

5. Sarah Ferguson, "No Justice, No Work: Immigrants Tap May Day's Radical Roots," *Village Voice,* April 28, 2006, http://www.villagevoice.com/news/0618,ferguson,73040,6.html.

6. Milkman, *L.A. Story,* 133.

7. Fernando Gapasin and Michael Yates, "Organizing the Unorganized: Will Promises Become Practices?" in *Rising from the Ashes? Labor in the Age of "Global" Capital,* ed. Ellen Meiksins Wood, Peter Meiksins, and Michael Yates (New York: Monthly Review Press, 1998), 80–81.

8. Enid Eckstein, "Putting Organizing Back into Labor Councils," *WorkingUSA* 5, no. 1 (2001): 124.

9. Stephanie Luce, "Building Political Power and Community Coalitions: The Role of Central Labor Councils in the Living-Wage Movement," in *Central Labor Councils and the Revival of American Unionism,* ed. Immanuel Ness and Stuart Eimer (Armonk, NY: M. E. Sharpe, 2001), 141.

10. Quote and subsequent information from David Reynolds and Jen Kern, "Labor and the Living-Wage Movement," *WorkingUSA* 5, no. 3 (2002): 30.

11. Quoted in ibid., 31.

12. Ibid., 37–42.

13. Ibid., 45.

14. Jonathan Rosenblum, "Building Organizing Capacity: The King County Labor Council," in *Central Labor Councils and the Revival of American Unionism,* ed. Immanuel Ness and Stuart Eimer (Armonk, NY: M. E. Sharpe, 2001), 182–83.

15. Reynolds and Kern, "Labor and the Living-Wage Movement," 35.

16. Steven Kest, "ACORN and Community-Labor Partnerships," *WorkingUSA* 6, no. 4 (2003): 95–99.

17. *New York Times,* quoted in ibid., 99.

18. Quote and subsequent information from Eckstein, "Putting Organizing Back into Labor Councils," 138.

19. Rosenblum, "Building Organizing Capacity," 182–85; Fernando Gapasin and Howard Wial, "The Role of Central Labor Councils in Union Organizing in the 1990s," in *Organizing to Win,* ed. Kate Bronfenbrenner et al. (Ithaca, NY: ILR Press, 1998): 63–64.

20. Tiffany Ten Eyck, "A New Alliance: Workers Centers and Unions," Counterpunch, http://www.counterpunch.org/teneyck01052007.html.

21. Gapasin and Wial, "The Role of Central Labor Councils," 63.

22. Eckstein, "Putting Organizing Back into Labor Council," 132.

23. Quoted in ibid, 133.

24. Ibid, 135.

25. Gapasin and Yates, "The Role of Central Labor Councils," 80; Immanuel Ness, "From Dormancy to Activism: New Voice and the Revival of Labor Councils," in *Central Labor Councils and the Revival of American Unionism,* ed. Immanuel Ness and Stuart Eimer (Armonk, NY: M. E. Sharpe, 2001); David Moberg, "Union Cities," *The American Prospect,* September 11, 2000, 35–37.

26. Fantasia and Voss, *Hard Work,* 110; AFL-CIO, "Building a Strong Union Movement in Every State and Community," http://www.aflcio.org/aboutus/thisistheaflcio/convention/2001/ecreport/building.cfm#unioncities.

27. AFL-CIO, "Building a Strong Union Movement"; Bronfenbrenner and Hickey, "Changing to Organize," 34.

28. See Jeff Grabelsky, "A New Alliance in New York State: A Progress Report on the Labor Movement's Restructuring, Capacity Building, and Programmatic Work," *WorkingUSA* 10, no. 1 (2007) for the success of CLCs in New York state.

29. Janice Fine, "Moving Innovation from the Margins to the Center," in *A New Labor Movement for the New Century,* ed. Gregory Mantsios (New York: Garland Publishing, 1998), 156.

30. Tait, *Poor Workers' Unions,* 130.

31. Gordon, quoted in "Toward a Cohesive Labor Movement: Worker Center and Union Collaboration in Los Angeles" (ILE Graduate Research Conference, February 21–22, 2003), 21.

32. Moody, "Immigrant Workers and Labor/Community Organization in the United States," 21–22.

33. Ibid., 22–25; Janice Fine, *Worker Centers* (Ithaca, NY, and London: ILR Press, 2006), 9–11, 16.

34. Jennifer Gordon, *Suburban Sweatshops* (Cambridge and London: The Belknap Press of Harvard University Press, 2005), 70–71.

35. Janice Fine, "Worker Centers: Organizing Communities at the Edge of a Dream" (EPI briefing paper 159, 2005, http://www.epinet.org/content.cfm/bp159); Janice Fine, *Worker Centers: Organizing Communities at the Edge of a Dream,* Neighborhood Funders Group Executive Summary, April 2005, 8; Gordon, *Suburban Sweatshops,* 243; "Organizing Low-Wage Immigrants—The Workplace Project: Interview with Jennifer Gordon," *WorkingUSA* 5, no. 1 (2001): 88. See Fine, *Worker Centers,* 162–79 for other examples of worker centers helping to enact labor-friendly laws.

36. Tait, *Poor Workers' Unions,* 131, 143.

37. Fine, "Worker Centers," briefing paper.

38. Tait, *Poor Workers' Unions,* 143; Quoted in Milkman, *L.A. Story,* 128.

39. May Chen and Kent Wong, "The Challenge of Diversity and Inclusion in the AFL-CIO," in *A New Labor Movement for the New Century,* ed. Gregory Mantsios (New York: Garland Publishing, 1998), 227–29.

40. Jeremy Brecher, "Labor Update: Organizing the New Workforce," *Zmagazine*, July/August 1998, http://zena.secureforum.com/Znet/zmag/zarticle.cfm?Url=articles/brecherjulyaug98.htm.

41. Tait, *Poor Workers' Unions*, 145–50.

42. Fine, "Worker Centers"; Moody, "Immigrant Workers," 29–30; Lisa Lowe, "Work, Immigration, Gender: New Subjects of Cultural Politics," *Social Justice* 25, no. 3 (Fall 1998): 40–41.

43. Ibid; Moody, "Immigrant Workers," 26–27; Elly Leary, "Immokalee Workers Take Down Taco Bell," *Monthly Review*, October 2005, 12–13, 19–20.

44. Janice Fine, "Moving Innovation from the Margins to the Center," 156; Tait, *Poor Workers' Unions*, 144.

45. Gordon, *Suburban Sweatshops*, 90.

46. Fine, *Worker Centers*, 122–24.

47. Gordon, *Suburban Sweatshops*, 293–94, 345.

48. Fine, *Worker Centers*, 217–18.

49. Immanuel Ness, *Immigrants, Unions, and the New U.S. Labor Market* (Philadelphia: Temple University Press, 2005), 158.

50. Gordon, quoted in "Toward a Cohesive Labor Movement," 23.

51. Fine, *Worker Centers*, 156.

52. Ibid., 247.

53. Quoted in Moody, *Workers in a Lean World*, 178.

54. Aparicio, quoted in Gordon, *Suburban Sweatshops*, 127; Saru Jayaraman, "La Alianza Para La Justicia: A Team Approach to Immigrant Worker Organizing," in *The New Urban Immigrant Workforce*, ed. Sarumathi Jayaraman and Immanuel Ness (Armonk, NY, and London: M. E. Sharpe, 2005), 99–100.

55. Kim Moody, "The Rank and File Strategy: Building a Socialist Movement in the US," Solidarity, http://www.solidarity-us.org/rankandfilestrategy.

56. Judy Atkins and David Cohen, "A Proposal for a Twenty-First-Century Trade Union Education League; An Attempt to Solve the Crisis of Organizing the Unorganized," posted at *Non-Majority Union Website* http://unity.caamwu.org/Articles/TUEL.htm.

57. Ibid.

58. David Johnson, "US, Mexican Unions Are Teaming Up," *Labor Notes*, September 1993, 8.

59. Greg Smithsimon, "Transnational Labor Organizing," *Socialist Review* 27, no. 3–4 (1999): 66.

60. Quoted in Terry Davis, "Cross Border Organizing Comes Home," *Labor Research Review* 23 (1995): 28.

61. Atkins and Cohen, "A Proposal."

62. CWA, "IUE-CWA Rolls Out WAGE Campaign at GE," http://www.cwa-union.org/news/cwa-news/page.jsp?itemID=27367968; Wade Rathke, "A Wal-Mart Workers Association? An Organizing Plan," in *Wal-Mart: The Face of Twenty-First Century Capitalism*, ed. Nelson Lichtenstein (New York and London: The New Press, 2006), 276–77.

63. Rathke, "A Wal-Mart Workers Association," 269.

64. Charles J. Morris, *The Blue Eagle at Work* (Ithaca, NY, and London: ILR Press, 2006), 210.

65. Quote and subsequent information from Rathke, "A Wal-Mart Workers Association," 272–76.

66. Quoted in Ibid., 282.

67. Leary, "Immokalee Workers," 21.

CHAPTER 7

1. Lichtenstein, *State of the Union*, 260.

2. Robinson, "Does Neoliberal Restructuring Promote Social Movement Unionism?" 199.

3. J. M. Barbalet, "Social Movements and the State: The Case of the American Labour Movement," in *Politics of the Future: The Role of Social Movements*, ed. Christine Jennet and Randal G. Stewart (Melbourne: The MacMillan Company of Australia, 1989), 255.

4. Zieger, *The CIO*, 145; Filippelli and McColloch, *Cold War in the Working Class*, 80; Matles and Higgins, *Them and Us*, 127; Report of the General Officers to the 8th UE Convention, reprinted in *UE News*, September 12, 1942, 5.

5. Matles and Higgins, *Them and Us*, 163.

6. Zieger, *The CIO*, 145; Matles and Higgins, *Them and Us*, 162, 164.

7. Stepan-Norris and Zeitlin, "Union Democracy, Radical Leadership, and the Hegemony of Capital," 839–40.

8. Ibid., 844.

9. Judith Stepan-Norris and Maurice Zeitlin, "Red Unions and 'Bourgeois' Contracts?" *American Journal of Sociology* 96, no. 5 (March 1991): 1172.

10. Halliday, *Revolution and World Politics*, 172.

11. Karl Marx, "The Eighteenth Brumaire of Louis Bonaparte" [1852], in *The Marx-Engels Reader*, 2nd edition, ed. Robert C. Tucker (New York: W. W. Norton & Company, 1978), 595.

12. Robinson, "Does Neoliberal Restructuring Promote Social Movement Unionism?" 221.

13. Lois A. West, "U.S. Foreign Labor Policy and the Case of Militant Political Unionism in the Philippines," *Labor Studies Journal* 16, no. 4 (Winter 1991): 69.

14. Unnamed KMU leader, quoted in ibid.

15. Lois A. West, *Militant Labor in the Philippines* (Philadelphia: Temple University Press, 1997), 195–96.

16. Moody, *An Injury to All*, 257; Ness, *Immigrants, Unions, and the New U.S. Labor Market*, 42 (emphasis in original).

17. Lichtenstein, *State of the Union*, 90.

18. Ruth Milkman, "Labor Organizing among Mexican-Born Workers in the U.S.: Recent Trends and Future Prospects," *Labor Studies Journal* 32 (1) 2007: 8–9.

19. Voss and Sherman, "Breaking the Iron Law of Oligarchy," 316.

20. Quoted in ibid., 329.

21. Quoted in ibid., 330–31.

22. Robinson, "Does Neoliberal Restructuring Promote Social Movement Unionism?" 223–24. As I argued before, due to the difference between what is labeled social movement unionism in America and social movement unionism in Brazil, the Philippines, South Africa, and South Korea, I prefer to use the term *social justice unionism* although I use the terms interchangeably.

23. Peter Waterman, "Social Movement Unionism: A New Union Model for a New World Order?" *Review* 26, no. 3 (Summer 1993): 251.

24. Mark Langevin, "Replacing the State: New Directions in Brazilian Labor Education," *Labor Studies Journal* 19, no. 1 (Spring 1994): 70. The new directions in Brazilian labor education involve the attempted linkage between "the articulation of workers' demands with the formulation and pursuit of political strategies to advance class-wide interests" (ibid., 61).

25. CAW, "Statement of Principles: Education," http://www.caw.ca/whoweare/CAWpoliciesandstatements/policystatements/cawedu_index.asp.

26. Reuben Roth, "The Canadian Auto Workers and Paid Education Leave: Social Unionism in Practice," The Ontario Institute for Studies in Education of the University of Toronto, http://www.oise.utoronto.ca/~rroth/1131.htm.

27. Ibid.

28. Sam Gindin, "Socialism 'with Sober Senses': Developing Workers' Capacities," in *Socialist Register 1998,* ed. Leo Panitch and Colin Leys (London: Merlin Press, 1998), 90–91.

29. Ibid., 97.

30. D. W. Livingstone and Reuben Roth, "Workplace Communities and Transformative Learning: Oshawa Autoworkers and the CAW," *Convergence* 31, no. 3 (1998): 17, 19–20.

31. For examples of US unions using worker education programs in an effort to revitalize Locals, see Voss and Sherman, "Breaking the Iron Law of Oligarchy," 322–24. Worker education programs have often been used throughout the US labor movement. For examples of successful worker education programs in the early part of the twentieth century, see Clyde W. Barrow, "Counter-Movement within the Labor Movement: Workers' Education and the American Federation of Labor, 1900–1937," *The Social Science Journal* 27, no. 4 (1990).

BIBLIOGRAPHY

Adler, Glenn, Judy Maller, and Eddie Webster. "Unions, Direct Action and Transition in South Africa." In *Peace, Politics and Violence in the New South Africa,* edited by Norman Etherington, 306–43. London: Hans Zell Publishers, 1992.

AFL-CIO. "Building a Strong Union Movement in Every State and Community." http://www.aflcio.org/aboutus/thisistheaflcio/convention/2001/ecreport/building. cfm#unioncities.

———. "Right to Work for Less." http://www.aflcio.org/issues/legislativealert/stateissues/ work/.

———. "What's the Difference." http://www.aflcio.org/aboutus/difference.cfm.

Alexander, Robin, and Peter Gilmore. "The Emergence of Cross-Border Labor Solidarity." *NACLA Report on the Americas* 28, no. 1 (July/August 1994): 42–51.

Aronowitz, Stanley. *From the Ashes of the Old: American Labor and America's Future.* Boston: Houghton Mifflin Company, 1998.

Atkins, Judy, and David Cohen. "A Proposal for a Twenty-First-Century Trade Union Education League; An Attempt to Solve the Crisis of Organizing the Unorganized." http://unity.caamwu.org/Articles/TUEL.htm.

Babson, Steve. "Cross-Border Trade with Mexico and the Prospect for Worker Solidarity: The Case of Mexico." *Critical Sociology* 26, no. 1–2 (2000): 13–35.

———. "UAW, Lean Production, and Labor-Management Relations at AutoAlliance." In *North American Auto Unions in Crisis,* edited by William C. Green and Ernest J. Yanarella, 81–100. New York: State University of New York, 1996.

Bacon, David. "Globalization: Two Faces, Both Ugly." *Dollars and Sense,* March/April 2000, 18–20, 40–41.

———. "Partnership in a War Zone." http://dbacon.igc.org/Unions/07kaiser.htm.

———. "Unions without Borders: A New Kind of Internationalism Is Challenging Neoliberal Globalism." *The Nation,* January 22, 2001, 20–24.

———. "West Coast Janitors Get Ready to Fight." *Z Magazine,* April 1997, www.zmag. org/ZMag/articles/apr97bacon.html.

———. "World Labor Needs Independence and Solidarity." *Monthly Review* 52, no. 3 (July–August 2000): 84–102.

Barbalet, J. M. "Social Movements and the State: The Case of the American Labour Movement." In *Politics of the Future: The Role of Social Movements,* edited by Christine Jennet and Randal G. Stewart, 237–61. Melbourne: The MacMillan Company of Australia, 1989.

Barrow, Clyde W. "Counter-Movement within the Labor Movement: Workers' Education and the American Federation of Labor, 1900–1937." *The Social Science Journal* 27, no. 4 (1990): 395–417.

Bayes, Jane H. "Globalization from Below: U.S. Labor and Social Movement Unionism." Paper presented to the Western Political Science Association Meetings, Las Vegas, NV, March 15–17, 2001.

Belzer, Michael H., and Richard Hurd. "Government Oversight, Union Democracy, and Labor Racketeering: Lessons from the Teamsters Experience." *Journal of Labor Research* 20, no. 3 (Summer 1999): 343–65.

Benson, Herman. "AFL-CIO Split Poses the Question: Must Labor Bureaucratize to Organize?" *Union Democracy Review* 157 (2005), http://bensonsudblog.blogspot.com/2005_08_01_archive.html.

Brecher, Jeremy. "Labor Update: Organizing the New Workforce." *Zmagazine,* July/August 1998, http://zena.secureforum.com/Znet/zmag/zarticle.cfm?Url=articles/brecherjulyaug98.htm.

Brecher, Jeremy, and Tim Costello. "Concluding Essay: Labor-Community Coalitions and the Restructuring of Power." In *Building Bridges: The Emerging Grassroots Coalition of Labor and Community,* edited by Jeremy Brecher and Tim Costello, 325–45. New York: Monthly Review Press, 1990.

Breitenfellner, Andreas. "Global Unionism: A Potential Player." *International Labour Review* 136, no. 4 (Winter 1997): 531–55.

Brenner, Aaron. "Rank-and-File Teamster Movements in Comparative Perspective." In *Trade Union Politics: American Unions and Economic Change, 1960–1990s,* edited by Glenn Perusek and Kent Worcester, 110–39. Atlantic Highlands, NJ: Humanities Press, 1995.

Broad, Dave. "Globalization and the Casual Labor Problem: History and Prospects." *Social Justice* 22, no. 3 (Fall 1995): 67–91.

Brody, David. *Workers in Industrial America: Essays on the Twentieth Century Struggle.* 2nd edition. Oxford: Oxford University Press, 1993.

Bronfenbrenner, Kate. "Changing to Organize." *The Nation,* September 3, 2001, 16–20.

Bronfenbrenner, Kate, and Robert Hickey. "Changing to Organize: A National Assessment of Union Strategies." In *Rebuilding Labor: Organizing and Organizers in the New Union Movement,* edited by Ruth Milkman and Kim Voss, 17–61. Ithaca, NY: Cornell University Press, 2004.

Bronfenbrenner, Kate, and Tom Juravich. "It Takes More Than House Calls: Organizing to Win with a Comprehensive Union-Building Strategy." In *Organizing to Win,* edited by Kate Bronfenbrenner et al., 19–36. Ithaca, NY: ILR Press, 1998.

Burgmann, Verity. *Power and Protest.* Sydney, Australia: Allen & Unwin, 1993.

"Business: The Strange Life of Low-Tech America." *The Economist,* October 17, 1998, 73–74.

Campbell, Duncan. "Foreign Investment, Labour Mobility and the Quality of Employment." *International Labour Review* 133, no. 2 (1994): 185–204.

Cassidy, John. "Why Karl Marx Was Right." *The New Yorker,* October 27, 1997, 248–59.

Castree, Noel. "Geographic Scale and Grass-Roots Internationalism: The Liverpool Dock Dispute, 1995–1998." *Economic Geography* 76, no. 3 (July 2000): 272–92.

CAW. "Membership Overview." http://www.caw.ca/whatwedo/bargaining/cbpac/2002 program/chapter1.asp.

———. "The CAW Constitution: Your Democratic Rights Guaranteed." http://www.caw.ca/jointhecaw/organizinglaws/canada/fact11.asp.

———. "CAW Covering Letter on the Campaign against Ontario Child Care Cuts." http://www.caw.ca/campaigns&issues/ongoingcampaigns/carecuts/coverletter.asp.

———. "CAW National Executive Board Statement on the Crisis of Homelessness." http://www.caw.ca/campaigns&issues/ongoingcampaigns/homelessness/nebstatementcrisis.asp.

———. "Statement of Principles." http://www.caw.ca/whoweare/CAWpoliciesandstatements/policystatements/cawprin_index.asp.

———. "Statement of Principles: Education." http://www.caw.ca/whoweare/CAWpoliciesandstatements/policystatements/cawedu_index.asp.

Change to Win. *Constitution.*, http://www.changetowin.org/fileadmin/pdf/Constitution.pdf (2005).

Chavez-Thompson, Linda. "Communities at Work: How New Alliances Are Restoring Our Right to Organize." *New Labor Forum* 3 (Fall/Winter 1998): 110–17.

Chen, May, and Kent Wong. "The Challenge of Diversity and Inclusion in the AFL-CIO." In *A New Labor Movement for the New Century*, edited by Gregory Mantsios, 185–201. New York: Garland Publishing, 1998.

Chomsky, Noam. *Profit Over People: Neoliberalism and the Global Order*. New York: Seven Stories Press, 1999.

"Citizens' Groups: The Non-governmental Order—Will NGOs Democratise, or Merely Disrupt, Global Governance." *The Economist*, December 11, 1999, 20.

Clawson, Dan. *The Next Upsurge*. Ithaca, NY, and London: ILR Press, 2003.

Cleaver, Harry. "Computer-Linked Social Movements and the Global Threat to Capitalism." Global Solidarity Dialogue. http://www.antenna.nl/~waterman/cleaver2.html.

Cockburn, Alexander. "Counterpoint: 'Dear Jim': What Ron Carey Should Tell the Boss of UPS." *The Wall Street Journal*, August 14, 1997, A13.

Cohen, R. "Transnational Social Movements: An Assessment." Paper to the Transnational Communities Program, University of Oxford, June 19, 1998 posted at www.transcomm.ox.ac.uk/working%20papers/cohen.pdf4.

Cooper, Marc. "Say It Ain't So, Miguel", L.A. Weekly, July 2002 posted at http://www.consumerwatchdog.org/healthcare/nw/?postId=560.

Crosby, Jeff. "Can Anything Good Come from This?" *New Labor Forum* 15, no. 1 (Spring 2006): 29–37.

———. "Democracy, Density, and Transformation: We Need Them All." *WorkingUSA* 8 (2005): 733–53.

Crowe, Kenneth C. *Collision: How the Rank and File Took Back the Teamsters*. New York: Charles Scribner's Sons, 1993.

CWA, "IUE-CWA Rolls Out WAGE Campaign at GE." http://www.cwa-union.org/news/cwa-news/page.jsp?itemID=27367968.

Davis, Terry. "Cross Border Organizing Comes Home." *Labor Research Review* 23 (1995): 23–29.

Demirovic, Alex. "NGOs and Social Movements: A Study in Contrasts." *Capitalism, Nature, Socialism* 11, no. 4 (December 2000): 131–40.

Demoro, Rose Ann. "Turmoil in the AFL-CIO: A Dollars & Sense Roundtable (Service Employees International Union and International Brotherhood of Teamsters Withdraw from AFL-CIO)." *Dollars & Sense*, September 1, 2005, http://www.dollarsandsense.org/archives/2005/0905demoro.html.

Downs, Peter. "Unsung Heroes of Union Democracy: Rank-and-File Organizers." In *The Transformation of US Unions: Voices, Visions, and Strategies from the Grassroots*, edited by Ray M. Tillman and Michael S. Cummings, 117–35. London: Lynne Rienner Publishers, 1999.

Early, Steve. "Book Review: A Country That Works: Getting America Back on Track—By Stern, Andy; America Needs a Raise: Fighting for Economic Security and Social Justice—By Sweeney, John." *WorkingUSA* 10, no. 1 (2007): 141–49.

————. "Membership-Based Organizing." In *A New Labor Movement for the New Century*, edited by Gregory Mantsios, 95–119. New York: Garland Publishing, 1998.

————. "Turmoil in the AFL-CIO: A Dollars & Sense Roundtable (Service Employees International Union and International Brotherhood of Teamsters Withdraw from AFL-CIO." *Dollars & Sense*, September 1, 2005, http://www.dollarsandsense.org/archives/2005/0905early.html.

Eckstein, Enid. "Putting Organizing Back into Labor Councils." *WorkingUSA* 5, no. 1 (2001): 124–45.

Edwards, Michael, and David Hulme. "Introduction: NGO Performance and Account-ability." In *Beyond the Magic Bullet: NGO Performance and Accountability in the Post-Cold War World*, edited by Michael Edwards and David Hulme, 1–20. Bloomfield, CT: Kumarian Press, 1996.

Eimer, Stuart. "From Business Unionism to 'Social Movement Unionism': The Case of AFL-CIO, Milwaukee County Labor Council." *Labor Studies Journal* 24, no. 2 (Summer 1999): 63–81.

Eisenscher, Michael. "Is the Secret to Labor's Future in Its Past?" *WorkingUSA* 5, no. 4 (2002): 95–122.

————. "Labor: Turning the Corner Will Take More Than Mobilization." In *The Trans-formation of US Unions: Voices, Visions, and Strategies from the Grassroots*, edited by Ray M. Tillman and Michael S. Cummings, 61–85. London: Lynne Rienner Publishers, 1999.

Epstein, Barbara. "Anarchism and the Anti-Globalization Movement." *Monthly Review*, September 2001,: 1–14.

Erickson, Christopher L., Catherine L. Fisk, Ruth Milkman, Daniel J. B. Mitchell, and Kent Wong. "Justice for Janitors in Los Angeles: Lessons from Three Rounds of Ne-gotiations." *British Journal of Industrial Relations* 40, no. 3 (2002): 543–67.

Estreicher, Samuel. "Disunity with the House of Labor: Change to Win or to Stay the Course?" *Journal of Labor Research* 27, no. 4 (Fall 2006): 505–11.

Eyck, Tiffany Ten. "A New Alliance: Workers Centers and Unions." Counterpunch. http://www.counterpunch.org/teneyck01052007.html.

Fantasia, Rick, and Kim Voss. *Hard Work*. Berkeley and Los Angeles: University of California Press, 2004.

Feeley, Dianne. "Teamster Trouble II." *International Viewpoint* 297 (February 1998): 18–20.

Fennell, Tom. "Upbeat on the Line." *MacLean's*, October 28, 1996, 36.

Ferguson, Sarah. "No Justice, No Work: Immigrants Tap May Day's Radical Roots." *Village Voice*, April 28, 2006, http://www.villagevoice.com/news/0618,ferguson,73040,6.html.

Feurer, Rosemary. "William Senter, the UE, and Civic Unionism in St. Louis." In *The CIO's Left-Led Unions*, edited by Steve Rosswurm, 95–117. New Brunswick, NJ: Rut-gers University Press, 1992.

Filippelli, Ronald L. "UE: An Uncertain Legacy." *Political Power and Social Theory* 4 (1984): 217–52.

Filippelli, Ronald L., and Mark D. McColloch. *Cold War in the Working Class: The Rise and Decline of the United Electrical Workers*. New York: State University of New York, 1995.

Fine, Janice. "Building Community Unions." *The Nation*, January 1, 2001, 18–22.

————. "Debating Labor's Future." *The Nation*, August 1, 2005, http://www.thenation.com/doc/20050801/fine.

————. "Moving Innovation from the Margins to the Center." In *A New Labor Move-ment for the New Century*, edited by Gregory Mantsios, 139–69. New York: Garland Publishing, 1998.

————. *Worker Centers*. Ithaca, NY, and London: ILR Press, 2006.

————. "Worker Centers: Organizing Communities at the Edge of a Dream." EPI briefing paper 159, 2005. http://www.epinet.org/content.cfm/bp159.

————. "Worker Centers: Organizing Communities at the Edge of a Dream." *Neighborhood Funders Group Executive Summary,* April 2005, 1–32.

Fisk, Milton. *Socialism from Below in the United States.* Ohio: Herra Press, 1977.

Frankel, Boris. *The Post-Industrial Utopians.* Oxford, UK: Polity Press, 1987.

Frost, Ann C. "Union Involvement in Workplace Decision Making: Implications for Union Democracy." *Journal of Labor Research* 21, no. 2 (Spring 2000): 265–86.

Ganz, Marshal, Kim Voss, Teresa Sharpe, Carl Somers, and George Strauss. "Against the Tide: Projects and Pathways of the New Generation of Union Leaders, 1984–2001." In *Rebuilding Labor: Organizing and Organizers in the New Union Movement,* edited by Ruth Milkman and Kim Voss, 150–94. Ithaca, NY, and London: Cornell University Press, 2004.

Gapasin, Fernando, and Howard Wial. "The Role of Central Labor Councils in Union Organizing in the 1990s." In *Organizing to Win,* edited by Kate Bronfenbrenner et al., 54–68. Ithaca, NY: ILR Press, 1998.

Gapasin, Fernando, and Michael Yates. "Organizing the Unorganized: Will Promises Become Practices?" In *Rising from the Ashes? Labor in the Age of "Global" Capital,* edited by Ellen Meiksins Wood, Peter Meiksins, and Michael Yates, 73–86. New York: Monthly Review Press, 1998.

Gibb, Robert. "Leadership, Political Opportunities and Organisational Identity in the French Anti-racist Movement." In *Leadership and Social Movements,* edited by Colin Barker, Alan Johnson, and Michael Lavalette, 60–76. Manchester, UK: Manchester University Press, 2001.

Gindin, Sam. "Breaking Away: The Formation of the Canadian Auto Workers." *Studies in Political Economy* 29 (Summer 1989): 63–89.

————. "The CAW: The Birth and Transformation of a Union." http://www.caw.ca/whoweare/ourhistory/cawhistory/index.html.

————. "Socialism 'with Sober Senses': Developing Workers' Capacities." In *Socialist Register 1998,* edited by Leo Panitch and Colin Leys, 75–101. London: Merlin Press, 1998.

Goldfield, Michael. "Race and Labor Organization in the United States." In *Rising from the Ashes? Labor in the Age of "Global" Capital,* edited by Ellen Meiksins Wood, Peter Meiksins, and Michael Yates, 87–99. New York: Monthly Review Press, 1998.

Gordon, Jennifer. *Suburban Sweatshops.* Cambridge and London: The Belknap Press of Harvard University Press, 2005.

Gouldner, Alvin W. "Metaphysical Pathos and the Theory of Bureaucracy." *American Political Science Review* 49, no. 2 (1955): 496–507.

Grabelsky, Jeff. "A New Alliance in New York State: A Progress Report on the Labor Movement's Restructuring, Capacity Building, and Programmatic Work." *WorkingUSA* 10, no. 1 (2007): 9–25.

Gray, John. *False Dawn.* London: Granta Books, 1998.

Greer, Ian. "Business Union vs. Business Union? Understanding the Split in the US Labour Movement." *Capital & Class,* Autumn 2006, 1–6.

Gwynne, Peter. "The Myth of Globalization?" *MIT Sloan Management Review* 44, no. 2 (Winter 2003): 11.

Halliday, Fred. *Revolution and World Politics.* London: MacMillan Press, 1999.

Hanisch, Carol. "Struggles over Leadership in the Women's Liberation Movement." In *Leadership and Social Movements,* edited by Colin Barker, Alan Johnson, and Michael Lavalette, 77–95. Manchester: Manchester University Press, 2001.

Harvey, Pharis. "Buying Time or Building a Future: Labor Strategies for a Global Economy." *Labor Research Review* 23 (1995): 89–101.

Hassan, Khalil. "The Future of the Labor Left." *Monthly Review,* July-August 2000, 60–83.

Helleiner, Eric. "Freeing Money: Why Have Some States Been More Willing to Liberalize Capital Controls Than Trade Barriers." *Policy Sciences* 27, no. 4 (1994): 299–318.

Henwood, Doug. "Talking about Work." In *Rising from the Ashes? Labor in the Age of "Global" Capital,* edited by Ellen Meiksins Wood, Peter Meiksins, and Michael Yates, 17–27. New York: Monthly Review Press, 1998.

Herzenberg, Stephen. "Whither Social Unionism? Labor and Restructuring in the US Auto Industry." In *The Challenge of Restructuring: North American Labor Movements Respond,* edited by Jane Jenson and Rianne Mahon, 314–36. Philadelphia: Temple University Press, 1993.

Hirschsohn, Philip. "From Grassroots Democracy to National Mobilization: COSATU as a Model of Social Movement Unionism." *Economic and Industrial Democracy* 19 (1998): 633–66.

Hirst, Paul. "The Global Economy—Myths and Realities." *International Affairs* 73, no. 3 (1997): 409–25.

Holmes, John, and A. Rusonik. "The Break-up of an International Labour Union: Uneven Development in the North American Auto Industry and the Schism in the UAW." *Environment and Planning A* 23 (1991): 9–35.

Hoxie, Robert. *Trade Unionism in the United States.* 2nd edition. New York: Appleton, Century, Crofts, 1966.

"How a Union Saved 1500 Jobs, a $2,000,000 Payroll and the Business They Create for St. Louis." *St. Louis Star-Times.* March 1940. United Electrical, Radio and Machine Workers of America Archive [UEA], University of Pittsburgh, Box 1430, FF6.

Huber, Sonya, and Stephanie Luce. "Jobs with Justice at 14: Building Social Movement Unionism." *Labor Notes,* October 2001, 14

Hulme, David, and Michael Edwards. "Conclusion: Too Close to the Powerful, Too Far from the Powerless?" In *NGOs, States and Donors: Too Close for Comfort?* edited by David Hulme and Michael Edwards, 275–84. New York: St. Martin's Press, 1997.

———. "NGOs, States and Donors: An Overview." In *NGOs, States and Donors: Too Close for Comfort?* edited by David Hulme and Michael Edwards, 3–22. New York: St. Martin's Press, 1997.

Hurd, Richard W. "Contesting the Dinosaur Image: The Labor Movement's Search for a Future." *Labor Studies Journal* 22, no. 4 (Winter 1998): 5–30.

———. "The Failure of Organizing, the New Unity Partnership, and the Future of the Labor Movement." *WorkingUSA* 8 (September 2004): 5–25.

Hyclak, Thomas, and Michael G. Kolchin. "The Drive for Autonomy by Canadian Auto Workers." In *Industrial Relations Research Association Series,* edited by Barbara D. Dennis, 265–71. Proceedings of the Forty-First Annual Meeting, New York, December 28–30, (Madison, WI: The Association, 1988).

Hyman, Richard. *Marxism and the Sociology of Trade Unionism.* London: Pluto Press, 1971.

International Brotherhood of Teamsters. "Highlights of the Tentative UPS National Agreement." http://www.trakups.org/materials/upshighlights.pdf.

———. "Letter to John Sweeney." July 25, 2005, http://www.rtands.com/breaking_news_archive.shtml.

———. "Teamsters Overwhelmingly Ratify Contract with UPS." 2002, http://www.trakups.org/News/nr_020829_1.htm .

———. *Union Negotiating Proposals National Master United Parcel Service Agreement,* Article 22, Section 3, 2002.

———. "UPS Contract Campaign Update: Whatever It Takes." October 1, 2001. http://www.teamster.org/01newsb/hn_011001_4.htm.

Jayaraman, Saru. "La Alianza Para La Justicia: A Team Approach to Immigrant Worker Organizing." In *The New Urban Immigrant Workforce,* edited by Sarumathi Jayaraman and Immanuel Ness, 85–104. Armonk, NY, and London: M. E. Sharpe, 2005.

Johnson, David. "US, Mexican Unions Are Teaming Up." *Labor Notes,* September 1993, 8–13.

Jonas, Andrew E. G. "Investigating the Local-Global Paradox." In *Organizing the Landscape: Geographical Perspectives on Labor Unionism,* edited by Andrew Herod, 325–50. London: University of Minnesota Press, 1998.

———. "Labor and Community in the Deindustrialization of Urban America." *Journal of Urban Affairs* 17, no. 2 (1995): 183–99.

Kagarlitsky, Boris. *The Return of Radicalism: Reshaping the Left Institutions.* London: Pluto Press, 2000.

Kelly, John. *Trade Unions and Socialist Politics.* London and New York: Verso, 1988.

Kest, Steven. "ACORN and Community-Labor Partnerships." *WorkingUSA* 6, no. 4 (2003): 84–100.

Kutalik, Chris. "A Play for Power?" *Labor Notes,* September 2005, 9.

———. "What Does the AFL-CIO Split Mean?" *Labor Notes,* September 2005, 7.

Kwik, Phill. "It's a New Day in the Teamsters." *Labor Notes,* August 1991, 1, 10, 12.

La Botz, Dan. "The Fight at UPS: The Teamsters' Victory and the Future of the 'New Labor Movement.'" http://www.solidarity-us.org/ups.

———. "Making Links across the Border." *Labor Notes,* August 1994, 7–10.

———. *Rank-and-File Rebellion: Teamsters for a Democratic Union.* London: Verso, 1990.

———. "Rank and File Teamsters Fight for Labor's Future." *Dollars and Sense,* September/October 1998, 16–20.

———. "Why Is It So Hard to Reform the Teamsters?" *Dollars and Sense,* November/December 1998, 26–41.

La Luz, Jose, and Paula Finn. "Getting Serious about Inclusion: A Comprehensive Approach." In *A New Labor Movement for the New Century,* edited by Gregory Mantsios, 187–211. New York: Garland Publishing, 1998.

Lambert, Rob, and Eddie Webster. "Southern Unionism and the New Labor Internationalism." In *Place, Space and the New Labor Internationalisms,* edited by Peter Waterman and Jane Wills, 33–58. Oxford: Blackwell Publishers, 2001.

Langevin, Mark. "Replacing the State: New Directions in Brazilian Labor Education." *Labor Studies Journal* 19, no. 1 (Spring 1994): 56–71.

Larkin, Jim. "Teamster Tragedy." *The Progressive,* January 1998, 20–22.

———. "Which Way for the Teamsters?" *The Nation,* October 8, 2001, 20–24.

Leary, Elly. "Immokalee Workers Take Down Taco Bell." *Monthly Review,* October 2005, 11–25.

Lerner, Stephen. "Taking the Offensive, Turning the Tide." In *A New Labor Movement for the New Century,* edited by Gregory Mantsios, 79–93. New York: Garland Publishing, 1998.

Lichtenstein, Nelson. *State of the Union: A Century of American Labor.* Princeton, NJ: Princeton University Press, 2002.

Livingstone, D. W., and Reuben Roth. "Workplace Communities and Transformative Learning: Oshawa Autoworkers and the CAW." *Convergence* 31, no. 3 (1998): 12–22.

Lopez, Steven Henry. *Reorganizing the Rust Belt.* Berkeley, Los Angeles, and London: University of California Press, 2004.

Lowe, Lisa. "Work, Immigration, Gender: New Subjects of Cultural Politics." *Social Justice* 25, no. 3 (Fall 1998): 31–49.

Luce, Stephanie. "Building Political Power and Community Coalitions: The Role of Central Labor Councils in the Living-Wage Movement." In *Central Labor Councils and the Revival of American Unionism,* edited by Immanuel Ness and Stuart Eimer, 140–62. Armonk, NY: M. E. Sharpe, 2001.

Madrick, Jeff. "Goodbye, Horatio Alger," *The Nation,* February 5, 2007, 20–24.

Mantsios, Gregory. "What Does Labor Stand For?" In *A New Labor Movement for the New Century,* edited by G. Mantsios, 51–74. New York: Garland Publishing, 1998.

Marx, Karl. "The Eighteenth Brumaire of Louis Bonaparte." 1852. In *The Marx-Engels Reader,* 2nd edition, edited by Robert C. Tucker, 594–618. New York: W. W. Norton & Company, 1978.

Marx, Karl, and Frederick Engels. *The Communist Manifesto.* 1848. London: Penguin Books, 1967.

Masters, Marick F., Ray Gibney, and Tom Zagenczyk. "The AFL-CIO v. CTW: The Competing Visions, Strategies, and Structures." *Journal of Labor Research* 27, no. 4 (Fall 2006): 473–504.

Matles, James J., and James Higgins. *Them and Us: Struggles of a Rank-and-File Union.* Upper Saddle River, NJ: Prentice-Hall, 1995.

Mazur, Jay. "Labour's New Internationalism." *Foreign Affairs* 79, no. 1 (January–February 2000): 79–93.

McVay, Kay. "Undemocratic Moves." *California Nurse,* August 2002, 3, 5.

Meiksins, Peter. "Same as It Ever Was? The Structure of the Working Class." In *Rising from the Ashes? Labor in the Age of "Global" Capital,* edited by Ellen Meiksins Wood, Peter Meiksins, and Michael Yates, 28–40. New York: Monthly Review Press, 1998.

Meyerson, Harold. "Labor's Civil War." *American Prospect,* June 2005, http://www.prospect.org/web/page.ww?section=root&name=ViewWeb&articleId=9771.

Michels, Robert. *Political Parties.* New York: Dover Publications, 1959.

Milkman, Ruth. "Female Factory Labor and Industrial Structure: Control and Conflict over 'Women's Place' in Auto and Electrical Manufacturing." *Politics & Society* 12, no. 2 (1983): 159–203.

———. "Labor Organizing among Mexican-Born Workers in the U.S.: Recent Trends and Future Prospects." *Labor Studies Journal* 32, no.1 (2007), http://www.soc.ucla.edu/faculty/milkman/lsjarticle.pdf.

———. *L.A. Story.* New York: Russell Sage Foundation, 2006.

Miller, Paul. "UPS Strike Watch Is On." *Catalog Age* 19, no. 5 (April 1, 2002): 1, 16.

Moberg, David. "Reforming the Teamsters." *The Nation,* September 2–9, 2002, 30.

———. "Union Cities." *The American Prospect,* September 11, 2000, 35–37.

———. "The UPS Strike: Lessons for Labor." *WorkingUSA,* 1, no.3, September/October 1997, 11–29.

Moody, Kim. "American Labor: A Movement Again?" In *Rising from the Ashes? Labor in the Age of "Global" Capital,* edited by Ellen Meiksins Wood, Peter Meiksins, and Michael Yates, 57–72. New York: Monthly Review Press, 1998.

———. "Immigrant Workers and Labor/Community Organization in the United States." *Union Ideas Network,* (2006): 1–34, http://uin.org.uk/content/view/186/66/.

———. *An Injury to All: The Decline of American Unionism.* London: Verso, 1988.

———. "The Rank and File Strategy: Building a Socialist Movement in the US." Solidarity. http://www.solidarity-us.org/rankandfilestrategy.

———. "Who Reformed the Teamsters?" *Against the Current* 7, no. 1 (new series, March–April 1992): 24–27.

———. *Workers in a Lean World.* London: Verso, 1997.

Moody, Kim, and Mary McGinn. *Unions and Free Trade: Solidarity vs. Competition.* Detroit, MI: A Labor Notes Book, 1992.

Morris, Charles J. *The Blue Eagle at Work.* Ithaca, NY, and London: ILR Press, 2006.

Mulhern, Francis. "Towards 2000, or News from You-Know-Where." *New Left Review* 148 (November–December 1984): 5–30.

National Master United Parcel Service Agreement for the Period: August 1, 2002 through July 21, 2008, 2002. http://www.nmfalibrary.org/nmupsindex.htm.

Ness, Immanuel. "From Dormancy to Activism: New Voice and the Revival of Labor Councils." In *Central Labor Councils and the Revival of American Unionism,* edited by Immanuel Ness and Stuart Eimer, 13–34, Armonk, NY: M. E. Sharpe, 2001.

———. *Immigrants, Unions, and the New U.S. Labor Market.* Philadelphia: Temple University Press, 2005.

Nissen, Bruce. "Alliances across the Border: U.S. Labor in the Era of Globalization." *WorkingUSA* 3, no. 1 (1999): 43–55.

———. "Alternative Strategic Directions for the U.S. Labor Movement: Recent Scholarship." *Labor Studies Journal* 28, no. 1 (Spring 2003): 133–55.

———. "What Are Scholars Telling the U.S. Labor Movement to Do?" *Labor History* 44, no. 2 (2003): 157–65.

Nissen, Bruce, and Seth Rosen. "Community-Based Organizing: Transforming Union Organizing Programs from the Bottom Up." In *Which Direction for Organized Labor?* edited by Bruce Nissen, 59–73. Detroit, MI: Wayne State University Press, 1999.

"Notes on Current Labor Statistics," *Monthly Labor Review,* July 2002, 61–127.

"Notes on Current Labor Statistics," *Monthly Labor Review,* July 2006, 60–79.

O'Brien, Robert. "The Agency of Labour in a Changing Global Order." In *Political Economy and the Changing Global Order,* 3rd edition, edited by Richard Stubbs and Geoffrey R. D. Underhill, 222–32. Oxford and New York: Oxford University Press, 2007.

———. "Workers and World Order: The Tentative Transformation of the International Union Movement." *Review of International Studies* 26 (2000): 533–55.

OECD. "Canada." *OECD Economic Outlook,* June 1997, 73–77.

OECD. "United States." *OECD Economic Outlook,* June 1997, 43–48.

Offe, Claus. "Reflections on the Institutional Self-Transformation of Movement Politics: A Tentative Stage Mode." In *Challenging the Political Order,* edited by Russell J. Dalton and Manfred Kuechler, 232–50. New York: Oxford University Press, 1990.

Omvedt, Gail. *Reinventing Revolution: New Socialist Movements and Traditions in India.* Armonk, NY: M. E. Sharpe, 1993.

"Organizing Low-Wage Immigrants—The Workplace Project: Interview with Jennifer Gordon." *WorkingUSA* 5, no. 1 (2001): 87–102.

Oshinsky, David. "Labor's Cold War: The CIO and the Communists." In *Major Problems in the History of American Workers: Documents and Essays,* edited by Eileen Boris and Nelson Lichtenstein, 510–24. D.C. Lexington, Massachusetts: D.C. Heath and Company, 1991.

Parker, Mike, and Martha Gruelle. *Democracy Is Power: Rebuilding Unions from the Bottom Up.* Detroit, MI: Labor Notes, 1999.

Petras, James. "Globalization: A Critical Analysis." *Journal of Contemporary Asia* 29, no. 1 (1999): 3–37.

———. "Imperialism and NGOs in Latin America." *Monthly Review* 49, no. 7 (December 1997): 10–26.

———. "NGOs: In the Service of Imperialism." *Journal of Contemporary Asia* 29, no. 4 (October 1999): 45–56.

Porter, Russell B. "The C.I.O." In *American Labor since the New Deal,* edited by Melvyn Dubofsky, 97–105. Chicago: Quadrangle Books, 1971.

Rachleff, Peter. "Why Participation? Lessons from the Past for the Future: A Response to Charles Hecksher's Article 'Participatory Unionism.'" *Labor Studies Journal* 25, no. 4 (2001): 9–26.

Rathke, Wade. "A Wal-Mart Workers Association? An Organizing Plan." In *Wal-Mart: The Face of Twenty-First Century Capitalism,* edited by Nelson Lichtenstein, 261–83. New York and London: The New Press, 2006.

Reynolds, David, and Jen Kern. "Labor and the Living-Wage Movement." *Working USA* 5, no. 3 (2002): 17–45.

Robinson, Ian. "Does Neoliberal Restructuring Promote Social Movement Unionism? U.S. Developments in Comparative Perspective." In *Unions in a Globalized Environment,* edited by Bruce Nissen, 189–235. Armonk, NY: M. E. Sharpe, 2002.

———. "Neoliberal Restructuring and U.S. Unions: Toward Social Movement Unionism." *Critical Sociology* 26, no. 1–2 (2000): 109–38.

Rosenblum, Jonathan. "Building Organizing Capacity: The King County Labor Council." In *Central Labor Councils and the Revival of American Unionism,* edited by Immanuel Ness and Stuart Eimer, 163–87. Armonk, NY: M. E. Sharpe, 2001.

Ross, Stephanie. "Is This What Democracy Looks Like? The Politics of the Anti-Globalization Movement in North America." In *Socialist Register 2003,* edited by Leo Panitch and Colin Leys, 281–304. London: Merlin Press, 2002.

Roth, Reuben. "The Canadian Auto Workers and Paid Education Leave: Social Unionism in Practice." The Ontario Institute for Studies in Education of the University of Toronto, http://www.oise.utoronto.ca/~rroth/1131.htm.

Rothstein, Richard. "Union Strength in the United States: Lessons from the UPS Strike." *International Labour Review* 136, no. 4 (Winter 1997): 469–91.

Rubinstein, Saul A., and Thomas A. Kochan. *Learning from Saturn: Possibilities for Corporate Governance and Employee Relations.* Ithaca, NY, and London: ILR Press, 2001.

Rubinstein, Saul, Michael Bennet, and Thomas Kochan. "The Saturn Partnership: Co-Management and the Reinvention of the Local Union." In *Employee Representation: Alternatives and Future Directions,* edited by Bruce E. Kaufman and Morris M. Kleiner, 339–70. Madison, WI: Industrial Relations Research Association, 1993.

Ruigrok, Winfried. "Multinational Corporations in the Global Economy." In *Political Economy and the Changing Global Order,* 3rd edition, edited by Richard Stubbs and Geoffrey R. D. Underhill, 197–210. Oxford and New York: Oxford University Press, 2007.

———. "Why Nationality Is Still Important." *Financial Times,* January 5, 1996, 12.

Savage, Lydia. "Justice for Janitors: Scales of Organizing and Representing Workers." *Antipode* 38, no. 3 (June 2006): 645–66.

Schatz, Ronald. "The End of Corporate Liberalism: Class Struggle in the Electrical Manufacturing Industry, 1933–1950." *Radical America* 9 (July-August 1975): 187–205.

Schenk, Christopher. "Social Movement Unionism: Beyond the Organizing Model." In *Trade Unions in Renewal: A Comparative Study,* edited by Peter Fairbrother and Charlotte A. B. Yates, 244–62. London and New York: Continuum, 2003.

Schiavone, Michael. "Social Movement Unionism in North America: An Evaluation of Kim Moody's Account." PhD diss., Australian National University, 2004.

Scholte, Jan Art. "Global Civil Society: Changing the World?" CSGR Working Paper 31/99, University of Warwick, May 1999.

Schou, Nick. "Nursing a Grudge." *OC Weekly,* May 16 2003, http://www.consumerwatchdog.org/nw/?postId=661&pageTitle=Nursing+A+Grudge.

Schrecker, Ellen. "McCarthyism and Organized Labor." *WorkingUSA* 3, no. 5 (January/February 2000): 93–101.

Sciacchitano, Katherine. "Finding the Community in the Union and the Union in the Community: The First-Contract Campaign at Steeltech." In *Organizing to Win,* edited by Kate Bronfenbrenner et al., 150–63. Ithaca, NY: ILR Press, 1998.

Scipes, Kim. "AFL-CIO in Venezuela: Déjà Vu All Over Again." *Labor Notes,* April 2003.

Seidman, Gay W. *Manufacturing Militance: Workers' Movements in Brazil and South Africa, 1970–1985.* Berkeley: University of California Press, 1993.

SEIU. "Janitors' Victory in Houston Sparks Hope for New Era of Economic Gains for Families in America." http://seiu.org/media/pressreleases.cfm?pr_id=1354.

SEIU. Press Release: July 25, 2005. http://www.seiu.org/media/pressreleases.cfm?pr_id=1237.

Simmons, P. J. "Learning to Live with NGOs." *Foreign Policy* 112 (Fall 1998): 82–96.

Slaughter, Jane. "Shrinking Auto Union Beats Back Reformers." *Labor Notes,* July 1992, 1, 15.

———. "UPS and Detroit Newspaper Strikes." *Monthly Review,* January 1998, 53–57.

Smithsimon, Greg. "Transnational Labor Organizing." *Socialist Review* 27, no. 3–4 (1999): 65–93.

Stepan-Norris, Judith, and Maurice Zeitlin. *Left Out: Reds and America's Industrial Unions.* Cambridge: Cambridge University Press, 2003.

———. "Red Unions and 'Bourgeois' Contracts?" *American Journal of Sociology* 96, no. 5 (March 1991): 1151–1200.

———. "Union Democracy, Radical Leadership, and the Hegemony of Capital." *American Sociological Review* 60, no. 6 (December 1995): 829–50.

Strange, Susan. "The Defective State." *Daedalus* 124, no. 2 (1995): 55–74.

Swinney, Dan. "Strategic Lessons for Labor from Candyland." *New Labor Forum* 55 (Fall/Winter 1999).

Tait, Vanessa. *Poor Workers' Unions.* Cambridge, MA: South End Press, 2005.

Teamsters for a Democratic Union. "Best Contract Ever." http://www.tdu.org/UPS/Best_Contract_Ever.pdf.

———. "Central States Pension Fund: No Pension Increase—Members Fight Back." http://www.tdu.org/Convoy/CSPF_Anger/CSPF_Freeze/cspf_freeze.html.

———. "Contract Bulletin, 8." http://www.tdu.org/UPSBulletin8.pdf.

———. "Contract Bulletin, 14." http://www.tdu.org/UPSBulletin14.pdf.

———. "Detroit Area UPSers Vote No; Hoffa Says Yes." http://www.tdu.org/UPS/UPS_Contract_411/UPS_Detroit_rider/ups_detroit_rider.html.

———. "Hoffa Uses 'Mystery Math' to Sell Agreement." http://www.tdu.org/UPS/UPS_Contract_411/UPS_Mystery_Math/ups_mystery_math.html.

———. "Survey Results: UPS Teamsters Say Conditions Are Worse Today Than at Start of Contract." http://www.tdu.org/UPS/upssurveyresults/upssurveyresults.html.

———. "UPS Rank & File Network Contract Bulletin." http://www.tdu.org/UPS_Bulletin_3.pdf.

Tillman, Ray M. "Reform Movement in the Teamsters and United Auto Workers." In *The Transformation of US Unions: Voices, Visions, and Strategies from the Grassroots,* edited by Ray M. Tillman and Michael S. Cummings, 137–66. London: Lynne Rienner Publishers, 1999.

"Toward a Cohesive Labor Movement: Worker Center and Union Collaboration in Los Angeles." ILE Graduate Research Conference, February 21–22, 2003.

Turner, Lowell, and Richard W. Hurd. "Building Social Movement Unionism." In *Rekindling the Movement: Labor's Quest for Relevance in the Twenty-First Century,* edited by Lowell Turner, Harry C. Katz, and Richard W. Hurd, 9–26. Ithaca, NY, and London: Cornell University Press, 2001.

UAW. "Departmental Reports, 33rd Constitutional Convention." http://www.local2209.org/pdf/01977.pdf.

———. "Who We Are." http://www.uaw.org/about/uawmembership.html.

UNCTAD. *World Investment Report, 2006.* New York and Geneva, Switzerland: United Nations, 2006.

Verma, Anil, and Joel Cutcher-Gershenfeld. "Joint Governance in the Workplace: Beyond Union-Management Cooperation and Worker Participation." In *Employee Representation: Alternatives and Future Directions*, edited by Bruce E. Kaufman and Morris M. Kleiner, 197–234. Madison, WI: Industrial Relations Research Association, 1993.

Voss, Kim, and Rachel Sherman. "Breaking the Iron Law of Oligarchy: Union Revitalization in the American Labor Movement." *American Journal of Sociology* 106, no. 2 (September 2000): 303–49.

Wade, Robert. "Globalization and Its Limits: Reports of the Death of the National Economy Are Greatly Exaggerated." In *National Diversity and Global Capitalism*, edited by Suzanne Berger and Ronald Dore, 60–88. Ithaca, NY, and London: Cornell University Press, 1996.

Waldinger, Roger, Chris Erickson, Ruth Milkman, Daniel J. B. Mitchell, Abel Valenzuela, Kent Wong, and Maurice Zeitlin. "Justice for Janitors: Organizing in Difficult Times." *Dissent* 44, no. 1 (Winter 1997): 37–44.

Waterman, Peter. "Social Movement Unionism: A New Union Model for a New World Order?" *Review* 26, no. 3 (Summer 1993): 245–78.

———. "Whatever Happened to the 'New Social Unionism'?" Paper for workshop on "International Trade Unionism in a Network Society: What's New about the 'New Labor Internationalism'?" Organized by the Leeds Working Group on International Labor Networking and hosted by Leeds Metropolitan University, Leeds, UK, May 2–3, 2003.

Webster, Eddie. "The Rise of Social-Movement Unionism: The Two Faces of the Black Trade Union Movement in South Africa." In *State, Resistance and Change in South Africa*, edited by Philip Frankel, Noam Pines, and Mark Swilling, 174–96. New York: Croom Helm, 1988.

Weinbaum, Eve S., and Gordon Lafer. "Outside Agitators and Other Red Herrings: Getting Past the 'Top-Down/Bottom-Up' Debate." *New Labor Forum* 10 (Spring-Summer 2002): 26–35.

Weiss, Linda. "Globalization and the Myth of the Powerless State." *New Left Review* 225 (September/October 1997): 3–27.

Wellman, David. *The Union Makes Us Strong*. Cambridge and New York: Cambridge University Press, 1995.

Wells, Donald M. "When Push Comes to Shove: Competitiveness, Job Insecurity and Labour-Management Cooperation in Canada." *Economic and Industrial Democracy* 18, no. 2 (1997): 167–200.

West, Lois A. *Militant Labor in the Philippines*. Philadelphia: Temple University Press, 1997.

———. "U.S. Foreign Labor Policy and the Case of Militant Political Unionism in the Philippines." *Labor Studies Journal* 16, no. 4 (Winter 1991): 48–75.

Williams, Jane. "Restructuring Labor's Identity: The Justice for Janitors Campaign in Washington, D.C." In *The Transformation of US Unions: Voices, Visions, and Strategies from the Grassroots*, edited by Ray M. Tillman and Michael S. Cummings, 203–17. London: Lynne Rienner Publishers, 1999.

Witt, Matt, and Rand Wilson. "Part-Time America Won't Work." In *Not Your Father's Union Movement: Inside the AFL-CIO*, edited by Jo-Ann Mort, 179–86. London: Verso, 1998.

———. "The Teamsters' UPS Strike of 1997: Building a New Labor Movement." *Labor Studies Journal* 24, no. 1 (Spring 1999): 58–72.

Witwer, David. *Corruption and Reform in the Teamsters Union*. Urbana and Chicago: University of Illinois Press, 2003.

"Working Poor." *Monthly Labor Review* 129, no. 7 (July 2006): 2.

Wright, Carter. "A Clean Sweep: Justice for Janitors." *Multinational Monitor,* January/February 2001, 12–14.

Wulkan, Fred "Facing Movement for Democracy, SEIU Gives Massachusetts Members to Teachers Union." *Labor Notes,* February 2006, 3–4.

Yates, Charlotte. *From Plant to Politics: The Autoworkers Union in Postwar Canada.* Philadelphia: Temple University Press, 1993.

———. "The Internal Dynamics of Union Power: Explaining Canadian Autoworkers Militancy in the 1980s." *Studies in Political Economy 31* (Spring 1990): 73–105.

———. "Unity and Diversity: Challenges to an Expanding Canadian Autoworkers' Union." *The Canadian Review of Sociology and Anthropology* 35, no. 1 (1998): 93–118.

Yates, Michael. "Does the U.S. Labor Movement Have a Future?" *Monthly Review* 48, no. 9 (1997): 1–18.

———. "'Workers of All Countries Unite': Will This Include the U.S. Labor Movement?" *Monthly Review* 52, no. 3 (July-August 2000): 46–59.

Zappone, Chris. "Congress Oks Minimum Wage Boost." CNN Website, http://money.cnn.com/2007/05/24/news/economy/minimum_wage/index.htm?postversion=2007052422.

Zieger, Robert H. *The CIO 1935–1955.* Chapel Hill and London: The University of North Carolina Press, 1995.

NEWSPAPERS/WIRE SERVICES

AP Online
Associated Press Newswires
Atlanta Constitution
Automotive News
The Boston Globe
Business Wire
Canada News-Wire
The Canadian Press
Chicago Sun-Times
Chicago Tribune
The Commercial Appeal
Convoy Dispatch
The Dallas Morning News
Dow Jones Business News
Dow Jones News Service
The Financial Post
Financial Times
The Globe and Mail
Houston Chronicle
The International Teamster
Knight-Ridder News Service
Knight-Ridder Tribune Business News
Labor Notes
Los Angeles Daily News
Los Angeles Times
The Manila Chronicle
The Milwaukee Journal

The Milwaukee Journal Sentinel
National Post
People's Press
People's Press (Schenectady Edition)
PR Newswire
Seattle Times
St. Petersburg Times
The Toronto Star
The Wall Street Journal
The Wall Street Journal Europe
The Washington Post
UE News

INDEX

About the Author

MICHAEL SCHIAVONE is Lecturer and Visiting Fellow at Flinders University, Australia, where he runs a master's program jointly with a Chinese university. He has written articles and encyclopedia entries on unionism and globalization for Greenwood Press and other publishers.